Edges of Loss

THEATER: Theory/Text/Performance

Enoch Brater, Series Editor

Edges of Loss

From Modern Drama to Postmodern Theory

Mark Pizzato

Ann Arbor

The University of Michigan Press

to my aunt
Helen Hammack Hogan
whose sense of loss
returning to hope
has always inspired
my writing

Copyright © by the University of Michigan 1998
All rights reserved
Published in the United States of America by
The University of Michigan Press
Manufactured in the United States of America
⊚ Printed on acid-free paper

2001   2000   1999   1998   4   3   2   1

A CIP catalog record for this book is available from the British Library.

Library of Congress Cataloging-in-Publication Data

Pizzato, Mark, 1960–
    Edges of loss : from modern drama to postmodern theory / Mark
Pizzato.
        p.   cm. — (Theater : theory/text/performance)
    Includes bibliographical references and index.
    ISBN 0-472-10914-6 (acid-free paper)
    1. Drama—Psychological aspects. 2. Theater—Psychological
aspects. I. Title.
PN1631 .P58   1998
809'.001'9—dc21   98-8955
                                                                        CIP

Acknowledgments

Earlier versions of chapters 2, 5, and 6 have been published as "Redressing the Chorus: Nietzsche in Eliot," *Journal of Ritual Studies* 6, no. 2 (summer 1992): 1–25; "Genet's Violent, Subjective Split into the Theatre of Lacan's Three Orders," *Journal of Dramatic Theory and Criticism* 5, no. 1 (fall 1990): 115–30; and "Mourning at a Distance: Brecht's Repression of the *Chora*," *Essays in Theatre/Études Théâtrales* 11, no. 1 (November 1992): 41–67. I appreciate the permission from the editors of these journals to republish my essays.

I also appreciate the advice of Kathleen Woodward, Gregory S. Jay, Patrice Petro, Bernard Gendron, and especially Herbert Blau—as I developed the initial drafts of this book at the University of Wisconsin–Milwaukee. Professor Blau's passionate, yet careful responses were crucial to my work, beyond mourning and melancholia, toward confidence as a writer. I also want to thank my colleagues Anne Davis Basting, Ann Johnson, Jan Michael Joncas, Michal Kobialka, Tullio Maranhão, David Penchansky, and my "Modern Drama" students, who discussed many of the book's issues with me as I revised it in St. Paul, Minnesota. The University of St. Thomas helped as well with a Research Assistance Grant in the summer of 1994. The editors and readers (including LeAnn Fields and Anthony Kubiak) at the University of Michigan Press also influenced the ultimate version of this work. Finally, I must thank my wife, Patricia Stevenson Pizzato, who helped me at home—like Herb Blau at the university—to face my own peculiar symptoms at the edges of loss. During the time I "birthed" the initial version of this book, Pattie was pregnant with my first son, Luke, who continues now to educate me in the joys and terrors of loss—as does his baby brother, Peter, still in his "mirror stage" as I polish off these pages.

Contents

Introduction

O! How this mother swells up toward my heart:
Hysterica passio! down, thou climbing sorrow!
—*King Lear* 2.4.54–55

Theater shows loss. As "live" performance, theater exists only for a moment, demonstrating the mortality of both actor and spectator. Theater also stages dramatic conflict, which articulates particular moments of loss in and between characters—while the audience watches. As Herbert Blau puts it: "The body in performance is dying in front of your eyes. Unceasing process is out there in the flesh. Or hangs, perceptually, on the audience's breath" (*Audience* 366). Whether the play is tragic, comic, or melodramatic, loss onstage creates a tentative tie between actors and spectators, though each experiences something different while sharing something together. The communal (yet individual) experience of theater as a live art form thus reflects the theater of ordinary life: the roles we each play, the plots we act out, the masks and costumes we wear—and the internal staging of desires, perceptions, and dreams. In such everyday, external/internal theater, the loss of certain persons, places, and things, of events and opportunities, of identities and abilities, fuels further dramas, which we act out and observe. Theater (as art) intensifies, expresses, and allows us to share the critical losses and creative powers of life's theatricality, both social and personal, external and internal.

But theater today is more and more upstaged by the popular dramatic media of film and television (both fictional and journalistic). My own involvement in theater, as artist and scholar, derives—I now realize—from watching TV at home and going to the movie theater, while growing up in southern California. My first experience of professional live theater (in San Diego and then in London) did not come until the end of high school. This is also true for many of the college students I now teach. With current video technology, they may be raised seeing themselves perform on the TV screen

at home—yet rarely attend live theater. What is the value, to each new generation, of the increasingly lost art of theater—when we are inundated by
daily drama on the home TV and intoxicated by the bigger-than-life stars
on our neighborhood cineplex screens?

My interest in theater, as reflected in this study, focused early on its
live, ritual, communal elements, which paradoxically involve a haunting
mortality, a strong suspicion of ritual submission, and the experience of
alienation despite communion. This eventual love for theatrical paradox
grew not only from a lack of live entertainment in my early years, but also
from a crucial event of personal loss. My mother died of breast cancer when
I was nine years old. I turned then more fervently to the Catholic Church
and its ritual faith, in which I'd been raised by both of my parents. My
father and I started going to daily mass in order to find a communal and
metaphysical sense to our loneliness. (I was also an only child.) Eventually,
though, in another nine years or so, I began to discover theater as an alternative (or supplement) to church.

In contrast to the communal boundaries and metaphysical demands of
religious ritual, theater expresses the twists of fate to a broader audience of
tentative believers and provokes more extensive questions about the drama
of life. And yet, theater has its own rituals (however distinct from its religious
origins), ordering current communities, for better and worse—even in the
general sense of repeated rehearsals and new performances of the same
drama. While teaching at two Catholic colleges in recent years, I often recon-
sidered, with the help of my students, this dialectic of theater and ritual. I
now find that theater helps to bridge the gap between traditional forms of
communal transcendence and new diverse fusions of mass-media epiphany.
That is the value I find in the experience and study of theater today—especially in relation to our culture's current modern/postmodern shift.

So, in the chapters ahead, I will focus on the modernist nostalgia for
transcendent meaning (in all four dramatists of my survey) and the postmodern passion for perverse, diverse play (in the various theorists used).[1]
Both of these desires demand certain sacrifices to make more of loss, to
make loss more sublime. The power of loss to fuel such sacrificial ecstasy,
in modern and postmodern directions, makes me wary of theatricality—
whether on the page, onstage, in church, in the media, or on the streets.
Yet, I believe that modern drama reveals a great deal about the potential
dangers and joys of theater in everyday life—particularly in relation to
postmodern theories of our current hypertheatrical society.[2] As Mária
Minich-Brewer warned a decade ago: "Theatricality carries with it lures
and seductions that, if unexamined, will continue to be a regressive blind

spot of theory, an automatic reflex, and a diffuse and misunderstood figure of modernity" (14).

Hopefully then, this study will help to show the current potential of theater, given the insights of modern drama, to illuminate our postmodern condition. For the Cartesian "I think, therefore I am" (at the beginning of modernity) is increasingly fractured today by the TV screen's multiple channels and remote controls. "I'm not onscreen, therefore I am not"—except when parts of me can identify with those players that millions are watching right now (as we all consume their buy-products). The modern certainty of universal truth, firm reality, and a definite past—with man as the measure of all things and God as absolute principle of order—has shifted increasingly toward multiple truths, virtual reality, and various subjective histories (and her-stories), with machines computing all things and chaos as the order of the day.[3]

Thus I (or the parts of me writing this) begin this exploration of theatrical loss under the rubric of "psychohistory": the psychological interplay of recent and retrospective historical stages. I am mostly concerned with the climax of modernity (the last several hundred years of Euro-American culture) in high modernism (the dominant art movement of the first half of this century)—and the new postmodern era or art movement "nascent" within the modern (Lyotard, *Postmodern* 79). But I do not make claims for any distinct definition of such periods. In fact, I hope to show how they continue to interweave, like classicism and romanticism, in the current theater of the mind, from the relevance of modern drama to the play of postmodern theory.

I take T. S. Eliot as representative of high modernism, with his passion (Romantic and classical) to resurrect a lost ritual chorus—through the symbolism and historical/domestic realism of his own poetic drama. First I will present the religious and scientific sides of high modernism, by rehearsing Eliot's debate with I. A. Richards about belief in poetry. Then, for the next two chapters, I will turn to Eliot's sacred and secular drama, juxtaposed with the early theories of Friedrich Nietzsche on the birth of tragedy, which mirror Eliot's desires in a perversely poststructuralist direction.[4] The main concern of this initial section on psychohistory will be the interplay of modernist belief(s) and postmodern perversity, in relation to theater's originary site of loss: the ancient ritual chorus.

The second half of this book uses details of "psychobiography" from several other modern playwrights, to diagnose the significance of their work in relation to various postmodern theorists. Hence, the personal loss of the maternal bond becomes more prominent in my analysis of each dramatist's work, though that still relates to the cultural loss of a ritual communal bond.[5] For in both sections I use the theories of Jacques Lacan to illuminate the cultural issues of poststructuralist theory (greatly influenced by his work) and to explore the mental theaters of each playwright.[6] But I do not claim to treat the real person behind the dramatist's name and work. That person is lost to us, even though his plays remain. Something from that writer's psyche, invested with current life, plays on in the drama—theatrically and theoretically—although the "playwright" becomes, through the stages of history, as much a character that we project onto his work as a true figure of authorial intentions.

Despite the death of the Author, announced by postmodern theorists in the late 1960s (Barthes, *Image* 142–48, and Foucault, *Language* 113–38)—or the New Critics' warning in the 1940s about an Intentional Fallacy, especially regarding Eliot's poetry (Wimsatt and Beardsley)—I find it is time now to reconsider the character of specific modern playwrights, because of the significance of their writings to the postmodern. But in doing so I admit that we actually recreate the figure of each author, for current display, as we analyze his corpus and life. (Similarly, Jacques Derrida in *Of Grammatology* deconstructs "Rousseau" for postmodern relevance, especially in his/their suspicion of theatrical representation.) Two of the dramatists I have chosen for the second half of this book are at the extreme ends of the modern avant-garde, opposed to Eliot's high modernism, as well as to each other. They thus point further ahead, toward a full spectrum of the postmodern revolution: Bertolt Brecht, with his rational, political use of personal alienation, and Antonin Artaud, with his cruel dream of sacred, cathartic violence onstage. But I will also address the work of a third, more recent avant-gardist (whom Martin Esslin calls absurdist), Jean Genet, because he in my view brings together the antithetical theaters of Brecht and Artaud, toward the polymorphous playfulness of the postmodern.

These practitioners continue to influence current trends, especially reactions against modern "realism." For their work reflects the perverse edges of theatrical belief in many previous periods, which point toward today's transcendent concerns. Eliot tried to revive both classical verse drama and the medieval mystery play, then displaced the hysteria of his ritual chorus in a postmodern direction (with the offstage martyrdom of Celia haunting the comic edges of *The Cocktail Party*). Artaud returned to the cruelty of Roman tragedy, Jacobean revenge plays, and Romantic closet drama, as well as oriental conventions and tribal rituals, stimulating recent environmental and paratheatrical experiments. Brecht adapted Shakespeare and non-Western ritual drama for his own anti-Aristotelian purposes, turning theater into an instrument for social change, and inspiring subsequent practitioners of sacred and political performance, from Grotowski to Boal. Genet, like Brecht and Artaud, reached beyond the limits of the Western tradition, with its gender and colonial oppressions, to show the hypocritical, yet repetitive mechanism of violence, which continues, of course, today.

There are many dramatists of loss who are missing in the stages of this book, due to the limits of its mirror. But hopefully the modern drama that is in the limelight here will suggest a new value for theater in relation to other forms of art and various academic disciplines. From its ambiguous origins in prehistoric ritual to its fundamental significance for models of human consciousness (Freud, Lacan, Klein, Winnicott) and social activity (phenomenologist Gadamer, sociologist Goffman, and anthropologist Turner), theater still bears much paradigmatic meaning, despite—and through—its loss of popular appeal to the current rites of film and TV spectatorship. My study will concentrate initially on the relationship between theater and literary theory, particularly in the tension between modern and postmodern stages. It will continue then with a distinct psychoanalytic bent, examining various permutations of loss and desire in modern drama. Perhaps the issues raised will indicate further applications of theatrical perspectives throughout the humanities and social sciences, as well as in art—especially regarding today's metahistorical critique of our Western tradition.

Because of my psychoanalytic approach, I will refer to certain elements of theater architecture as archetypal structures of the mind. I want to use the terms of Western theater's predominant spatial conventions—especially its stage edges—to trace the psychospatial dynamics of actor and watcher, within the mind and society, as shown in modern drama and postmodern theory. Such architectural conventions did develop historically, of course, from ancient Greek and Roman, to medieval, to Renaissance (or early modern) proscenium theater. Also, the stability of a fixed stage edge has been contested by postmodern experiments in "environmental staging"[7]—a recent return to something more like medieval mansions and Renaissance dispersed decor, which created more flexible and fluid positioning of spectators. Today there are many varieties of thrust and arena stages, along with flexible or mobile staging, which alter proscenium dynamics to recover different possibilities in the Euro-American tradition and to borrow from other cultures as well. The pages that follow will likewise show how various modern dramatists revise proscenium conventions to stress distinct psychological dynamics in theatrical space.[8]

With this focus on the proscenium paradigm, I will make two phenomenological claims. First, there is a crucial separation between performer and audience that defines theater—as the threshold of the "stage edge" helps to describe. That edge also distinguishes onstage from offstage space, vertically as well as horizontally, as shown by the proscenium frame. Yet the edges of the stage often evoke a larger dramatic world (like the "diegesis" of film theory). The cutoff creates a surplus of illusion at the edge, as with the infinite vistas of perspective scenery or the closed wings of the box set. While such proscenium devices may extend the spectacle beyond the acting area, the offstage edge remains tied to the primary threshold between actor and spectator. Even if that edge and those identities are momentarily crossed—with, for example, the fluidity of environmental performance, the ambiguities of guerrilla theater, or the redefinition of a "spect-actor" (Boal)—there must be some sense of a stage edge to display performance. As psychoanalyst André Green says, diagnosing the return of the spectator's gaze at the stage edge (downstage and wings): "We may try to eliminate this edge; it is only reconstituted elsewhere" (3). In any theatrical event, the spectator may perform and the actor may watch, to some degree; but the roles of each (and the border between them) must be distinguished, even if they shift, to create a common consciousness of theater.

Second, there is the "choral womb" of theater, which I will define through Eliot's drama and Nietzsche's theoretical archaeology. This ghostly site may still be glimpsed in the empty proscenium "pit" or in the repressed space beneath the stage surface. For it derives from the lost ground of ritual origins—in theater's "birth" from the ancient Dionysian chorus and medieval monks' tropes, according to Nietzsche and the Cambridge anthropologists. While this evolutionary model could be historicized as a Victorian and modernist fantasy, it persists in an uncanny way in the postmodern nostalgia for alternative ethnic origins. Phenomenologically, however, theater also precedes ritual, as the awareness of a psychospatial separation between watcher and watched, which religious or ethnic communion promises to overcome. (Theater may even precede Derridean *écriture,* as Anthony Kubiak has argued [151–52].) While I use the stage edge to mark that separation, I also refer to the gap between spectator and performer—figured by the orchestra pit as remnant of the ancient choral space. Unlike the stage edge that visibly marks a taboo boundary (although sometimes blurred), the choral womb only appears as empty space, as the place of former symbiotic contact now lost. Or perhaps such nostalgic space merely evokes the déjà vu of a dream—the projection of personal loss upon the historical memory of primal ritual. Either way, the affective gap at the stage edge becomes the womblike source of theater's creative power. For the loss of communal and maternal origins, haunting performer and spectator, folds under the lip of the stage, beneath its "apron," producing the force onstage of theatrical presence, however elusive and illusory.

The edge between actor and audience thus reflects the Lacanian "split subject," which has been instrumental in the postmodern deconstruction of the modern self. The gap at that edge is akin to Lacan's definition of the human being as *manque-à-être:* lack of being, or want to be—exemplified in the "mirror stage" (*Écrits* 1–7). While Lacan relates the infant's image in the mirror to the reflection of identity in the mother's eyes and the discrepancy between the imaginary ego *(moi)* and the real body, he does not call that gap a choral womb. My use of that term is inspired more by Julia Kristeva's theory of the *chora* (Platonic "Receptacle of Becoming"), as abject, repressed, semiotic womb of language, law, and psyche, which I apply to the performance (con)text.[9] Yet Lacan's description of the primordial site of personal loss does evoke a ritual stage edge, not only in the mirror stage, but also with the Freudian *fort/da* (when the infant plays "gone" and "here" with a reel [and the real] as toy). "For the game of the cotton-reel is the subject's answer to what the mother's absence has created on the frontier of his domain—the edge of his cradle—namely, a *ditch,* around which one can only play at jumping" (*Four* 62). This orchestra pit at the cradle's edge, in the mother's absence, marks the separation from, yet re-creation of, a choral womb, like theater's separation from and bearing of ritual space—in the playful response to a painful loss at the origins of personal/cultural history.

Lacan's theory of the Desire of the Other, as constituting our lacking being, will also be employed here regarding the desire of audience/actor, in both directions, across the stage edge. But I prefer to use the term *loss* more often than lack or gap, because I want to stress the affective and temporal dimensions in theatrical re-presentation. For I also see the stage edge (especially with Brecht and Genet) as gaping between actor and character, as the one performs the other, making, yet losing identity—and thus playing out more visibly and audibly the death-drive friction between real body, imaginary face, and symbolic name. Hence, the real body, which seems more and more lost in our postmodern simulacrum, is momentarily recovered through live stage communion, only to be lost again in the very same moment of death—between actor and character, performance and audience.

I will also use the term *stage edge* for the edge between modern and postmodern stages, because I see those as reciprocal attitudes toward loss, rather than as distinct periods in a linear progression. As Ihab Hassan remarks: "We are all, I suspect, a little Victorian, Modern, and Postmodern, at once" (*Postmodern* 88). While it may be necessary, or at least normative, for thespians and children to separate from ritual and mother—in order to have a distinct presence onstage and identity in society—this cut is by no means easy, nor ever really complete. Actors and adults are drawn toward the vertiginous edge of ritual and maternal communion, though that means a loss of present identity. From the modern or the postmodern side, that stage edge abyss looks quite different; this difference shows the modern/postmodern shift in response to loss. There is the postmodern leap into the loss of faith, "the Nietzschean *affirmation*—the joyous affirmation of the freeplay of the world and without truth, without origin," even to the point of transcending loss: "*This affirmation then determines the non-center otherwise than as loss of the center.*" Or, the modernist leap into the lost center, as "one seeks to decipher, dreams of deciphering, a truth or an origin which is free from freeplay and from the order of the sign, and lives like an exile the necessity of interpretation" (Derrida, "Structure" 265). Through such leaps of modernist belief in universal truth or of postmodern play in polymorphous diversity, the theater of theory appears—to interpret loss.

My first section, staging the modern and postmodern senses of loss, begins with a debate on poetic belief between Eliot and Richards, rehearsing the New Criticism of literary communion. But the second chapter, on the choral desires of Nietzsche and Eliot, will move between theories of literature and the anthropological dimension of current performance theory (using Victor Turner and Richard Schechner), as well as the more theologically oriented ritual theory of Ronald Grimes and the psychoanalytic theory of Lacan/Kristeva. Whereas this chapter ties the Nietzschean edges of Eliot's choral return to Kristeva's theory of a maternal *chora,* the third chapter shows a postmodern hysteria moving through Eliot's dramatic corpus, in relation to current feminist critiques of Freud and Lacan. These chapters and their interdisciplinary approach complete the section on ritual loss and return but also initiate the main concern of the next section: personal, maternal loss as inspiring various modern/postmodern revolutions of theater and theory.

Derrida's own essays on Artaud will be used then—along with psychoanalyst Melanie Klein's theory of epistemophilic aggression—to analyze the theater of cruelty as a powerful response to ontological loss. For Artaud's psychotic expressions of impossible belief have greatly influenced not only environmental theater and performance art, but also postmodern theory, particularly Derridean deconstruction and Deleuze and Guattari's "schizoanalysis." (Kristeva has also pointed to Artaud's writings as exemplary of the chora's abject, horrifying power.) Likewise, Genet's perverse theater responds with criminal and terroristic violence to the historical loss of familial or cultural identity. Thus, the belief/perversion dialectic of the first section, showing modern and postmodern reactions to psychohistorical loss, will continue into the chapters on Artaud, Genet, and Brecht, though the investigation shifts toward psychobiography, with the mother as originary site of loss.

The multiple mirroring of violence and alienation in Genet's drama, with symptomatic perversions of belief, morality, and beauty, will be analyzed through Lacan's view of an Oedipal theater within the human mind and social psyche (and through Irigaray's view of Plato's cave). This reveals significant differences, as well as similarities, between Artaud and Genet. While Artaud's theatrical violence aims at an ultimate revolutionary truth, behind the mirror of material illusion (and before the infant's mirror stage that Lacan theorizes), Genet finds the truth of violence and revolution in the mirror, subverting all rebellious dreams and acts with the inevitable reality of role-playing. Brecht, on the other hand, holds to a dream of theater as real instrument for social change. He thus perverts its lost, yet lingering, ritual edge toward alienated acting and a critical, thoughtful community of distanced spectators. Artaud's homeopathic medicine/poison is cruelty; Brecht's is alienation. But I will show in the work of both, and in Genet's as well, an originary loss and repressed mourning, which drives their (im)moral ideals of theatrical martyrdom. Hence, the work of mourning exposed within the alienation effect of Brecht's drama will reflect back from my final chapter through the others—to the sublimated loss of ritual in Nietzsche and Eliot.

Among today's many theoretical concerns, certain ones will get special attention here. With all four dramatists and their works, recent feminist critiques of patriarchy will be engaged and questioned. Postcolonial discourse will also be echoed with the borrowing of stories and techniques from non-Western cultures by Artaud, Genet, and Brecht. This reflects, too, an increasing concern of theater today with ethnically diverse performance. Prominent issues of literary and cultural theory, along with those of theatrical and personal history, are thus intertwined in the present account of various creative reactions to a fundamental sense of loss in being human.

The power of loss—to illuminate and delude theatrically—also evokes the theme of martyrdom in modern drama: from Eliot's Thomas and Celia to Artaud's Beatrice (or Artaud himself as viewed by Derrida) and the various revolutionary hero(in)es of Genet and Brecht. Each author's martyrs bear distinct (anti)metaphysical meanings that have particular postmodern edges. In pointing out the tragic reasons for such theatrical victims, I mean to understand critically, but not simply to blame: our patriarchal society and its history, the dramatists' own mothers, or cinema and television as murderous media (theater's patricidal offspring). Rather than figuring such systems and ghosts as melodramatic villains, my juxtaposition of various martyrs of modern drama will question (1) the appeal of victimization, (2) the pleasure of heroic suffering, and (3) the lure of revenge as loss's due—all of which tempt the postmodern as well.

While I do not investigate the biographies of Eliot and Nietzsche in the first section, the choral womb that they desire does reflect a personal relation to the mother (or chora) as originary site of loss. Of course, the patriarchal order of theater and society plays a role, too, in that painful identity, as do fathers in real life. With Artaud, "maternal loss" does not mean a child's ordinary separation from the mother, but rather his inheritance of her loss: her mourning the early death of his siblings, his consequent closeness to her and to her mother, the distance of his father, and other significant details of his personal theater of cruelty. With Genet the orphan, the loss of both parents, and then of a surrogate mother, also reveals much about his hollow rituals onstage and his own antimartyrdom (or perverse holiness as split subject) through theater. Finally, Brecht's repression of mourning after the death of his mother, when he was a young playwright, catalyzes the power of his antiritual theater: his effect of making alien *(Verfremdungseffekt)* rather than feeling alienated *(Entfremd)*,[10] as a rational cure for social ills. But it is not the actual mother of these dramatists that I am blaming or crediting for such pain and creativity.[11] Rather, her role in their lives—as a character in that story—helps to figure the revolutionary power of their drama, as they react to her loss.

Therefore, I hope I am not read as misogynistic when I focus at times on the cruel creativity of the womb (or chora), behind and within the work of the male playwrights in my study. As a man I have little right to speak of the womb as a woman experiences it. Nor would I identify women only with motherhood. And yet, becoming a father recently has increased my appreciation of the physical and emotional burden of a woman's body, as well as the difficult role of patriarchal Other. Even for those of us who do not become mothers, the burden of our own mother's womb haunts us. Whether or not we have that organ in our bodies, we bear a psychic womb related to the physical one we came from[12]—and its many layers of meaning through the psyches of mother, father, dead relatives, and the living society around us. These edges of loss haunt modern drama and postmodern theory, as well as the pages that follow.

Psychohistory
Ritual Returns

Chapter 1

Belief in Poetry
Eliot and Richards

To many postmodern theorists, *belief* is a term bearing the taint of religion. Yet today's critical theory also expresses a belief in the value of questioning all beliefs and truths. It even wants to question itself, "to undo the closures constituted by theory *from within*" (Carroll 3). In common usage, belief refers not only to institutional religion or the supernatural, but also to any sort of conviction, trust, persuasion, expectation, or even tentative opinion. I propose to use the term through the paradigm of theater, specifically in relation to the meeting point of perspectives at the stage's edge—and the sense of loss in that meeting. Such a theatrical encounter involves both belief and disbelief, complicity and questioning, traditional conventions and their perversion, to greater or lesser degrees. It also includes affect in relation to the body as well as intellect. So does belief in the realm of theory, whether that of modern New Critics or of postmodern critical theorists, though the character of belief changes considerably among them. (The plot changes as well, even more so as postmodernists claim not to have any master narrative.) Thus, as I recast the modern/postmodern debate in terms of belief and perversion, I am not simply aligning modernism with belief and postmodernism with perversion. For I want to view, too, the perversity within belief (and vice versa) of both stages.[1]

The term *perversion,* in its most general sense, means a turning away from the dominant social order, from what is considered to be (or has been) "normal" in belief and action. Yet the normality and orthodoxy of any order of belief requires a perverse edge to substantiate it. (Elaine Scarry has recently described how pain inflicted upon the body of a tortured victim substantiates belief in religious and capitalist systems.) Hence perversion delimits belief and also exists at the center of it. Theater, as underground or avant-garde political force, and even sometimes as official institution, locates itself at this perverse, "liminoid" edge of dominant social views (Turner, *From Ritual* 54) but also reflects perversity at the center of society.

For theater often displays the potential acting out of conflict beyond the limits of current law.

So, too, do some postmodern believers. Gay and lesbian theory, for example, tends to embrace the "perverse" label, with intentional, activist irony. I will use the term with regard to the specific psychosexual traits of theater: fetishism, voyeurism, exhibitionism, and sadomasochism. But I will also use it in a more general sense to show a partisan mirror (perverse image) at the modern/postmodern stage edge: a perspective upon the other side's beliefs, or responses to loss, as perverse to one's own ideology. That is why I begin with the debate between two New Critics, T. S. Eliot and I. A. Richards, on the issue of belief in reading poetry. Not only does this relate to Eliot's own poetic drama, which I will analyze in the next two chapters; it also shows the tension between religious and scientific beliefs (or between religious and sexual concerns) within high modernism—as it moves toward postmodern theatricality. Furthermore, this debate illuminates Eliot's specific desire for theatrical community, as he resurrects (then displaces) a ritual chorus in his plays.

Eliot's theories of belief and community continue to influence more recent debates. For example, William Corlett desires the emancipatory extravagance of deconstruction, to undo the hierarchical subjugation (which Eliot valued) implicit in the unity of community. Richard Shusterman, on the other hand, advocates an Eliotic, structured freedom versus the "empty essentialism" of poststructuralist emancipation (218).[2] A half century ago, Eliot himself faced a similar dilemma. He became dissatisfied with the appeal to divine authority in his early dramas, because they structured communal perception through exclusivity—alienating the secular spectator to the degree that they involved the ritual believer. Eliot's own double bind of theatrical desire for divine and human realities, sacred and secular orders, elite and popular audiences thus elucidates a crucial tension between metaphysical and ethical drives—which has become a paradigmatic agon of modern drama and postmodern theory. Yet, one can already see the beginnings of this in Eliot's debate with Richards on poetic belief.

The Perverse Sharing of Belief

Two years before his play *Murder in the Cathedral* was performed at Canterbury, T. S. Eliot gave the Charles Eliot Norton lectures at Harvard University (published as *The Use of Poetry and the Use of Criticism*). In them he credits I. A. Richards for "having done the pioneer work in the problem of Belief in the enjoyment of poetry" (90–91). Eliot then refers to his own essay on Dante (from 1929), in which he described, *pace* Coleridge, a suspension of belief as well as disbelief in the enjoyment of reading the *Divine Comedy* (*Selected Essays* [*SE*] 219). In that earlier essay, Eliot had insisted upon a separation between the reader's and author's beliefs, between aesthetic enjoyment and the sharing of beliefs with an author (229). In the 1932–33 lectures at Harvard, however, Eliot alters his own earlier theory of belief in literature and elaborates it in contrast to Richards's.

In *Practical Criticism* Richards had rejected Coleridge's famous remark on the willing suspension of disbelief,[3] claiming that "the question of belief or disbelief, in the intellectual sense, never arises when we are reading well" (qtd. in Eliot, *Use* 95). But Eliot, in opposition to Richards and to his own earlier view on Dante, describes how an author's belief, as presented in a poem, can indeed block the reader's enjoyment of it. Eliot uses as an example his own intoxication with Shelley's poetry at the age of fifteen (when Richards's statement did apply, he says) and contrasts that with his current distaste for the same poetry because of its author's untenable beliefs (96–97).

As Eliot continues to articulate a theory of belief in relation to poetry—against that of Richards—he reveals the crucial paradox of his own future theatrical works. Eliot mocks the secular technique of meditation that Richards proposes as a "ritual for heightening sincerity" in the reading of poetry (qtd. in *Use* 131). Eliot calls this contemplative program "sentimental," a mere "modern substitute for the *Exercises* of St. Ignatius" (Eliot 134). But Eliot's own plays and late poetry will demand that a secular audience and readership enter a modern ritual space based on certain religious traditions and the author's own belief in their specific sense and meaning. Actually, Eliot is judging inadequate in Richards's theory what he himself will attempt in lyric and drama. The result will be an irresolvable tension between sacred and secular, between temporal community and eternal communion, between inclusion or exclusion of the reader/spectator, particularly in the performance of his plays onstage.

When Eliot praises Dante's poetry (in the earlier essay) as "the one universal school of style for the writing of poetry in any language" (*SE* 228–29), he betrays his own admiration for the long history and tradition of the Roman Catholic Church, despite his recent conversion to the Church of England. He calls Dante's writing "safer to follow" as a model for poetry than that of "any English poet, including Shakespeare" (229). To allow for this preference, he must insist on the potential of a non-Catholic to perceive as much or more than a Catholic in reading Dante's poetry. "I will not deny that it may be in practice easier for a Catholic to grasp the meaning, in many places, than for the ordinary agnostic; but that is not because the Catholic believes, but because he has been instructed" (219). Eliot had made his own public profession of faith in the Church of England two years before, not as an "Anglican" but as an "Anglo-Catholic." He thus expresses his own partial exclusion from the poetic and religious tradition he so much admires. *Murder in the Cathedral* attempts to close the gap by presenting the drama of a Roman Catholic saint martyred in the cathedral that would later become the center of the Church of England. But it also reproduces—and theatrically plays with—this gap between the character of a twelfth-century Thomas à Becket and his twentieth-century author and audience.

Communal Hierarchy

Eliot's later essays in *The Idea of a Christian Society* (1940) and *Notes towards the Definition of Culture* (1948) bind together ideals of society, culture, and faith, to a degree that might be seen (especially in the secularity of today's academia) as perverse.[4] In the latter book he declares: "no culture has appeared or developed except together with a religion." And he speaks of "Christian culture as the highest culture . . . that the world has ever known" (15). In the former book he describes "a vertical as well as a horizontal measurement" for the capability of believing anything (37). Yet this is not a new perversity in Eliot's thought. It reflects and extends his earlier vision of theater, particularly the hierarchical belief structure of *Murder in the Cathedral.*

In his Norton lectures, two years before that play appeared onstage, Eliot mentions a verse play that he had already designed with

> one character whose sensibility and intelligence should be on the plane of the most sensitive and intelligent members of the audience. . . . There was to be an understanding between this protagonist and a small number of the audience, while the rest of the audience would share the responses of the other characters in the play.

These characters Eliot describes as "material, literal-minded and visionless" (*Use* 153). But the Jamesian condescension in this proposed design does not go as far as Yeats's "aristocratic theater" for an elite few. Eliot remains enamored of theater's potential for connecting with mass culture, as suggested by his *Criterion* commentaries of the 1920s, particularly in his eulogizing of music hall performer Marie Lloyd.[5] With his 1933 Norton lectures,

Eliot continues to convey this desire for a mass audience: "The ideal medium for poetry, to my mind, and the most direct means of social 'usefulness' for poetry, is the theater" (*Use* 153). Yet, his later project to define culture through the idea of a Christian society finds its prototype here: the ideal social poetry of a modern sacred theater—with hierarchically ordered audience—that Eliot realized to some extent at Canterbury.

The "different degrees of consciousness" in Eliot's 1933 depiction of a theater audience (*Use* 153) corresponds to his 1948 description of "cultural levels." In the latter he reminds his readers "that we should not consider the upper levels as possessing *more* culture than the lower, but as representing a more conscious culture" (*Notes* 48). He admits, however, that "the more conscious becomes the belief, so the more conscious becomes unbelief: indifference, doubt and scepticism appear" (67). And yet, Eliot values the connection between a more conscious belief and doubt, between orthodoxy and protest, between Catholicism and Protestantism. For although an apparently heretical element may grow into a separate faith, it remains tied to its parent tradition: "every sub-culture is dependent upon that from which it is an offshoot. The life of Protestantism depends upon the survival of that against which it protests" (75).[6] On the other hand, the older dominant belief needs its dissenters as well. "As in the relation between social classes . . . a constant struggle between the centripetal and the centrifugal forces is desirable" (82).[7]

In Eliot's Neoplatonic, Christian republic, as in his modern sacred theater, class divisions are necessary (35). Yet continued tensions, mutations, and perversions between classes are also necessary to avoid "the danger of development into a *caste* system" (45). A healthy intersection of belief and perversion is implied at the selvage of Eliot's definition of culture—in the theater of his ideal society. This ideal of theater involves varying degrees (and classes) of cultural consciousness, with both belief and unbelief emanating, horizontally and vertically, from the incarnation of a saintly character onstage, and reverberating in verse and spirit throughout the audience and surrounding community.

Sex, Science, and Purity

Perhaps T. S. Eliot would see as perverse my use of that term for his ideal of belief and unbelief in culture and theater, particularly with its sexual connotations. In his Norton lectures, Eliot takes issue with Richards's interpretation of sex in *The Waste Land*. While he agrees with Richards that Canto XXVI of the *Purgatorio* illuminates his own poem, he disagrees that it "illuminates his persistent concern with sex, the problem of our generation, as religion was the problem of the last" (Richards, *Principles* 292). Or rather, Eliot disputes only the last phrase in that comment, leaving his own sexual concerns, and their possible persistence, unexamined (*Use* 126–28). "My contemporaries seem to me still to be occupied with it [religion], whether they call themselves churchmen, or agnostics, or rationalists, or social revolutionists" (128).[8]

Today it is clear that Richards was correct. Sex is a characteristically modern concern, though that began, as Michel Foucault has demonstrated, in the Victorian period, in both a repression of overt sexual activity and an obsession with it in discourse. Of course, the concern with sex continues into, and is amplified by, postmodern discourse, both in the revolutions of recent theory and the explicit perversions of avant-garde performance art. Thus Foucault describes, from a postmodern perspective, the earlier development of perversity in the modern: "Modern society is perverse, not in spite of its puritanism or as if from a backlash provoked by its hypocrisy; it is in actual fact, and directly, perverse" (*History* 47). But it is my contention in the following pages that Eliot was also correct, that modern theater continues to be occupied, too, with problems of belief and unbelief, as manifestations of a fundamental loss, although not always in Eliot's overtly religious way. I will also show postmodern theory continuing that concern today—though it may wish at times to deny or repress it, that is, to lose the belief in the lost.

While admitting a certain leap of faith, Richards insisted on differentiating intellect from emotion in the experience of art, separating "scientific beliefs" from "emotive beliefs."[9] He describes the former as "grounded in fact" (*Principles* 280), whereas emotive beliefs are "parasitic" because they will, "as is shown by certain doses of alcohol or hashish, . . . readily attach themselves to almost any reference, distorting it to suit their purpose" (279). Bertolt Brecht, in his *Short Organum* of 1949, criticized audiences who "look at the stage as if in a trance: an expression which comes from the Middle Ages, from the days of witches and priests" (*Brecht on Theatre* 187). He demands the exact opposite from the actor and audience of his epic theater: "Aiming not to put his audience into a trance, he must not go into a trance himself" (193). In 1926 Richards had also tried to proclaim the end of such religious and magical elements, though he admitted that they persist in art, even as the world turns away from a dominant "Magical View," involving "belief in Inspiration and the beliefs underlying Ritual," toward a more scientific view (*Science* 57–58). According to Richards, it is so important to separate scientific knowledge from emotive belief that he describes "the intermingling of knowledge and belief [as being] indeed a perversion" (*Principles* 282–83). He calls this intermingling "the most insidious perversion to which the mind is liable" (282).

Neither scientific nor religious belief is involved for Richards in the reading of *King Lear* (*Principles* 282; *Science* 72–73)—a point that Eliot addressed in his 1927 review of Richards's *Science and Poetry*. Eliot notes there (as he will again in 1933) the paradox of Richards's own belief in salvation through poetry. "Mr. Richards thinks that the only thing that can save us from 'mental chaos' is poetry, a poetry of the future detached from all belief" ("Literature" 242–43)—from all belief, that is, except for the belief in science.[10] In criticizing Richards, Eliot emphasizes, too, the parallel between religious and scientific belief. "If one is going to consider philosophically the nature of Belief, it is as dangerous to be a scientist as to be a theologian; the scientist, still more—in our time—than the theologian, will be prejudiced as to the nature of Truth" (241).

The parallel, though contrary, prejudices of each of these modern critics—in scientific and theological directions—sets the stage for our current investigation of theater and theory, of the "nature of truth" onstage and in perspectives upon art and culture. While Eliot's belief in theological truth may seem perverse by today's heterodox standards,[11] Richards's hope for a poetry purified from belief is just as extreme. Thus, our differences from them must be seen against the historical backdrop of their debate. Eliot ends his *Idea of a Christian Society* with a postscript dated September 6, 1939. He says that "the possibility of war, which has now been realised, was always present"; but he adds that "the alignment of forces which has now revealed itself should bring more clearly to our consciousness the alternative of Christianity or paganism" (66). Eliot is trying to rally his society against the pagan forces gathering in Germany, to find a renewed, collective belief to save European culture from the powers of Nazism,[12] the way that Richards had sought a purified poetry to defend against the insidious perversion of emotive belief. From our vantage point upon the past, we see today that neither Christianity nor science can claim to have been purely against those forces in Europe that led to such obvious evil. Yet we also face the impurity of our own beliefs in art, theory, and culture—be they emotive, scientific, or theological—and the difficulty of discerning what mode of perversity is creative or virulent.

German theory since World War II has mostly avoided Nietzsche and Heidegger, because both were implicated in the workings of Nazism. French theory, however, has picked up the writings of both, as well as those of Marx and Freud, and elaborated them (through its own philosophical tradition) in relation to religion, morality, language, Being, culture, sexuality, and art. Jean-François Lyotard, for example, uses Marx and Freud to announce, like I. A. Richards, the end of a predominantly religious world, in which art (and culture itself) "functions as a religion, as something that joins people by permitting them to communicate" (*Postmodern* 71). He champions instead the modern, revolutionary, moral function of "anti-art" (using a theatrical trope): "What art does—what it ought to do—is always to unmask all attempts to reconstitute a pseudo-religion" (72). He also privileges libidinal desire as antitheory, "play[ing] Marx and Freud off against each other" (Carroll 43). Foucault, too, praises the power of the perverse. The postmodern stage of his "theatrum philosophicum" displays a new sense of metaphysics, "freed from its original profundity as well as from a supreme being" (*Language* 171). Yet, the new freedom of the "phantasmaphysics" (described by Deleuze) springs not only from the dead God that Nietzsche proclaimed, but also from "the epidermic play of perversity," which Foucault sees in Freud and Artaud, as they "exclude each other and give rise to a mutual resonance" (171–72).[13]

I shall explore this postmodern belief in perversity further in chapter 4, through Derrida's essays on Artaud. Derrida elaborates the "end of metaphysics" that Heidegger announced by investigating the "fate of representation" in Artaud's dream of theater, and believes he discovers there a "nontheological space." But I will show, in a Freudian deconstruction of Derrida's dream of Artaud, that this involves a postmodern nostalgia, or mourning, for what Ned Lukacher has termed "the lost metaphysical object" (90)—similar to Eliot's modernist longing for the lost communion of cultural belief.[14] Some of today's Marxist theorists, such as Fredric Jameson (following Ernst Bloch), have also expressed a belief in the future return of their lost object of "primitive communism" (*Political* 290–91). The desire for and belief in a renewal of a lost order can be seen, too, in feminist theorists who follow Luce Irigaray's deliberate perversion of Lacanian theory and Western philosophy—which I shall investigate in chapter 5. Like Genet's theatrical desire within the prison of his outlaw identity and maternal void, Irigaray seeks a way out of the theater of Plato's cave through a return to lost, feminine origins, before the Name and No of patriarchal intervention. In a different Lacanian vein, mined throughout the coming chapters, but especially in the sixth regarding Brecht, Julia Kristeva looks to the semiotic (and amniotic) chora of language, and to the abject in literature, for the power of poetic revolution and feminine *jouissance*. I will thus demonstrate, too, a fundamental Oedipal/theatrical dynamic in postmodernism (or at least in its core, disseminating movement of poststructuralism), though many feminists have used Lacan and Derrida to repudiate Freud's confidence in the Oedipus complex. Even the anti-Oedipal schizo-analysis of Gilles Deleuze and Félix Guattari betrays a persistent tie between such purposely perverse theories and the parent tradition and beliefs they are rebelling against.

The dynamics of a theater of liberation in postmodern theory may seem antithetical to the theological and scientific concerns of Eliot and Richards. Yet they share, despite conspicuous differences, a vital dialogue between belief and perversion, as they struggle to redefine the lost Other in the shifting ideological borders of a modern/postmodern stage. Even Eliot valued the "perverse" genius of Baudelaire's "Satanism," in which he saw a rediscovery of Christianity "at the beginning" (SE 373–74). Here, as in his own early drama, Eliot's desire parallels the fascination of postmodern theory with Nietzsche and Artaud, and their rediscovery of perverse energies at the origins of Western theater. This I shall specifically relate to current views on the feminine and maternal versus the masculine and patriarchal. For the "insidious perversion" that Richards denounced in emotive belief takes a positive charge in the more polymorphous inclinations of postmodernism. Yet it also serves to illustrate a critical difference between Artaud and Brecht, whose influence upon both theater and theory continues to this day. It indicates, too, a psychopathological edge to the gap between performer and spectator, as we see in the radical theodicies of Eliot and Artaud, the criminal passions of Genet, and even the scientific gestures of Brecht.

The Eliot/Richards debate on poetic faith reveals a dangerous horizon to the most compelling energies of postmodern theory. Yet we must enhance the irresolvable dialectic between speculative perversions and ideological beliefs.[15] For the creative wound of theater's mythical birth returns to us not only through the ritual stages of Eliot, Artaud, and Genet—and the antiritual effects of Brecht. It is also summoned by today's antiaesthetic, avowedly secular, and counterphallocentric theories. These are now creating new communal heroes, villains, and victims, despite (and through) their rebellion against older hierarchical orders. Thus, the modern desire for tragic meaning, sacrifice, and scapegoats persists,[16] even with the satyr play of postmodern loss.

Chapter 2

Redressing the Chorus
Nietzsche in Eliot

Friedrich Nietzsche has had as profound and pervasive an influence upon postmodern theory as T. S. Eliot did upon modernist New Criticism. Particularly through the French poststructuralists, who pulled Nietzsche out of Nazi uniform, his Dionysian energy, under other guises, has come to typify much of the newer critical theories in North America. Not only deconstruction, but also the Marxist New Historicism and the many varieties of post-Lacanian feminism show a distinctive revolutionary spirit traceable to Nietzschean performance. In the current battle between such rebel theorists and formerly dominant critics, a reevaluation of Nietzsche's first philosophical work, *The Birth of Tragedy,* along with Eliot's early religious drama, becomes highly significant. Both involve a return to lost ritual sources, especially to the transformative power of a liminal chorus—but for very different reasons.

Whether or not the dithyrambic chorus is the historical source of ancient Greek tragedy will not be debated here—though that has become an important bone of contention in recent decades, through various critiques both of the Cambridge School, seminal to Eliot, and of Nietzsche.[1] Instead, I am analyzing the ritualization[2] of desire, within Eliot's drama, for a Nietzschean choral womb, as it reflects the larger social drama of conflicting generations in twentieth-century literature and theory. For example, Nietzsche's critique of metaphysics in his later works (so influential upon poststructuralist theory), particularly his attack on the "ascetic priest" in *On the Genealogy of Morals,* would appear to be completely antithetical to Eliot's transcendental Christian drama, especially to the ascetic hero of *Murder in the Cathedral.* Yet even in that later work, Nietzsche expresses his own ascetic idealism. "All my honor to the ascetic ideal *insofar as it is honest!* so long as it believes in itself and does not play tricks on us" (158).[3] It is this anti-Christian ascetic ideal, from Nietzsche's Dionysian Apollo to his later, messianic Zarathustra (*Genealogy* 96)[4] that I find mirrored (as perverse image) in Eliot's *Murder* chorus and Saint Thomas.

Eliot, for his part, mostly ignored Nietzsche in his own critical writings (Leavell 111). However, in a book review, twenty years before *Murder in the Cathedral,* Eliot stated: "one does not receive the impression that Nietzsche held any consistent moral policy in regard to the cosmic flux." Yet he also expressed "regret for the omission of any account of Nietzsche's views on art" in the book he was reviewing (427). This suggests that the shadow of Nietzsche's Dionysus haunts the moral politics of Eliot's Thomas and the sacred, cosmic flux of his chorus.

Christian Drama and Anti-art

According to the *Oxford English Dictionary,* the word *modernism*—aside from all its recently explored meanings—was used early in the twentieth century to describe a progressive, theological movement in the Roman Catholic Church that tried to modify traditional beliefs in accordance with modern criticism. In his own modern theological turn, Eliot chose the Anglo-Catholic movement (in the Church of England) that John Henry Newman had headed in the previous century. In "Lancelot Andrewes" Eliot praised the same Elizabethan theologians that Newman had invoked in his *Apologia Pro Vita Sua* sixty years before. Eliot saw them as the basis for England's greatest playwrights: "if the Church of Elizabeth is worthy of the age of Shakespeare and Jonson, that is because of the work of Hooker and Andrewes" (*SE* 301). While Eliot did not follow Newman into the Roman Catholic Church,[5] his attempt at a ritual drama looked to that older Christian tradition, through which formal Western theater had found its medieval rebirth. Eliot's revival of the chorus also recalls the (theoretical) origins of theater in ancient Greece. Yet he was not alone in trying to create a modern sacred drama. Eliot headed a burgeoning movement that continued for several decades to hold much promise for believers in both Christianity and theater.[6]

In the preface to his 1967 study of this movement, William Spanos details a "curious irony . . . [in the] conventional critique of the Christian attitude toward art." He insists that it is not the "modern Christian imagination . . . [that is] inimical to temporality," but rather the radical disillusionment of the humanistic imagination (from Descartes through Wittgenstein and Sartre), which "is perilously close to hatred of the phenomenal world and is objectified in a militant aesthetic of anti-art" (*Christian* x).

Here one sees a modernist theological defense against the postmodern vein of humanism: a threatening, "antistructural communitas" (Turner, *From Ritual* 45–49) developing through existentialist philosophy and avant-garde art into the rebellious perversity of postmodern theory. Jean-François Lyotard (writing in 1970) also calls this militant aesthetic "anti-art." But he praises it as the power to reveal ideological (and normative) communitas on the other side: "to unmask all attempts to reconstitute a pseudo-religion [in art and culture] . . . as ideological" (*Driftworks* 72).

The antistructural ideal of what Turner calls spontaneous communitas (*From Ritual* 47–48) also becomes apparent in the work of other postmodern theorists, as they unmask explicit ties between belief and ideology. For example, New Historicist Stephen Greenblatt has pointed to such a connection in Renaissance "self-fashioning" and colonial "improvisation" (227–29). More recently, Marxist theorist Terry Eagleton has delineated the double power of belief and perversion (or subversion) in the ideology of the aesthetic, from the eighteenth through the twentieth centuries. "The aesthetic, then, is from the beginning [with Baumgarten's *Aesthetica* in 1750] a contradictory, double-edged concept"—both "a genuine emancipatory force" and "a supremely effective mode of political hegemony" (*Ideology* 28).[7] As we investigate the overtly theological transcendentalism of Eliot's drama, we shall also discover a sublimated perversity in his tragic choruses, their rapture for a double-edged aesthetic reason. This is not the anti-art that Lyotard admires, but it could be viewed retrospectively as an anti-anti-art, unmasking the belief in perversion of today's postmodern theories.

The Communal Wound

Using Erich Auerbach's theory of the *figura*, Spanos explains that Eliot's modern verse interpretation of the historical murder of Thomas à Becket is "a *figura Christi*, a sacramental action, [both] itself and other than itself."[8] In the historical intersections of cyclical, kairological time, such a figure of God's purpose fulfills the previous, "real and archetypal sacrifice of Christ" and also points to a future "fulfillment of the eternal pattern" (*Christian* 94). One could add (in a somewhat Bakhtinian vein) that each reenactment of Eliot's play dialogically incarnates this sacrifice in theatrical time and space onstage.[9] Spanos's analysis, however, diminishes the role of the chorus. He briefly mentions that the chorus "mediates between the audience and the action"; yet he calls this "the least direct link" in connecting the natural time of the audience to the sacramental significance of the play

(*Christian* 100–101). Spanos does describe the submission of Thomas "to a passive activeness" and the parallel consent of the chorus "to an active patience" (90), but he gives no indication of the perversity between them.[10]

In my investigation of the modern/postmodern stage edge, the chorus is of prime importance: particularly as it marks the correlatives between Eliot's incarnation of modernist desire and Nietzsche's theatrical impact upon postmodernism. But rather than taking the *figura* of the to-be-martyred Thomas as an archetypal, theological *donnée* (as Spanos does), I shall examine how the chorus plays its role between spectators and stage to create this ritual fetish figure. For there is also a perversely negative theology in Eliot's play, through which libidinal and providential economies intersect. The chorus, having "smelt them, the death-bringers," consents with Becket to his murder/martyrdom, according to God's purpose (*Complete Poems and Plays* [*CPP*] 207). Yet they must struggle, along with (and against) him,[11] to perfect their desire for his death. Their fetishizing of his impending demise can then sublimate a collective death drive toward his transcendent saintliness and their conjoining *jouissance*.

The Apollonian *figura* of St. Thomas needs his Dionysian chorus, the anonymous women of Canterbury, who sacrifice their own particular, ordinary sufferings in order to fetishize his.

> We know of oppression and torture,
> We know of extortion and violence,
> Destitution, disease,
> The old without fire in winter,
> The child without milk in summer,
> Our labour taken away from us,
> Our sins made heavier upon us.
> We have seen the young man mutilated,
> The torn girl trembling by the mill-stream.
> And meanwhile we have gone on living,
> Living and partly living.
>
> (*CPP* 195)

But this refocusing of daily communal loss, toward sublime meaning in the martyr's destiny, also requires the investment of the reader/spectator—a personal cathexis that paradoxically combines faith and despair, love and hate, naive hope and painful knowledge. For the fetish, as substitute for the lost maternal phallus (according to Freud), becomes a ritual surrogate in the writer's, reader's, and spectator's double bind of desire. As J.-B. Pontalis has pointed out (72–76), Freud elucidates a passionate clash of belief and knowledge regarding the fetish:[12] I know she does not have the phallus (nor do I, insists Lacan), yet I believe she does. I empower the fetish, as substitute for maternal/personal loss—and as expression of the womb's fearful power. Thus, the maternal "labour" of Eliot's chorus (as uterine chora, not just phallic lack) gives birth to the fetish-hero onstage, by evoking the creative tension of belief and disbelief in the spectator.

The twentieth-century audience is not immune to this holy psychopathology of the play (depending, of course, on the acuity of performance). Eliot's drama implies that modern spectators do participate, through varying degrees of belief and unbelief (investment or detachment), in the ritual sacrifice of the fetish—in the murder of Thomas and the violation of the chorus. Thomas himself suggests this at the end of part 1 (*CPP* 197). And the Third Knight reemphasizes it in the play's postritual, Brechtian ending.[13] "I am going to appeal not to your emotions but to your reason," he says to the audience (216). Then he directly confronts them with their retroactive role in the killing, both theatrically and historically. "We have served your interests; we merit your applause; and if there is any guilt whatever in the matter, you must share it with us" (218). This applied particularly well to the play's original performance in the chapter house adjacent to Canterbury Cathedral in 1935. For the spectators of the play at that time were also the "sightseers" that the chorus mentions in their final verses. Some of these modern Canterbury pilgrims (with the aid of Eliot's chorus) found their contemporary beliefs, as well as voyeuristic, fetishistic desires, engaged in the play's ritual recreation of martyrdom upon the same "holy ground" (221) that was inseminated by a martyr's blood eight hundred years before. But to what degree the play's ritual (shifting from liminal to liminoid, in Turner's terms) would infect the blood of a mostly secular audience at a different location—and on what grounds—remains a crucial issue in our excavation.

E. Martin Browne remarks that the purpose of *Murder in the Cathedral* in its first performance at Canterbury (which he directed) "was to be the same as that of most Greek tragedies—to celebrate the cult associated with a sacred spot by displaying the story of its origin" (*Making* 37). Nietzsche also points to the geography of ancient Greek theater in his *Birth of Tragedy*. But it is the mythical shapes and powers of nature that Nietzsche sees in the originating architecture of Western theater, rather than any ecclesiastical story.[14]

The form of the Greek theater recalls a lonely valley in the mountains: the architecture of the scene appears like a luminous cloud formation that the Bacchants swarming over the mountains behold from a height—like the splendid frame in which the image of Dionysus is revealed to them. (63)

Here the bacchants, the worshipers of Dionysus, would seem to correspond to the Greek theater audience, who were actually seated in a *theatron* cut into the hillside.

But the spectators do not become worshipers of Dionysus simply by taking their seats near a sacred spot. Nietzsche focuses his analysis on the dithyrambic "satyr chorus," from which, he says, Attic tragedy originally arose, as the crucial binding element between performer and spectator (56).[15] Adapting A. W. Schlegel's formulation of the chorus as "ideal spectator" *(Idealische Zuschauer),* Nietzsche tries to expel from it the contemporary sense of a "public of spectators" (62). He depicts the ancient Greeks seated in their *theatron* as imaginatively merging into the chorus, as they watch the play onstage "in absorbed contemplation" (63). The chorus for Nietzsche is not just the ideal spectator, but indeed the only spectator: "the only beholder . . . of the visionary world of the scene" (62). Nietzsche thus rejects Schiller's "ideal" distancing function in Schlegel's formula (Carlson 179). He shifts the organic unity and genius of the author (in Schlegel's extension of Goethe's theory) to nature itself, or rather to the Dionysian in nature and human culture—breaking through both the satyrs and citizens who surround the stage.

Here, too, Nietzsche gives as evidence the geography and architecture of Attic theater: "the terraced structure of concentric arcs made it possible for everybody to actually *overlook* the whole world of culture" (63). For Nietzsche both Western culture and Christian religion are overlooked and overcome in this willful return to the ancient roots of theater, to the communal wound of a single chorus of spectators. Nietzsche, as anti-Christian spectator/speculator, thus makes a Pascalian wager upon theater's eternal return: not merely as the celebration of a sacred spot, but as the omphalos (navel of the earth) in his dream of a future, Dionysian reality.[16] Although Nietzsche loses the bet historically (through his later disillusionment with Wagnerian opera), his dream of the Greek stage and belief in its choral edge bleeds into his later views of the will to power, death of God, and eternal repetition/return—which have in turn stimulated the theatricality of postmodern theory.

Chorus as Lens and Womb

Browne describes the chorus of *Murder in the Cathedral* as the play's "true protagonist" and explicitly connects it to the Dionysian chorus of ancient Greek theater ("Christian" 132–33). R. P. Blackmur, writing in 1935, the year of the Canterbury premiere, stressed the literary importance of the chorus's lines as "the finest poetry" in the play and as a more successful "fusion of interests" than the chorus of Eliot's previous play, *The Rock* (145). However, Hugh Kenner, writing thirty years later, called the *Murder* chorus "a poetic embarrassment" (244). Kenner speculates that Eliot discovered with *The Rock* that "crisp and athletic" choral verses become "unintelligible" in performance, hence the "ululating logorrhea" and "reduplication of epithets" in his next chorus (242–43). Kenner also criticizes the *Murder* chorus's "absence of focus," condemning it, through Eliot's own attack on Shakespeare's *Hamlet,* as "lack[ing] an objective correlative" (243). But from a postmodern perspective, the ululating verses of the chorus in performance might be analyzed as the "echolalias" of an abject, semiotic chora (Kristeva, "Within" 37–38),[17] emerging from beneath the oppressive edge of a modernist stage and Kenner's crisp expectations. Yet, to the degree that it may work in performance as a fusion and focus of interest (over the diffused mycelium of an orchestral abyss), the chorus itself functions as an objective correlative to Thomas's passionate reason for dying,[18] as well as a Nietzschean lens for believing spectators to view his holiness and immortality onstage.

In his own 1951 critique of *Murder in the Cathedral,* T. S. Eliot mentions two "reasons for depending, in that play, so heavily upon the assistance of the chorus" (*Poetry* 28). Eliot says he wanted to concentrate the drama on Becket's death and martyrdom, through "a chorus of excited and sometimes hysterical women, reflecting in their emotion the significance of the action." He also states (with ostensible modesty about his inexperience in writing dramatic dialogue): "The use of a chorus strengthened the power, and concealed the defects of my theatrical technique." But it is not only "dramatic weaknesses" that are "covered up by the cries of the women" (29). His Canterbury bacchants, like those envisioned in ancient Greece by Nietzsche, (re)cover the theological and theatrical chasm between a twelfth-century saint being martyred onstage and the twentieth-century audience, watching him with varying degrees of complicity and faith. Thus, the semiotic hysteria of the chorus, along with the symbolic focus of their poetry, becomes crucial to the performative credibility of Eliot's modern tragedy.

The chorus begins the play by resisting Thomas's treasonous return from exile. Like Prufrock they would prefer not to force the moment to its crisis: "we are content if we are left alone" (*CPP* 176). Yet they clairvoyantly sense an impending, irresistible catastrophe that will not leave them alone, that will bring their voices and visions together into communal, transformative suffering. "Some presage of an act / Which our eyes are compelled to witness, has forced our feet / Towards the cathedral" (175). Here the chorus stimulates, to some degree, the fear and pity of a watching theater audience, particularly of the 1935 pilgrims. This would ostensibly be for moral, not perverse purposes; but there is also a Dionysian edge to Eliot's classical chorus. The hysterics of Canterbury intensify a ritual cathexis of belief and desire into the voyeuristic vortex that connects (at least some) spectators to the sacrifice onstage and gives birth to its modern meaning. In this sense the audience joins the chorus as liminal chora: "forced to bear witness" (175).

Nietzsche tried to (de)purify Aristotle's theory of catharsis from the "moral vision" of neoclassical aestheticians by insisting on a "pathological" element to such purgation/procreation. According to Nietzsche the "truly aesthetic listener" along with "the tragic artist . . . creates his figures like a fecund divinity of individuation." But this is not to be understood as a mere Aristotelian imitation of nature. Rather, a "vast Dionysian impulse then devours" the artist's and spectator's empirical "world of phenomena"; they "sense beyond it, and through its destruction, the highest artistic primal joy, in the bosom of the primordial One" (*Birth* 132). Paradoxically, the Nietzschean edges of Eliot's stage suggest opposite extremes: both the highest modernist desire for ritual potency and the deconstructive, antimetaphysical horizon ahead. But Eliot's drama did not go as far as Nietzsche's theory (toward antistructural, spontaneous communitas) in either the sacred or secular direction.

In addition to Aristotle's theories, Nietzsche criticizes the "new Socratic-optimistic stage world" of Sophocles' tragedies as "the first step toward the *destruction* of the chorus, whose phases follow one another with alarming rapidity in Euripides, Agathon, and the New Comedy." As Nietzsche sees it, Socrates' "dialectic drives *music* out of tragedy" and thus ruins tragedy's "visible symbolizing of music, as the dream-world of a Dionysian intoxication" (92). Eliot also mistrusted the emotive power of tragedy, unless it could be channeled through an objective correlative. His early, optimistic attempt to revive verse drama through modern tragedy does create a visible symbolizing of music, but not as intoxicating dream-world. Eliot's Christian dialectic resurrects a Greek-like chorus, yet makes the Dionysian more Socratic (from a Nietzschean perspective), tying it to the medieval morality play. For Eliot "kept in mind," he said, "the versification of *Everyman*" while writing *Murder in the Cathedral* (*Poetry* 27). The passion of its supposedly tragic hero ultimately obeys God's plan, rather than rebelling with hubris against the gods. Despite the knights' attempt at a Brechtian conclusion, the chorus intercedes with a final note: a kyrie eleison (*CPP* 221) intimating a future, happy end to the tragedy, as divine comedy.

According to Nietzsche, the Sophoclean chorus destroys the Dionysian "character" of the dithyrambic chorus by making it "almost co-ordinate with the actors, just as if it were elevated from the orchestra into the scene" onstage (*Birth* 92). After *Murder in the Cathedral* Eliot moves consciously in that direction, paralleling what Nietzsche had condemned as Socrates', Aristotle's, and Sophocles' perversion of the pre-Attic chorus. "Tracing out the route of exploration" in his previous drama, Eliot in 1951 acknowledges that audiences will "put up with verse from the lips of personages dressed in the fashion of some distant age"; but he despises such acceptance as that of a mere "poetry recital." Sounding anti-Nietzschean and nearly Brechtian, he states: "What we have to do is to bring poetry into the world in which the audience lives and to which it returns when it leaves the theater; not to transport the audience into some imaginary world totally unlike its own" (*Poetry* 31).

The intersection of Eliot's Nietzschean and anti-Nietzschean edges can be seen in his elegy to Marie Lloyd of 1923. Eliot admired the music-hall chorus, with which the "working man . . . joined" as he watched Lloyd onstage, "himself performing part of the act" (*SE* 407). This early admiration, prior to Eliot's own involvement with theater, parallels Nietzsche's vision of the ancient Greek audience joining the chorus as a single, active spectator. Yet it also illustrates Eliot's attraction to the popular, which will gradually turn him away from sacred plots and explicit choruses. In 1951, after seeing four of his plays produced onstage, the first two in religious settings and the latter two in secular theaters, Eliot still believes in a potential verse drama that would make "our own sordid, dreary daily world . . . suddenly illuminated and transfigured" (*Poetry* 32). But he has decided that this will not be achieved through a separate choral body at the edge of the stage, which reeks of poetry recitals and audiences that "expect to have to put up with poetry" (25–26). In fact, such a chorus worked in *Murder in the Cathedral* only because "it was a religious play, and people who go to a religious play at a religious festival expect to be patiently bored and to satisfy themselves with the feeling that they have done something meritorious"

(26). In his subsequent, more secular and Ibsenesque drama, Eliot will move the chorus "into the scene" (as Nietzsche had lamented about Greek drama) and dismember their communal voice into individuated characters. Such characters still seek a lost communion of divine order and reason, but with a larger, mundane audience in mind.

Nietzsche, like Eliot, desired illumination and transfiguration in theater, but through a different deifying mechanism than that in Eliot's later drama. Nietzsche treasured the lost ur-chorus of Greek drama and its dithyrambic song and dance, in which he glimpsed the "veil of *maya*" of his own daily world being "torn aside and . . . fluttering in tatters before the mysterious primal unity" (*Birth* 37). Nietzsche believed in this perverse transfiguration through the recovery of the divine power at theater's birth—in the "mythical maternal womb" of a modern Dionysian chorus's "destruction of the visible world of mere appearance" (136–40). With this sense of an orchestral edge, Nietzsche is both pre- and postmodern. His theory not only reflects Romantic *Sturm und Drang* (and what Nietzsche calls "the dark Heraclitus"), it also presages Derridean deconstruction, "the playful construction and destruction of the individual world as the overflow of a primordial delight" (142).

Jonas Barish sees an antitheatrical prejudice in Nietzsche's antimimetic theory of tragedy. "The moment the element of illusionism and portraiture begins to crystallize, the moment tragedy begins to consist of an action shown to onlookers—the moment, in short when it begins to resemble what for more than two millennia in western European history has passed for theater—Nietzsche's approval begins to cool" (404). Barish describes the change from Nietzsche's belief in 1873 in early Greek drama, and in Wagner's *Tristan*, to his attack in 1888 upon Wagner as "stretch[ing] out a hand to the puritanical Plato of the *Republic*" (405). He senses the fire of an inquisition on Nietzsche's breath in his later complaint against Wagner: "a faint theological aroma in the charge, a whiff of brimstone. Wagner is Lucifer, lighting souls the way to hell—even if that hell occupies a purely secular site" (406).

Though Barish somewhat distorts Nietzsche's theories on theater to fit them into his own thesis,[19] his perspective provides a locus for our present concerns. For one can see a similar disillusionment, although against his own theological desires, in Eliot's view of his own "progress in dispensing with the chorus" (*Poetry* 33). While Eliot does not criticize the failure of his choruses as passionately as Nietzsche does Wagner's, their dispensation shows the quixotic impossibility in Eliot's dream of uniting sacred communion with popular culture.[20] Yet, his failed return to the womb of tragic music, along with Nietzsche's deconstructiveness, also displays a persistent temptation to ritual belief that lies at the stage edge of both the modern and postmodern.

Of Woman, Will, and Wheel

In his critique in 1888 of the formerly promising Wagner, Nietzsche asserts that "the danger for artists, for geniuses . . . is woman: adoring women confront them with corruption" (161). Jacques Derrida has stated, regarding the spur of Nietzsche's writing style, that "the question of the figure is at once opened or closed by what is called woman" (*Spurs* 41).[21] Outside the theater, the Bacchic choruses of ancient Greece had mostly female members (as depicted in Euripides' *Bacchae*); their worship of Dionysus derived from earlier mother goddess religions.[22] Nietzsche himself connected "Dionysian art and its tragic symbolism" to this semiotic, maternal chora—or, in his terms, "the eternally creative primordial mother" (*Birth* 104).[23] Tragedy was born and will be reborn, according to Nietzsche, not only out of the spirit, but also out "of the womb of music" (82). "The *tragic myth* . . . leads the world of phenomena to its limits where it denies itself and seeks to flee back again into the womb of the true and only reality" (131). This for Nietzsche is the "tremendous historical need of our unsatisfied modern culture . . . the loss of myth, the loss of the mythical home, the mythical maternal womb" (136).

Eliot also felt the modern loss of, and tremendous need for, a return to the womb of tragic myth. In his *Murder in the Cathedral,* the chorus of hysterical women, as *hystera* (womb) of poetry, gives birth to the tragic figure of the martyr.[24] But this reborn body, while moving toward immortal sainthood, is not yet invulnerable to corruption, particularly through the Canterbury women's Dionysian adoration—and presentiment of divine loss. "God is leaving us, more pang, more pain, than birth or death" (*CPP* 195). This abject horror at a godless horizon becomes, in Eliot's drama, a rock and rack for saintly suffering and salvation. For the Nietzschean postmodern, however, it will twist into a different, perverse joy: a will to power beyond the martyr's metaphysics—opened or closed by what is called woman.

In the opening scene, the Canterbury women do not adore their martyr-to-be uncritically. They even hint at his ultimate temptation in the play: the Apollonian hubris of envisioning, through their adoration, his own identity beyond death. The chorus at first accuses Thomas, like the old men of Colonus with Sophocles' Oedipus, of "bringing death into Canterbury" (180). The Second Priest then tries to dismiss them (like Hugh Kenner) as "foolish, immodest and babbling women." He suggests (perhaps in a Kleinian sense) that if they continue "croaking like frogs," they might be "cooked and eaten." But Thomas, just offstage, sees the chorus mirroring and magnifying his own fears and convictions. Indeed, the chorus gives their *figura* a modern, existential premonition: "now a great fear is upon us, a fear not of one but of many, / A fear like birth and death, when we see birth and death alone / In a void apart" (181).

With this fear for their own Dionysian deconstruction, the chorus does not bear much Aristotelian pity for their holy hero. Instead, they cry out to the offstage archbishop with a working-person's complaint (similar to that posed by Brecht's Little Monk to Galileo [*Collected Plays (CP)* 5:56–57]): "secure and assured of your fate, unaffrayed among the shades, do you realise what you ask, do you realise what it means / To the small folk drawn into the pattern of fate . . . [into] the doom of the world?" (181). When Thomas enters, he honors their Nietzschean *ressentiment* and rebukes the Second Priest: "They speak better than they know, and beyond your [the Priest's] understanding. / They know and do not know, what it is to act or suffer" (182). Thomas here resists two choral temptations: corruption by their tragic adoration and sympathy for their existential despair. Instead, he uses their vision and bodily fear, their knowing and not knowing, as a fulcrum for his own transcendence.

Yet he thus promises to show them a paradoxical but salvific "pattern" that is both eternal action and personal suffering, submissive consent and the will to spiritual power. To substantiate this pattern, the martyr and his choral mirror, along with the theater audience (to varying degrees), must will a Nietzschean self-overcoming. But this will be in the direction of Christian grace and redemption, rather than the Nietzschean direction of postmodern freedom in a dead (or at least decentered) God[25]—though both involve a painful transcendence through the wheel of fate.

> In an eternal action, an eternal patience
> To which all must consent that it may be willed
> And which all must suffer that they may will it
> That the pattern may subsist, for the pattern is the action
> And the suffering, that the wheel may turn and still
> Be forever still.
>
> (182)

For Nietzsche the direction of self-overcoming through the Dionysian chorus is explicitly opposed to Christianity. In his preface to the 1886 edition of *The Birth of Tragedy*, entitled "Attempt at Self-Criticism," Nietzsche calls the Dionysian "purely artistic and *anti-Christian*" (24). Yet a parallel will to divine insight can be seen in the choruses of Eliot's early plays and Nietzsche's early theories of the pre-Attic Dionysian. There is also a parallel critique of empathy in the tragic will to power of Nietzsche's philosophy and Eliot's plays (and in his theory of artistic self-sacrifice in "Tradition and the Individual Talent"): an antisentimental, classical virility, and at times a misogynistic rigor. Hence, the disillusioned Nietzsche criticizes Wagner as not only being corrupted by the adoration of women, but also as "a seducer on a grand scale . . . [who] flatters everything Christian, every religious expression of decadence" (183).

While both Nietzsche and Eliot articulate a certain critique of empathy, the former criticizes (neo)Aristotelian fear and pity in order to purify his passionate will to the choral power of Dionysian truth (*Birth* 132).[26] Eliot takes a different route through the fundamental fantasy of ancient Greek theater. His will to have objective correlatives for expressing emotions (*SE* 124) and to separate "the man who suffers and the mind which creates" (8), in his early aesthetic essays, prefigures the revival and then gradual rejection (as we shall see in the next chapter) of an empathetic chorus in his own verse drama. In a later essay he expressed the view that "the ideal toward which poetic drama should strive . . . [is the] feeling of which we are only aware in a kind of temporary detachment from action." Like Nietzsche, Eliot ties this "perception of an order in life" (*Poetry* 42) to "the border of those feelings which only music can express." However, Eliot now insists that his ideal dramatic feelings, though detached from action, remain in "contact with the ordinary everyday world," perceiving the order of that life, by "imposing a credible order upon [the stage fiction of] ordinary reality" (43).

Yet both sides in Nietzsche's critique of Wagnerian empathy already appear in Eliot's *Murder in the Cathedral*. Adoration and seduction combine, as the archbishop and his flock together will a communal belief in divine will. Here the greatest temptation to "treason" that Thomas faces is the hubris of self-canonization: "To do the right deed for the wrong reason," that is, the corruption of imagining future, eternal adoration from the poor women of Canterbury and from the rest of the Church (the Bride of Christ)—represented by the theater pilgrims watching him (*CPP* 196). But his final tempter had already given the potential martyr some helpful advice on this, echoing Thomas's earlier description of his chorus: "You know and do not know, what it is to act or suffer" (193). Thomas must shed the tran-scendent deception of his imaginary knowledge of martyrdom in order to actually offer himself to God's will.

The chorus had thus, at the beginning of the play, mirrored to Thomas the Aristotelian "recognition" (anagnorisis) that he needs to purify his desire for martyrdom, a consciousness that he only reaches at the end of his four temptations. In Lacanian terms, Becket must enter the *passage à l'acte* of martyrdom as a split subject, stripped of his belief in his own holiness, yet believing in the sanctity of the act and the value of his suffering. The chorus at this point, however, mirrors further ahead and behind, to the "restless movement" of dithyrambic feet beneath Thomas's Christian confidence and grace. Perhaps they even hear and speak of a Dionysian mother goddess, "earth [that] is heaving to parturition of issue of hell." Likewise the chorus of four tempters describe a Nietzschean veil of maya: "all things become less real, man passes / From unreality to unreality" (194). The chorus's despair then reaches existentialist dimensions: "God is leaving us, more pang, more pain, than birth or death" (195). Hence, the turning yet still wheel of sacramental time is also a perverse rack, which cat-apults Eliot's Thomas to saintly *(figura)* status, through the existential despair and tragic adoration/seduction of the chorus—along with the labor invested by (at least some of) the audience.[27]

At the Twist of a Möbius Strip

When Nietzsche describes the chorus as a mirror to the spectator, an implied, narcissistic gap appears between them: "we may call the chorus in its primitive form, in proto-tragedy, the mirror image in which Dionysian man contemplates himself" (*Birth* 63). And yet, through this choral mirror, Nietzsche envisions the prebirth place of Western theater, the liminal dream/womb of music and myth.[28] There Nietzsche glimpses the phallic mother goddess in Dionysian parturition of the *figura* (fetish) as Apollo-nian mask. Such a Nietzschean vision of this bloody show, the primal scene of theater history, thus reveals a perverse edge to Eliot's belief in a modern Christian drama that would return to ancient Greek and medieval ritual.

The semiosis of Nietzsche's revolution in theatrical language corre-sponds, too, with Eliot's pre-*Murder* pageant play, *The Rock*. Browne, who was also the first director of *The Rock,* ties the chorus of this play not only to the medieval *Quem quaeritis,* but also to Yeats's No drama, specifically *Calvary* and *Resurrection*. Both begin with the ritual folding and unfolding of a cloth (or proscenium curtain) by musicians. Browne converts this idea into a chorus of worshipers as human curtain, folding and unfolding between scenes (*Making* 20). Whereas the chorus of *Murder in the Cathedral* must wait, according to Thomas, for God's purpose to be revealed, the practical purpose of the initial production of *The Rock* was clear from the start (and critiqued by its Agitator): to raise money for the building of forty-five new churches in the Greater London area. Its chorus members were conceived as "stone-like figures, growing out of the rock on which they stood" (Browne, *Making* 17). They also stood around the central figure of the play, "the Rock"—which, Eliot stressed, was not to be identified only with St. Peter (Browne, *Making* 26–27). The chorus of *The Rock*, half-masked and costumed with "stiff robes of hessian draped in statuesque folds" (29), became a human stone curtain, an unfolding hymen revealing the maternal phallus of the Rock, symbolizing the rebirth/rebuilding of churches and Church.

This exhibition of the Rock as fetish, through the spectacle and music of the chorus, to the voyeuristic audience of contributors to the church-building fund, sublimates the perverse pleasures of theater toward spiritual edification. It also commodifies the sufferings of unemployed and homeless contemporaries (in the chorus) into an objet d'art, for the divine purpose of future edifices of stone signification. I do not mean this critique as a dismissal of the play, nor of T. S. Eliot; for such a fetishizing, commodifying process is inherent to the staging of any play—and also of any theory, particularly as modern or postmodern. However, Eliot's choruses do make this confluence of sexual, spiritual, and economic forces more apparent, through their evocation of and submission to communal belief in the hero.

The objective correlative of the chorus's passion is this erection of the Rock onstage—and of future churches in London. Likewise, in *Murder in the Cathedral*, the chorus, along with sympathetic believers in the audience, wills a re-creation, in verse and vision, of the saint's martyrdom onstage. This sadomasochistic ritual of objectification for the pleasure of another also operates in the other direction across the stage edge.[29] Both actors and choral performers, as "self-sacrific[ing] artists" (in Eliot's antisentimental sense), submit to the bondage of the artwork and its audience, to a "depersonalization" that separates "the man who suffers and the mind which creates" (*SE* 7–8). Eliot used these terms to define the dialogue between "tradition and the individual talent," in his essay of that title from 1919. But they can also be applied to a performer's "concentration" of emotions and experiences, in acting out the refined feelings of his subsequent drama. Eliot is explicitly anti-Romantic in that essay. Contra Wordsworth, he states that "experiences are not 'recollected,' and they finally unite in an atmosphere which is 'tranquil' only in that it is a passive attending upon the event." He abjures the eccentric "search for novelty" in poetic emotion as being "perverse" (10). Yet, Eliot's plays of the 1930s try not only to recollect, but also incarnate a sacred Other onstage, an *Übermensch* whose tranquillity transcends mortal suffering. They thus reveal a perverse, nearly Nietzschean *jouissance*—a "painful joy,"[30] as Thomas promises his chorus—within Eliot's neoclassical morality and Christian mysticism. Yet one finds such Romantic (and deconstructive) perversity not only at the limit edge of Eliot's modernist belief in verse drama, but also at the crux of his sacrificial wheel.

Eliot's sense of an ordered literary tradition producing (and being slightly altered by) "monuments" of individual talent (4–5), parallels his early theatrical belief in a timeless, yet temporal, interaction between chorus and tragic hero. In "Tradition and the Individual Talent," Eliot even comes close to the positivism of his later adversary, I. A. Richards. With the "depersonalization" of the artist into artwork, which Eliot expressly values, "art may be said to approach the condition of science."[31] Eliot uses the analogy of a chemical "catalyst" for this split subjectivity of the artist (7)—which is applicable to his later attempts to revive a tragic chorus as catalytic converter of theater's perverse passions. But Eliot not only intersects the beliefs of Richards at certain points in this essay, he also approaches the subsequent generation of literary theorists, who rebelled against him, according to Harold Bloom ("Reflections"). There is even a foreshadowing of Bloom's influence theory in Eliot's demystifying of "the poet's difference from his predecessors." For Eliot claims that "not only the best, but the most individual parts of his [the poet's] work may be those in which the dead poets, his ancestors, assert their immortality most vigorously" (*SE* 4).

Though postmodernism (in art and theory) represses or explicitly rebels against modernist influences and predecessors, staging itself off of that previous period, it also continues prior perversities and beliefs, through inverted and explicit correlatives. In such metaphoric condensation and metonymic displacement, the latencies of one era create manifest dreams in the next, which then become apparent in the earlier one, retrospectively. One can thus depict the interaction of belief and perversion within each period—and between them—as a Möbius strip, twisting at the points (or edge) where theorists and artists attempt to frame their works, concepts, and periods as distinct from one another. The particular perversions of Eliot's stage, while "extimate"[32] to his own beliefs, illustrate this and more. Not just the "mechanism of sensibility" of his drama, but also an ontological friction in the persistent ritual structure of theatrical desire. Not only an interplay of orthodoxy and heresy in his high modernist views of culture, but a recurrent dialectic within and between successive periods. Eliot's use of the term "mechanism of sensibility" to align his own work with that of the metaphysical poets, rather than with more recent predecessors (247), exemplifies, too, the cycles of rejection and return over the course of several literary periods, as they each are reenvisioned by successive generations. However, the distinctive beliefs and perverse edges of any particular artwork do make a world of difference—as Eliot discovered with his religious and secular audiences.

Observer or Participant in the Choral Fetish

As performers submit to masochistic depersonalization, individual spectators may also dissolve into the collective audience, and then perhaps into the chorus itself, depending upon their degree of ritual investment. O. B. Hardison's study of the medieval rebirth of theater demonstrates this connection with ritual, though he takes an Aristotelian (rather than Nietzschean) view and follows the archetypal structuralism of Frazer and Frye (x–xi).[33] Hardison examines the writings of medieval interpreters, showing that the Mass itself was a "rememorative drama depicting the life, ministry, crucifixion, and resurrection of Christ" (44). And this was so even before the overtly theatrical *Quem quaeritis* trope emerged in the tenth century (41). Eliot emphasizes the liturgical and theological roots of his own rememorative mystery (and morality) play, *Murder in the Cathedral*.[34] He positions at the center of its formal symmetry a sermon by Archbishop Thomas à Becket, as if at a mass "on Christmas Morning, 1170" (CPP 198). Here modern spectators, along with the chorus, are supposed to play a role as worshipers (and choir) in Canterbury Cathedral. Ideally, this creates a still point in the dramaturgical wheel of the play, tying twelfth century to twentieth, and religious tradition to the temporary ritual of theater.

In "A Dialogue on Dramatic Poetry" (1928), Eliot describes a man who

> went to High Mass every Sunday, and was particular to find a church where he considered the Mass efficiently performed. And as I sometimes accompanied him, I can testify that the Mass gave him extreme, I may even say immoderate satisfaction. It was almost orgiastic. (*SE* 35)

This is the dialogical voice of Eliot's "B," responding to "E," who had just suggested that the "only solution" for modern drama, in the desert of its current prose realism, would be a "return to religious liturgy" (34–35). In the year previous to the publication of these voices, Eliot had been baptized into the Church of England—and then in 1928 declared himself "Anglo-Catholic" as well as "Classicist." So, it is highly possible, as Herbert Blau has commented ("Myth" 313), that Eliot expresses through B a suspicion about his own pleasure in the Mass, while accompanying himself to church on Sunday. For the classicist B accuses his churchgoing friend, and thus also E (who had described his "only dramatic satisfaction" as being "in a High Mass well performed"), of being "guilty of a *confusion des genres*" (35).

The bondage and depersonalization of the Mass, according to Eliot's B, requires a different "frame of mind"—a participating that is "supremely conscious of divine realities." The anti-Arnoldian B insists that literature "can be no substitute for religion," and vice versa, "because we need literature as well as religion." Here again Eliot's own guilt in pleasurably confusing the two creeps into B's moralizing tone: "you have no business to care about the Mass unless you are a believer. And even if you are a believer you will have dramatic desires which crave fulfilment otherwise . . . [in] some liturgy less divine . . . of which we shall be more spectators and less participants" (36). To whatever degree this voice represents the vengeful, repressed ghost of his grandfather (a Unitarian minister),[35] Eliot here elucidates the crucial tension between belief and perversion in his subsequent drama. B's view implies two distinctly perverse dramatic desires. For believers in the Mass, it is participatory sadomasochism; for believers in theater, it is the spectator's voyeurism. Hence, he suggests a chasm between the two types of community surrounding altar and stage: co-performing (or conforming) chorus and worshipers versus distanced observers. A few years later, however, the religious circumstances of Eliot's early plays would favor E's position over B's. He would attempt to join these two communities of altar and stage, as in theater's ancient and medieval (re)birth.

At the end of part 1 of *Murder in the Cathedral*, Thomas seems very much aware of the distanced observers and disbelievers in his twentieth-century congregation.

> I know
> what yet remains to show you of my history
> Will seem to most of you at best futility,
> Senseless self-slaughter of a lunatic,
> Arrogant passion of a fanatic.
>
> (*CPP* 196–97)

The historical meaning and theatrical pleasure of this hero's mad, arrogant passion varies from actor to choral member to each spectator (and from modern to postmodern). But ultimately the "consent" of all three psychospatial dimensions is required for the efficacy of his ritual remartyrdom, as the chorus shamefully voices, asking the archbishop's forgiveness for their complicity in his death (208). All three dimensions must conjoin—although, in the modern and postmodern periods, with different consciousness of, and craving for, the human or divine—to make the blade fall at the edge of the stage. Thomas, however, boasts an aloofness to such painful pleasure, in his classical obedience to a divinely ordered heroism. "But for every evil, every sacrilege, / Crime, wrong, oppression and the axe's edge," he tells his also complicit twentieth-century audience, "Indifference, exploitation, you and you, / And you, must all be punished. So must you. / I shall no longer act or suffer, to the sword's end" (197).

Thomas sees himself (in a choral mirror) as having reached the still point within the wheel of his fate. One might also see him as being at the twisting point of a Möbius strip on which belief and perversion are opposed, yet interwoven; polarized, but contiguous. From his own viewpoint within the wheel, Thomas predicts, for the chorus and audience surrounding him, a cathexis of guilt that will be required for their cathartic punishment and potential transcendence through faith in his martyrdom. This metaphysical confidence (game) seems perverse in the light of postmodern ethics and politics. As in Nietzsche's theory of Christian guilt (*Genealogy* 92–93), the archbishop pressures the chorus, and believing participants in the audience, to support his immortal status through their psychological self-punishment. Or, in Elaine Scarry's terms, the hysterical "body in pain" of the chorus "substantiates" the hollow "fiction of power" that is their "structure of belief" in a tragic saint.[36]

The sadomasochistic structure of Eliot's stage operates in several specific directions: between spectators and chorus, between chorus and actor(s) onstage, between actor and character being incarnated, and between audience and actor/character. Also involved are the more obvious theatrical perversities of voyeurism and exhibitionism, characteristic of spectator and performer. Yet fetishism is the most exemplary perversity in Eliot's theater, joining the participant's sadomasochism and observer's voyeurism. It is also, and perhaps less guiltily so, in Nietzsche's dream of an anti-Christian chorus creating Apollonian divinity onstage. The chorus as human/stone curtain in *The Rock* is itself a fetish, "a protective veil against the invisible, the intolerable . . . absence of a penis" (Pontalis 47) on the maternal body of the stage. But this curtain of the chorus, prophylactic hymen against (yet stimulating) the scopophilia of the spectators, then unfolds to reveal a greater fetish in the totemic Rock onstage.[37]

Taking the place of an original, lost womb of music, the chorus of *The Rock* becomes objectified as Eliotic correlative and Nietzschean mirror/lens. Such a chorus might be called an "acoustic lens,"[38] through which the audience views the rhetorical interplay of human and divine, mortality and immortality, in actor and character onstage. The chorus leader makes this clear early in the play, just before the Rock's first appearance.

> Silence! and preserve respectful distance.
> For I perceive approaching
> The Rock. The Watcher. The Stranger.
> He who has seen what has happened.
> And who sees what is to happen.
> The Witness. The Critic. The Stranger.
> The God-shaken, in whom is the truth inborn.

(8)

Through their leader the chorus becomes a lens for the theater audience to perceive the Rock. Through this choral lens the spectators, in varying degrees of belief/disbelief, see a reflection of themselves as watcher, stranger, witness, critic. They see, too, what has and is to happen, and perhaps even become God-shaken with an inborn Dionysian truth. Hence, the tripartite structure of audience/chorus/hero in Eliot's early plays—through a Nietzschean lens—becomes itself a Möbius strip, twisted at the choral edge of the stage.

Today's Redress

The Möbius strip of belief/perversion twists, too, at a choral edge between modern and postmodern stages. The issue of ritual participation versus voyeuristic observation typifies a double bind in both periods, as each is reborn from and against the other. For the postmodern is also premodern: modernism in its "nascent state" (Lyotard, *Postmodern* 79). This corresponds to Ronald Grimes's description of "unframed ritual" as being both nascent and decadent, as "gaining or beginning to lose its distinctions from ordinary actions" ("Turner's" 93). Grimes also refers to Turner's genealogy of genres, in which social drama is the grandparent, ritual the parent, and stage drama the child—a dialectical cycle as "narrative and drama, functioning as paradigms, provoke further social dramas" (Grimes, "Turner's" 80 or *Ritual* 175; Turner, *From Ritual* 72–82). But this genealogy leaves out what Grimes charts (in the earlier version of the essay) as "unframed ritual," paralleling the unframed/framed dialectic of social and stage drama ("Turner's" 92). Perhaps this is a role for Kristeva's semiotic chora, as the liminal womb between generations—the feminine body repressed by patriarchal fetishism and theatrical heroism, which the postmodern tries to recover.[39] And yet, this faithful and perverse, nascent and decadent, return to the womb appears, too, in Eliot's modernist stage drama—the child of Nietzsche's imagined Dionysian ritual, but also parent to today's social drama of critical theory.

"Simplifying to the extreme," says Lyotard (*Postmodern* xxiv), "I define *postmodern* as incredulity toward metanarratives." To this he connects "the crisis of metaphysical philosophy." Postmodern theory takes its cue in this skeptical role from Nietzsche's premodern genealogy of morals—born from a perverse genealogy of theater, driving through broken, metaphysical mirrors at the dawn and dusk of Western metanarrative. Today modernists fight for the transcendence of their ideals, whether sacred or secular, beyond what they see on the current theoretical stage as the perverse, antistructural communitas of newer generations. At the same time, the postmodern antithesis becomes normative and ideological, losing its spontaneous edge. Thus, in the breach and crisis of the modern/postmodern twist, a ritual redress and potential reintegration is sought by both sides,[40] as they each return, in different ways, to the semiotic, maternal chora.

For some, on either side, the term *ritual* seems not redressive, but regressive. Even Richard Schechner, a champion of reintegrating ritual within performance theory and practice (though in a less hieratic sense than I am tracing), insists on separating theater from the ritual of the Mass. He defines theater, like Eliot's B (and Brecht), as a separation of observing spectators from participating performers (*Performance* 126). Yet, like Eliot's E, Schechner sees a persistent, intimate relationship in this parent-child pair (*Performance* 120–52; *Between* 105, 130–48)—and in the parenting of social drama by the stage. "Theater and ordinary life are a möbius strip, each turning into the other" (14).[41]

But other theorists today, who are less ritually invested, stick to narrative as their paradigm. Lyotard, for example, despite his poststructuralist incredulity to metanarrative, points to the "little narrative" *(petit récit)* as the primary postmodern form (*Postmodern* 60). While modernity "cannot exist without a shattering of belief and without discovery of the 'lack of reality' of reality, together with the invention of other realities" (77); the postmodern "would be that which, in the modern, puts forward the unpresentable in presentation itself" (81). Thus, through disbelief in metanarrative and performance of absence, postmodernism finds a different ritual truth, putting both ritual and truth under erasure *(sous rature)*. It would playfully return, beyond the mirror edge of modernist mourning and sublime nostalgia to an always already lost and disseminating chora, as liminal void and original supplement within language, body, narrative, and theater.[42] For the Nietzschean postmodern quickens within and against, but also beyond, the Eliotic modern, along sacred and secular loops in their joint Möbius strip, as it snakes ahead through history.

Chapter 3

The Sacrificial Hyster(i)a of Eliot's Secular Drama

Aside from the Wooster Group's deconstruction of *The Cocktail Party* (in their 1978 *Nyatt School*), T. S. Eliot's drama has not been a favorite source for postmodern performance.[1] But this and others of his more secular plays—which turn away from, yet maintain (in differing experimental forms) the ritual framework of his earlier drama—offer much insight upon the sacrificial politics of postmodern theory. For this reason I will focus, through the theories of Nietzsche and Lacan, on Eliot's transformation of the hysterical chorus from his earlier plays into visionary and psychothera-peutic characters in the later ones. Particularly in relation to current femi-nism, Eliot's Celia, martyr of *The Cocktail Party,* discloses a perverse mir-roring of the Other's desire, between modern and postmodern stages.

Eliot's symptomatic sense of loss drove him from the Neoplatonic cor-respondences of Christian ritual—with separate orders of audience, chorus, and tragic hero—to a more Aristotelian/Sophoclean psychology of chorus as pitying and fearful characters (in *The Family Reunion*), and then to the hidden Greekness of ordinary "comedy" (as he called *The Cocktail Party*). The comedy of the latter's drawing room is still fed by tragic consequence,[2] but the hero is now female, and her martyrdom occurs offstage, in a far-away missionary land. Together with Nietzsche's earlier, visionary "rap-ture" (66) in a lost Dionysian choral womb, Eliot's swing from divine to ordinary reality exemplifies the modern play of a Western phallocentric stage between the ontology and teleology of Woman.[3] As with the fetishist's paradoxical love/hate and belief/disbelief,[4] the symptoms of Eliot's drama and Nietzsche's theory disclose a paradox at the heart of patriarchy. The violence of patriarchal oppression is fueled not only by a thrilling power over, but also by a horrible vulnerability toward, an unrepresentable stage (m)other.[5] And thus, the guilt of an absent father tragically repeats from generation to generation. Yet this is the key to change, according to Lacan-ian theory and Eliot's drama.

Displaced Chorus and Father

En route to the saintly Celia, as offstage tragic Woman for the comic *Cocktail Party*, Eliot's *The Family Reunion* diminishes the role of the chorus from *Murder in the Cathedral*. There are still a few lines written for the "Chorus"; but they are spoken by "minor personages, representing the Family," and by actors who perform "sometimes as individual character parts and sometimes collectively as chorus" (*Poetry* 33).[6] Only, in fact, at five brief points in the drama do they perform collectively. Yet they begin their collectivity in the play not unlike the Canterbury chorus, with an apprehensive waiting for the hero's (Harry's) entrance: "embarrassed, impatient, fretful, ill at ease, / Assembled like amateur actors who have not been assigned their parts" (*CPP* 231). Here they reflect a simpler, more amateur waiting than the profound, historical, and sacred pregnancy of the *Murder* chorus. But their minor embodiment of illness at ease will still reverberate at significant points in this family drama, voicing the curse of the House of Monchensey (and Wishwood).

Rather than being gathered by a divine Father's providence, it is the matriarch of the house who directs the *Family* chorus, despite their ironical disbelief in the Oresteian tragedy surrounding them: "we are gathered at Amy's command, to play an unread part in some monstrous farce, ridiculous in some nightmare pantomime" (231). And they continue to criticize the mimesis when they next collect (at the end of the first scene), still avoiding their possible role as tragic chorus, or even as Ibsenesque confidants: "Why should we stand here like guilty conspirators, waiting for some revelation / When the hidden shall be exposed . . . ?" (242). But this somewhat postmodern pose, parodic of the modernist rage for order, does not last long. After four separate lines, baring their individual distrust of one another, Ivy, Gerald, Violet, and Charles resume a single, fearful voice: "Hold tight, hold tight, we must insist that the world is what we have always taken it to be" (243). The matriarchal Amy (Lady Monchensey) has also "struggled to keep Wishwood going / And to make no changes before your return," as she tells her son, Harry, earlier in the first scene (233).

Harry bears within himself a generational necessity for change, and a painful vision of a newly credible order. Like Thomas à Becket, he carries a heavy burden of destiny. But his temptation is to guilt rather than pride: he believes he may have killed his wife. (She died while on a cruise with him, when she fell, or was pushed, overboard during a storm.) Yet Harry comes to realize during the course of the play that the Furies chasing him embody the curse of the House of Monchensey—from an ancestral sin, not solely his

own. "I am the old house . . . In which all past is present, all degradation /
Is unredeemable" (234). In this sense, Harry's flight from the Furies,[7] as
dark mother goddess(es), preceded the death of his wife. For he married her
to escape from his own phallic mother and absent father. Thus the circle of
sin, guilt, and fear comes to roost again at Wishwood, along with the
Furies, as the play's periodic chorus expresses it: "I am afraid of all that has
happened, and of all that is to come; . . . And the wings of the future darken
the past, the beak and claws have desecrated / History" (256).

The Furies appear in an Elizabethan-like discovery space: the cur-
tained window embrasure of the drawing room—a mythical/ritual proscenium within the proscenium (253). Eventually, this becomes the place of
Harry's cure, his identification with the *sinthome* (symptom)[8] of his familial curse. The Furies thereby turn into Eumenides within the domestic setting. Harry is not led to this passage, however, by the vision of the play's
chorus (as was Eliot's St. Thomas), but rather by his visionary aunt Agatha.
While the characters who make up the explicit *Family* chorus are also
Harry's aunts and uncles, Agatha plays a distinctive choral role *as* character. She becomes the cathartic catalyst (or analyst manipulating transference), helping him to cross his fundamental fantasy of familial guilt.[9]

Unlike the other family members, Agatha provides Harry with essential primal-scene information. She tells him that his father had plotted to
kill his mother while she was pregnant with Harry. (Agatha herself pre-
vented the double murder, she says [274].) Harry thus realizes the repetition
of compulsive fantasy in his own wish to murder his wife: "Perhaps / I only
dreamt I pushed her." It is then that Agatha expresses the oracular meaning
of the tragic hero's agony: "You are the consciousness of your unhappy
family, / Its bird sent flying through the purgatorial flame." At this point
Harry feels "happiness," glimpsing the end of his treatment (and the
drama) "in a different vision" (275). He sees the past more clearly, too: "I
have been wounded in a war of phantoms" (276). Harry and Agatha continue in their visionary duet as hero and choral figure, until the Other chorus of Furies/Eumenides appear again. "This time you are real," says Harry,
"this time you are outside of me, / And just endurable" (278). He professes
a willingness to follow them, to meet his difficult destiny, like Thomas,
through their choral power.

But Agatha shows Harry the empty place of this Other, by reopening
"in a somnambular fashion" the curtains covering the window, and thus
"disclosing the empty embrasure." She then embodies its oracular emptiness, stepping into the hollow wound, "the place which the Eumenides had
occupied." From this choral womb at the back of the stage, she pronounces

a Greco-Freudian axiom, which gives birth to a new identity for Harry. "A curse comes to being / As a child is formed" (278). Slavoj Žižek explains that the ultimate goal of Lacanian treatment is identification with such a primal curse—as symptom of the Other's lack. He clarifies this by extending Freud's formula, "Wo es war soll ich werden" (where it/id was I/ego ought to be): "you the subject must identify yourself with the place where your symptom already was; in its pathological particularity you must recognize the element which gives consistency to your being" (*Sublime* 75).

Critics of Freud and Lacan might well view such elemental recognition as being a symptomatic "phallacy," not unlike Eliotic salvation, in which high modernist rage for guilty submission leads to complicit support for the patriarchal order. For the Lacanian analyst, though, a cure of the patient, not of patriarchy, is the primary ethical goal. And yet, for Lacanian cultural theorists like Žižek, this may also mean—through each patient's subjective destitution and acceptance of the Other's nonexistence (*Sublime* 230–31)—a less oppressive patriarchy for all of us. Or, as Agatha puts it, during the chorus's ritual extinguishing of candles at the end of the play: "Each curse has its course / Its own way of expiation / Follow follow" (*CPP* 292). In Eliot's drama, as in its Greek models, a perverse resistance to, or flight from, the curse of parental sins makes for an even more impacted and oppressive patriarchal structure. It may be possible, however, to break the cycles of resistant repetition, which spread the violence and guilt from generation to generation, by following the full course of one's own particular curse.

In this way, Agatha's choral function on a secular stage continues to bear the mystical, hysterical vision of the *Murder* chorus, although the explicit *Family* chorus seems at times to mock that earlier play. Agatha's ethic of suffering is also a therapeutic response to Harry's modernist hysteria—through a more complete embodiment of the lacking Other. Harry describes how he might have been like his choral aunts and uncles (other than Agatha), holding tight to "the normal." But his own wounded life has come to seem more significant than "an isolated ruin, / A casual bit of waste in an orderly universe." It has become "part of some huge disaster"; it signifies "Some monstrous mistake and aberration / Of all men, of the world, which I cannot put in order" (268). A dozen years after Eliot's baptism into the orderly universe of the Church of England, his *Family Reunion* expresses a dramatic crisis of faith. Harry tries to flee the womb of Wishwood and the painful mystery of an absent father. But he carries the guilty hollowness within his body, hysterically hallucinating (or perhaps acting out) the patriarchal sin. So, he must return home to the phallic mother, pursued by the Furies of his fateful ancestry, in order to pass through the recurrent familial perversity of an Oresteian death wish.[10]

The non-Lacanian (although French) psychoanalyst Janine Chasseguet-Smirgel has theorized (borrowing from Pasche's theory of fetishism) that all perversion derives from the lack of proper idealization of the father by the child.[11] This is often caused, she says, by a mother encouraging her child to believe it can "be a satisfying partner to her," replacing its father (14–16).[12] Recently, American object-relations psychoanalyst Jessica Benjamin has used Chasseguet-Smirgel (and Melanie Klein) to assert, contra Freud, that both male and female children have a fundamental "fantasy of maternal power not maternal lack" (94).[13] I will not relate her full, feminist argument here; but Eliot's drama begins to open this postmodern wound, in his modernist, masculinist symptoms of an absent father (and God), lacking as phallic ideal, which could be used to "beat back" (Chasseguet-Smirgel, qtd. in Benjamin 94–95) the powerful, reengulfing mother (goddess). "We felt that he was always here," Harry says of his childhood memories of his lost father. "But when we would have grasped for him, there was only a vacuum / Surrounded by whispering aunts: Ivy and Violet— / Agatha never came then" (260). Indeed, Agatha, according to Harry's mother, took his father away when he was a child (282–83). In the course (and transferential treatment) of the drama, Agatha, as choral analyst, gives Harry his dead father's phallus to beat back his mother's dominance and separate from her for good. "I always wanted too much for my children, / More than life can give," Harry's mother confesses at his final exit—as she then goes offstage to die (287).

While such phallic beating back, or even beating to death, of the mother goddess might be criticized today as a return to phallocentrism, it is more centrifugal than centripetal. It sends Harry again out of Wishwood, but this time beyond the specter of dominating mother and aunts, through the ghost of a guilty father and raging Furies, even past the good witch, Agatha, to a cure of the curse somewhere offstage. Eliot thus reveals a spectral, pre-Oedipal mother[14] persistently haunting the stage edge, through various insufficient figures, from "Greek goddesses" to "modern spooks" (*Poetry* 37). But he also shows, beyond the failing horizon of ritual verse drama, a mystical alternative to modern realism, with postmodern political relevance. The offstage martyrdom of the missionary Celia in Eliot's next play, like Harry's escape from Wishwood, surpasses the Christian and matriarchal phallocentrism that structures its curse of guilt and course of atonement. Going further than Harry, Celia will perhaps subvert the patriarchal authority that forms her tragic character—by playing out her role within and beyond it. For some readers and spectators, the hysterical ecstasy of Celia's unrepresentable, offstage death might realize a postmodern *jouissance* beyond the phallus,[15] exploding the Christian sense that Eliot's play imposes upon her sacrifice. "I have thought at moments that the ecstasy is real," she says clairvoyantly (before leaving the stage and country), "Although those who experience it may have no reality" (*CPP* 363).

Choral Analyst and Offstage Heroine

With *The Family Reunion,* Eliot did not find a cure to his double-binding (schizophrenic) desire for popular audiences and metaphysical, verse drama. But with his next play, *The Cocktail Party* (written in 1949), Eliot dispensed with the chorus completely and achieved popular success on the secular stage, first in New York and then in London. Yet, he continued to borrow from Greek drama—this time from Euripides' *Alcestis*—and to use Christian themes. The visionary factor of the choruses in Eliot's earlier, ritual drama continues, too, in this play, though transformed even further into character. The chorus of *Murder in the Cathedral,* with its powerful, hysterical wound, becomes the Heraklean Harcourt-Reilly, who solves the painful riddles of various characters onstage and thus involves the audience as observing spectators more than participating believers. He wears an Apollonian mask of psychotherapeutic wisdom, like a veteran hero/saint (or perhaps bodhisattva), who has himself passed through tragic suffering and now helps others toward tragicomic salvation. Yet there is a lingering Dionysian hysteria just under the surface of his enlightened composure and verse. While *The Cocktail Party* marks a final point in Eliot's passage beyond the symbiotic temptation of a Nietzschean chorus, its initially "Unidentified Guest" still bears both heroic and choral functions.

Reilly is like Euripides' Herakles, as Eliot himself pointed out (*Poetry* 39); but he is also similar to Dionysus in *The Bacchae.*[16] Like Herakles, Reilly brings Edward's wife back from being dead to him (*CPP* 341). Yet Reilly also leads Edward to a horrifying vision of psychological dismemberment, like Dionysus does more literally to Pentheus (and Reilly does also to Celia). In addressing Edward, Reilly even becomes a clairvoyant lens upon the postmodern death of the subject. "You no longer feel quite human. / You're suddenly reduced to the status of an object" (307). Initially, Edward had tried to use his Unidentified Guest as a simple confidant, on whom he might unburden the mystery of his wife's disappearance (304). However, Reilly warns Edward "that to approach the stranger / Is to invite the unexpected, release a new force" (306).[17] As in much of the psychological realism of Ibsen and Chekhov, this confidant is a doctor. Yet his Christian counseling involves a nearly Lacanian alienation-effect. Rather than merely bolstering Edward's ego, by making him "feel important" (348), Reilly manipulates Edward's psyche through an *aphanisis* (fading)[18] of desire and ego: "I began to dissolve / To cease to exist" (349). This moves him toward a reunion with his wife, grounded on their having in common the "same isolation" (355). Lacan announced (in the 1970s) "the fact that love is impossible, and that the sexual relation founders in non-sense" (*Feminine* 158); Eliot's Reilly makes this into a comical, paradoxical "bond" between Edward and Lavinia (356).

As they leave the secular confessional of his consulting room, Reilly gives Edward and Lavinia a Christian-sounding blessing: "Go in peace. And work out your salvation with diligence" (357). Reilly gives the same final words to Celia, as he sends her toward missionary work and martyrdom; but here a different relationship is indicated: "Go in peace, my daughter. / Work out your salvation with diligence" (366). Between the two counseling sessions, a female power is shown behind Reilly's paternal wisdom. Julia, who had seemed to be only an ordinary party guest, is now revealed as a prime manipulator behind the scenes of Reilly's patriarchal control. She informs him that Celia "is ready / To make a decision" and even orders him to appear more energetic in his task: "Henry, get up. You can't be as tired as that" (358). Perhaps she represents the mother Goddess looming behind the stranger's unexpected force, as in the ancient rituals of Dionysus and the Marian cults within Catholicism. She would thus demonstrate the lost, primal chorus in Nietzsche's theory of tragedy becoming a repressed, mystical force in Eliot's secular, yet Christian, plays, particularly as they meet the modern death of God (the Father).[19]

In the comedy of *The Cocktail Party,* Celia's tragic salvation must be sought with an offstage diligence. But her cure also passes through the profound sense of alienation that Reilly evoked from Edward onstage. She goes further, though, crossing Eliot's own fundamental fantasy of theatrical communion. "They make noises, and think they are talking to each other; / They make faces, and think they understand each other. / And I'm sure that they don't" (360). With this play Eliot settles for the transitory illusion of community among secular spectators, or at most a Derridean "being-together as separation," rather than the ideal communion of believers implied by his early drama. Like Edward (with Lavinia), he finds that "we must make the best of a bad job" (356). And, as it turns out, it is not too bad a job as a popular play. It runs nine months in London, and when broadcast on television in 1952, it is seen by an estimated 3.5 million spectators (Ackroyd 308).[20] Yet Eliot holds onto a higher ideal in the play, of aesthetic and spiritual sacrifice beyond the common isolation of Edward and Lavinia—or of Broadway, West End, and TV audiences. While Celia would seem to fulfill this higher modernist ideal, she might also be seen to subvert it, through an excess of hysterical sacrifice.

In response to Edward's acquiescent words (about making the best of a bad job), Reilly says: "The best of a bad job is all any of us make of it— / Except of course, the saints" (356). There is a similar phrase in Thornton Wilder's *Our Town* (written a decade earlier). But its Stage Manager includes poets along with saints, as those very few who "realize life" while still alive, in anything like the nostalgic fervor of the dead Emily's perspective (62). Eliot the poet also reaches toward an immortal viewpoint on life, through the mystical visions of chorus, choral characters, and heroes. But he is caught, in the isolation of artistic sacrifice, between nostalgia and paranoia—between modern theatrical drives toward the sacred or secular, ritual or realistic, metaphysical or political. So he moves from the onstage Apollonian martyrdom of Thomas to the offstage Dionysian *sparagmos* and *omophagia* (ritual tearing apart and eating) of Celia by cannibals, merely reported during the play's concluding party.[21] Although Eliot tries to impose a right reason for Celia's rare choice of fatal, foreign ecstasy that would join sacred and secular in a modernist ritual realism, her hysteria ultimately escapes such symbolic ordering. Its real Otherness lies beyond the comical (and canonical) stage of *The Cocktail Party*. Her death can only be interpreted, or rather interpolated, as being out of reach.

Celia might have achieved popular success as an actress, the play suggests (as Eliot did as its author), had she stayed for its final party (379). But Reilly confesses (at that party) that he had a strange vision of Celia when he first met her at an earlier party, in the first scene of the play. He saw her face "five minutes after a violent death." Through this choral, cocktail vision, Reilly also foresaw his own role in her treatment: "to direct her in the way of preparation" (384) toward an offstage apotheosis as tragic heroine and Christian martyr. Thus, it is not inappropriate that Lavinia should accuse Reilly of taking sadistic "satisfaction" (Dionysus-like) in the report of Celia's death (383). He insists, though, that the high price she paid in being crucified was "part of the design" (384). Whether the design is complete within Eliot's play, or reaches beyond it, remains an open question, however.[22]

Postmodern Edges

The Cocktail Party shows, through the choral character of Reilly (with Julia behind him), two providential economies of alienation, sacrifice, and communion—at either the "normal" level or a sacred extreme.[23] Edward, much like Celia, is trapped in a fatal double-bind. "Hell is oneself," he says (contra Sartre), then adds: "One is always alone." Yet he finds a "practical" solution (342), much like his author's pragmatism in moving toward a more Chekhovian, tragicomic realism. Celia, however, has had a "vision" of her own higher destiny, as she confesses to Reilly in his consulting room. But she does not "know" yet what it is (364). The choral Reilly mediates between her present, unclear vision of destiny and her future act of sacrifice, which the audience will not see, only hear about. Celia is also aided by Reilly, like Thomas by his chorus, to see the distinctive wound of alienation in her choice, in contrast to Edward's. "Each way means loneliness—and communion," Reilly tells Celia. "But those who take the other / Can forget their loneliness. You will not forget yours" (365). Actually, neither Celia nor Edward has a choice between such ways. Like St. Thomas, their only choice for a Lacanian cure is to follow the preordained plot of their particular character, the right deed of their *sinthome*. Yet Edward's more "familiar" way does not demand the "courage" of Celia's (or Thomas's). Her "unknown" path to tragic death in a faraway land, unlike Edward's existential living on,[24] "requires faith," says Reilly, though it is the "kind of faith that issues from despair" (364).

Eliot tried to maintain this kind of transcendent faith in the potential of modern verse drama to reach a popular audience, despite the failure of his early choruses. Moving the martyrdom offstage with Celia, he increased its tragic brutality, and perhaps absurdity, in comparison with Thomas's onstage death. Also, she is not a high-ranking historical figure like Thomas, but an ordinary, contemporary character, except that she has an extreme sense of spiritual destiny. As in Arthur Miller's ostensible tragedies of the "common man," Celia rises to noble stature in the course of the play, through her tragic frailty and fall. Yet, the reaction of the cocktail party guests is unlike Reilly's choral confidence (and sadistic satisfaction) in her "triumphant" end (385). They first see and resent it as a great "waste" (381); then they begin to feel "guilty" for it (385). Though the religious framework is stronger here than in Miller's social realism, there is perhaps a greater ambiguity about the poetic justice of the hero(ine)'s sacrifice than in *Death of a Salesman* or *The Crucible*. This ambiguity leans in the direction of a postmodern desire for secular, ethical evaluation. For the guilt that lingers after her death threatens to perpetuate the patriarchal demand for sacred violence.

Eliot continued to seek the ideal of Christian community for society at large, though with neither too much diversity nor too much unity, in essays written after *The Cocktail Party*.[25] But the waste and guilt seen by the party guests in Celia's crucifixion, like the *Family* chorus's initial mocking of their own tragic role, points to a new order breaking through the modern death of tragedy, as reenacted by Eliot's drama. His project (along with that of Christopher Fry, Paul Claudel, and others) to revive a tragic verse drama may have been doomed from the start. Before Eliot's earliest plays, Joseph Wood Krutch identified (in 1929) a "tragic fallacy" in the desire to recover that ancient dramatic form. In 1961 George Steiner theorized that tragedy would always be incompatible with Christianity (though he sees its potential rebirth in Brecht's *Mother Courage*). Seen, however, through the metaphysical darkness and existential liberation of Nietzsche's death of God, Eliot's high modernist phallacy, his will to tragic power, also bears, at its repressed edges, the postmodern desire for satyr play and critical politics, as antihierarchical cure.

From a postmodern perspective, Edward is, as he says, more guilty for Celia's death than that "band of half-crazed savages" who killed her (385). He would also be criticized, from a postcolonial position, for viewing native people that way, even if they were cannibals who practiced crucifixion. There might even be some praise for these natives' sense of irony: taking the missionary oppressors' primary myth and turning it against them as hyperreal ritual.[26] Reilly, however, along with Edward, would bear the brunt of a feminist critique. Lavinia's attempt to share the blame and feel guilty with her husband, for being "unkind" and "spiteful" to Celia (385), might also indicate her own oppression by husband and doctor. While Lavinia did have an affair with Peter (who left her to pursue Celia), Edward not only made love to, but also rejected Celia, telling her: "You should have a man . . . nearer your own age" (325). His affair with her and condescending dismissal parallels the patriarchal manipulation of Reilly's cure, in which he orders her mind toward a missionary vocation and even arranges her trip to that "sanitorium" (366). (One might also see parallels here with Eliot's marriage to his much younger private secretary less than a decade after *The Cocktail Party* was written—as well as his flight in previous years from his first wife, Vivien, and her mental illness.)[27] The hysteria that Eliot himself analyzed in his *Murder* chorus migrates through the pursuit of Harry by the Furies in *The Family Reunion* (as he moves from dead wife back to dominating mother) to the visionaries, Reilly and Celia, and her Bacchae-like killers offstage from the chorus-less *Cocktail Party*. But without belief in a Christian order of temptation, sin, guilt, and ultimate redemption, a postmodernist may well see a dangerous perversity in Eliot's dramatic sublimation of hysteria[28]—especially if he or she feels a strong temptation to deconstruct the choral vision of Eliot's tragic metaphysics, which gives heroic value to the suffering of the Other.

The popularity of *The Cocktail Party*, in its initial New York and London productions, indicates that both the mundane making-do of Edward/Lavinia and the tragic heroism of Celia appealed to Eliot's audiences as (the illusion of) credible cures for modern despair. Yet the absurd waste expressed in such resolutions, along with the existential alienation of these characters, also leans toward the stylistically opposed edge, just over the midcentury horizon, of theater of the absurd. Such absurdity and alienation opens, too—at the edge of Eliot's still Christian stage—the wound of an absent chorus, whose communal hysteria had earlier (with *Murder in the Cathedral*) born a Nietzschean potential. This orchestral gap, compressed into the acoustic lens of certain choral characters in Eliot's later drama (including the "one-eyed" Reilly), carries today a cruel, postmodern truth—through the Nietzschean (re)vision of good and evil genealogies in the politics of sacrifice. All the crueler, perhaps, since Eliot's plays are now so rarely produced.

Transcendent/Revolutionary Hysteria

Recently, feminists have discovered a primal tragic scene in Freud's sacrifice of his hysterical patients, most notably Ida Bauer ("Dora"), to his experimental science of psychoanalysis.[29] Claire Kahane concludes her introduction to *In Dora's Case* by stating: "Although Freud's assertion that hysteria afflicted both men and women was a liberating gesture in the nineteenth century, contemporary feminists are reclaiming hysteria as the dis-ease of women in patriarchal culture" (31). The liberating gesture of Celia's martyrdom, through the visionary hysteria of Reilly, inverting the gender positions of chorus and hero from Eliot's previous plays, thus bears a postmodern edge: the dis-ease of women and men on the perverse side of patriarchal belief. One of the *In Dora's Case* essays, jointly written by five (male and female) authors, focuses upon Freud's (mis)interpretation of the Madonna figure and its importance to Dora in his unsuccessful treatment of her. Using Lacan's theory of the mirror stage, they reanalyze her and disagree with Freud: "Dora's deepest desire is not identification with the mother (in the sense of the assumption of the mother's role) but fusion with the mother, a return to that 'desperate paradise'" (Collins et al. 249).[30] They point out that Freud, too, late in his career, found a connection between "an unresolved attachment to the mother and the etiology of hysteria" (250). And they expand their revelation from Dora's case to "Freud's parallel occulting of the mother in the Oedipus complex," and even beyond that to "a perversion—the repression of the mother—which lies at the root of Western civilization itself" (251).

Nietzsche excavated the repressed womb of a dithyrambic chorus at the stage edge of Western theater. And he hoped in vain for a return to that desperate paradise of Dionysian fusion with Wagner's operas. Eliot began his playwriting career with a similar attempt to resurrect the chorus, even if one includes the unfinished *Sweeney Agonistes,* with its Kleinian erotics that resurface in the cannibalism reported by *The Cocktail Party.* His original desire for modern ritual drama involved, like Nietzsche's (and Yeats's), both music and dance (Howarth 307–9).[31] But Eliot's potentially dithyrambic choruses became immobilized (into a mere "poetry recital" [*Poetry* 31]) before the mirror-audience of Christian believers. So he transferred his choral verse visions from the acoustic lens of the orchestra pit to his onstage hysterical characters, embodying there the lack of the Other. Celia as missionary healer and female Christ-figure, pushed offstage by the mundane cocktail party and visionary Reilly, represents the final movement of this hysterical wound within Eliot's dramatic corpus—and the persistent attachment to the tragic (m)other, which he repressed in writing a popular drawing-room comedy. Today's feminism discovers an occulting of the mother at the heart of psychoanalysis, particularly in Freud's treatment of Dora, reflecting the current dis-ease of women (and men, too, I would argue). Similarly, the perverse traits in Reilly's and Celia's faith, issuing from hysterical as well as existential despair, disclose a postmodern womb in Eliot's writing: the creative dis-ease of future generations.

For the ancient Egyptians, Greeks, and Romans, hysteria was a disease of the womb (Greek *hystera*) moving within the body.[32] This monstrous migrating organ became associated with demonic possession under Christianity, initially through the writings of St. Augustine (who feared the theater for similar reasons). Such beliefs continued throughout the Middle Ages and into the Renaissance persecution of witches as the Church's perverse Other (Veith 46–47, 56–59). Celia alludes to this lingering belief and fear, in her view of Reilly's mysterious power (to bring Lavinia back and persuade Edward that he wants her again): "Then he *must* be the Devil! He must have bewitched you" (*CPP* 321). After working with Charcot, Freud also connected medieval terms and descriptions for witchcraft, such as *stigmata Diaboli* (wound/sign of the devil), to his own theories of hysteria and its symptoms (*SE* 1:11, 41, 45).[33] Freud, though, moved away from Charcot's theatrical demonstrations, hypnotic treatment, and hereditary sources for hysteria in developing his seduction theory, talking cure, and dream interpretations—along with his own hysterical symptoms and self-analysis.[34]

But in the confessional intimacy of his consulting room, the Freudian psychoanalyst becomes as devilish to many feminists today as Charcot was in directing the spectacular performances of hypnotized hysterics in his medical theater. Maria Ramas, for example, sees the sadomasochistic devil of modern patriarchy (and capitalism) exposed in Freud's treatment of Dora. Yet Dora's own homosexual desire—and "rebellion" against Freud's heterosexual ideology by refusing further treatment—becomes heroic for Ramas, as desiring spectator. The Victorian perversity in Dora's hysteria thus stimulates a postmodern feminist's faithful vision of revolutionary sacrifice.

Eliot's dramatic hyster(i)a, migrating from stage edge and central hero to choral characters and offstage heroine, continued to be masked by Christian faith and tragic ideals. But that Apollonian mask also contained a Dionysian drive toward the primal modern wound of existential alienation. As the Canterbury Cathedral fell to a drawing-room ceiling, the metaphysical heavens were collapsing, too, toward the postmodern horizon of patriarchal guilt. The martyr's divine intersection of eternity and temporality, at the center of a mortal wheel of being, thus rolls into this revisionary ambush. Today, rather than applaud the providential economy that selects a Thomas, Celia, or Dora to be sacrificed through the clairvoyant wisdom of a chorus, Reilly, or Freud, society is judged as perverse for demanding real suffering from actual women (and other historically oppressed peoples) through such evil agents. But as Eliot's drama shows, the facilitators of patriarchal sacrifice can also be female: the women of Canterbury; Amy, Agatha, and the Furies; Julia behind Reilly. Thus, the postmodern melodrama of guilty males and victimized females masks a more pervasive and perverse tragedy.

Celia, under Reilly's watchful eye, identifies with two highly significant modernist symptoms: not only existential aloneness, but also metaphysical guilt. Her sin of adultery (with Edward), like Harry's memory of murdering his wife, spurs her guilty self-questioning, but it is not the most fundamental fantasy that grounds her special symptoms and grandiose sacrifice. She sees everything around her as sinfully false, as hysterically hollow, as a

Nietzschean veil of maya:[35] "I have no delusions— / Except that the world I live in seems all a delusion!" Like Harry, though, she would prefer to see herself, rather than the entire world (or patriarchy), as perverse, because the latter would be "much more frightening" (*CPP* 359).

Unlike today's feminist fetishization of Dora as lost object and revolutionary heroine at the primal scene of psychoanalysis, Celia takes upon herself the original sin of alienation and the guilt of a hollow, perverse, patriarchal world. Rather than be a chorus that focuses the perspective of a worshipful Canterbury audience upon another character, Celia chooses to act out the fate of a tragic heroine. Even though she is a modern woman, who "had always been taught to disbelieve in sin" (361), she seeks out a metaphysical dimension to her suffering, instead of believing that historical and political blame lies with the Father.

Or is this merely Reilly's hypnotic indoctrination of her, manipulating her transference toward a cruel death, which he claims to have clairvoyantly foreseen? Such a view would figure Reilly not as a messianic Herakles or Dionysus, but as a modernist Agamemnon sacrificing his "daughter" to the metaphysical winds of Christian imperialism. He would thus perpetuate the curse of patriarchy, as Eliotic inheritor of Wishwood's Furies, beating back the hysterical chora (like Harry with his wife and mother) through the further, violent repression of women. But this potential superimposition of postmodern politics upon Eliot's metaphysics—like Clytemnestra's revenge upon Agamemnon—ignores the role of women (or of the goddess Artemis) in upholding patriarchal subjection when it is to their advantage. Hence, we are tempted to replay the symptomatic curse of our forefathers and foremothers, even as we pass to a stage beyond modernist regressions. The archetypes (and stereotypes) of tragedy and melodrama become repeated *through* the Oedipal fight to be liberated from them. In the "social drama" (Turner) of current theory, at the stage edge between modernism and postmodernism, the "sacrificial crisis" (Girard) of inherited guilt and lost historical victims demands new scapegoats to restore the illusion of justice. Power may shift, but ritual violence returns and refocuses—with each new generation of players and spectators.

Exemplifying this inheritance of guilt, Celia asks Reilly why she feels so guilty about her own alienation, as if it were her own (original) sin to be cut off from mother and womb by an imaginary mirror.

> Like a child who has wandered into a forest
> Playing with an imaginary playmate

And suddenly discovers he is only a child
Lost in a forest, wanting to go home.

(362–63)

The use of "he" for the child (in this analogy to herself) predicts Celia's later identification with the *sinthome* of a male tragic hero and Christ-figure. But, as of yet, she is still caught in a fundamental fantasy of lostness. In his response to Celia's lines, Reilly pushes her to cross that fantasy: "Disillusion can become itself an illusion / If we rest in it" (363).[36] He thus compels Celia to see her "salvation" not in a past injustice, but in her own future, sacrificial act.

Once permanently offstage, Celia becomes a nun, a missionary nurse, and a martyr (prefiguring the secular sainthood of today's Mother Teresa)—through her desire of the Other that speaks as the symptom of metaphysical guilt. Hence, the oracle of the *Murder* chorus also looks ahead to her heroism, prophesying through a moving, communal hyster(i)a: "What is woven on the loom of fate . . . Is woven like a pattern of living worms / In the guts of the women of Canterbury" (208). This translates to Celia's modern(ist) faith issuing from hysterical despair, through her feeling "of emptiness, of failure / Towards someone, or something, outside myself; / And I feel I must . . . atone—is that the word?" (362).

Today, many feminist theorists try to envision a reality for women other than sacrificial daughter, mother, or martyr. But Celia's question also challenges the anti-phallogocentric choice of political blame over existential at-one-ment. Both options require further sacrifice, in word and deed, to restore poetic justice, as personal and social cure. Yet, who should be sacrificed and how (among fathers and daughters, mothers and sons) remains a crucial factor in the postmodern equation. We are all patriarchal subjects cursed by loss in some particular, familial way—with a present guilt that we readily project or transfer. The hyster(i)a of Eliot's secular drama serves to remind us that a tragic temptation must still be faced, especially when the satyr plays and melodramas of the postmodern verge upon revolutionary violence, when alienated victims become communal (albeit secular) martyrs.[37] I now turn to three avant-garde dramatists, whose differences from Eliot's high modernism show other edges of power and vulnerability arising from patriarchal/maternal loss.

Psychobiography
Lost Stage Mothers

Chapter 4

Artaud's Womb in Derridean Re-presentation

While Eliot fashioned on- and offstage martyrs with his drama, Antonin Artaud became one himself, through his own heroic failure to re-present what he felt theater had lost. Hence, this famous phrase from *The Theater and its Double* reflects Artaud's own role in the history of theater: "And if there is still one hellish, truly accursed thing in our time, it is our artistic dallying with forms, instead of being like victims burnt at the stake, signalling through the flames" (13). Like Nietzsche, Artaud came to incarnate, physically as well as historically, certain "unbearable truths"—as he said of Nietzsche, van Gogh, and other predecessors in 1947, one year before his death. He saw each of them as a revolutionary individual, an "authentic lunatic," who provoked the universalizing conscience (of a particular society) to interrogate itself. Yet he also describes the painful alienation of such "lucid" individuals, becoming "overwhelmed by the powerful suction of the formidable tentacle-like oppression of a kind of civic bewitchment which soon openly expresses itself in the general conventions" ("Van Gogh" 47).[1]

Artaud saw himself—through the choral mirror of others viewing and manipulating his madness—as fighting valiantly against an octopus-like chora underlying the Other's symbolic order and civic conventions. Two decades after his death, Artaud also became a martyred hero for rebellious students in the Paris riots of 1968.[2] Through his eloquent, schizophrenic and paranoiac writings, Artaud has continued to be a great visionary of post-modern art and theory, sacrificed by society, like van Gogh, Nietzsche, and other geniuses he admired. Yet Artaud's genius was trapped during his own lifetime in his extreme sense of life's betrayal.[3] He played the role of martyr so well that he could not create the theater he theorized. He kept desiring beyond it, and losing it as soon as it became real: an activity outside his own body.

Nevertheless, Artaud's theories did crystallize into a few plays of his

own—though these are usually ignored today, with the greater regard given
to his directorial dreams and their iconoclasm against canonical texts. The
current chapter will analyze these somewhat forgotten dramas in relation to
Artaud's theories and childhood psychobiography. Again postmodern theory will be involved, particularly Jacques Derrida's interpretation of a
"nontheological" theater, which he finds in Artaud's final, encopretic writings. Thus, the vicissitudes of loss and power in various stages of Artaud's
life and afterlife will be displayed: primordial, infantile, psychosomatic,
performative, dramatic, schizophrenic, and postmortem/postmodern.

Like Nietzsche's theories of the birth of tragedy and Eliot's hysterical
choruses, Artaud tried to theorize and revive a lost power in theater. But
Artaud went farther theoretically than either Nietzsche or Eliot in breaking
the prophylactic barrier of the classical chorus. Whereas Eliot's dramatic
corpus bears, but cannot contain, a postmodern hyster(i)a, moving from
ritual chorus to offstage heroine, Artaud shattered the stage-edge mirror of
choral mimesis and psychological realism, eventually making his own body
into a theatrical womb—to be viewed through insanely lucid poetry. Nietzsche desired a return to the ancient chora of theater, as Dionysian womb
prior to the birth of Western tragedy, through a merging of spectators and
chorus that would "overlook" culture and reenvision a god onstage.
Artaud also rebelled against Western culture and the ossification of its theater by returning to ritual sources,[4] but in a much greater variety, both occidental and oriental. Thus, the Dionysian *sparagmos* in Artaud's theater of
cruelty became a rending of Western history and its corpus of canonical
drama, inspiring many revolutionary figures in postmodern theory and performance.

Gnostic Cruelty, Individual and Communal

In her introduction to the *Selected Writings (SW)* of Artaud, Susan Sontag
describes him as being primarily an individualist, with a firm gnostic faith
that developed from romantic genius toward a schizophrenic, yet heroic
shamanism.[5] For the same reason, Sontag points to Nietzsche along with
Artaud as paradigms for modern authorship, "by their effort to disestablish
themselves, by their will not to be morally useful to the community, by their
inclination as . . . seers, spiritual adventurers, and social pariahs" (xviii).
Postmodernism has now pushed this trickster *figura* of Nietzsche/Artaud to
a new stage. Despite the "death of the author" (according to Barthes and
Foucault),[6] these heroic writers continue to bear revolutionary spirit, mir-

rored in the choruses of current theorists. Artaud's case is at least as paradoxical as Nietzsche's, and more directly influential in his theories of theater. His life and writings refuse to be contained by Sontag's labels, helpful
as they are in explaining him. For, as she also shows, he is both gnostic and
materialist, individualist and communist (though not in the political sense),
social pariah and metaphysical moralist.

Nietzsche's dream of theater depended upon separate orders of audience, chorus, and actor. Artaud's theories also hope for spectator ecstasy,
but through a "direct communication" with the actor and spectacle (Theater 96). This gnostic communion of bodies would explode conventional,
historical divisions.[7] "I propose then a theatre in which violent physical
images crush and hypnotize the sensibility of the spectator seized by the theater as by a whirlwind of higher forces" (82–83). Unlike Brecht's aversion to
theatrical hypnosis (which I will examine in a later chapter),[8] Artaud wants
to create a theater "that induces trance," as with dancing dervishes or "certain tribal music cures" (83). Unlike Derrida's philosophical community
beyond metaphysical violence, with an ideal being-together as separation
(in his essay on Levinas), Artaud desires a violent, communal cure to the
desperate sense of separation within individual human beings, as well as
between them. And yet, Derrida adapts Artaud's gnostic theater of moral
cruelty for his own project of overcoming theological violence—which I
shall investigate later in this chapter.

Despite what Sontag shows of Artaud's heroic individualism, his plans
for theater attack the Western tradition of focusing on individual character
psychology. "The theater must make itself the equal of life—not an individual life, that individual aspect of life in which CHARACTERS triumph, but
the sort of liberated life which sweeps away human individuality and in
which man is only a reflection" (Theater 116). Artaud would transform
both spectacle and spectator (without Nietzsche's intervening choral lens)
into the immortal power of life, which man merely mirrors. Yet the cut of
this mirror in human life—in being human and divine, in feeling both mortal and immortal—is precisely the cruel stage edge of the Artaudian revolution. His hope that theater might attain the liberative power of life, "in the
gnostic sense of a living whirlwind that devours the darkness," is just the
other side of an excruciating, physical sense "of that pain apart from whose
ineluctable necessity life could not continue." Hence, his passion for a cruel
theater reflects and is empowered by the cruelty of life—by an acute consciousness of death in life: "It is consciousness that gives to the exercise of
every act of life its blood-red color, its cruel nuance, since it is understood

that life is always someone's death" (102). It is not the blood of the heroic martyr that makes the theater transcendent and hieratic for Artaud; it is the loss at the heart of life, the horror in beauty, the blood in birth.

Artaud's theater continues the liberative violence of the French Enlightenment, while destroying the epistemological barrier of the Cartesian proscenium. Yet his writings bear this revolutionary spirit as cyclical. They point ahead to the postmodern; they also return to the ancient tradition of gnosticism. Varieties of this faith recur in many different religions and cultures, although often marginalized as perverse.

> The leading energies of Gnosticism come from metaphysical anxiety and acute psychological distress—the sense of being abandoned, of being an alien, of being possessed by demonic powers which prey on the human spirit in a cosmos vacated by the divine. (Sontag xlv)

Artaud's stress upon physical spectacle and liberative communion reflects a crisis of divine emptiness in the universe and of evil forces within the body.[9] Through this severe, personal void and threat, Artaud connects the mystical elements of various traditions—those of repressed heresies in the West and of theatrical rituals maintained by the oriental Other—to formulate his own alchemical strategy.[10]

The Canon Exploded

Artaud prefigures the postmodern death of the author not only through playing the role of martyr in his own "abortive theatre" (*Collected Works* [*CW*] 2:22), but also by attacking the conventional reverence for dramatic text and playwright. He blames Renaissance drama, primarily that of Shakespeare and Racine, for the development of a "purely descriptive and narrative theater," with the actors on one side and the audience on the other, divided by the stage edge. This makes the spectators into perverse "Peeping Toms" of character psychology at a safe, "disinterested" distance—though all they really see is the "mirror" of themselves (*Theater* 76–77, 84). Even eroticism in theater "has lost its mystery." Thus, art for art's sake becomes "an unmistakable symptom of our power to castrate" (77). Here Artaud perceives, in theater, what Lacan later theorized as the "mirror stage" of infants, and the father's *père-version* in separating the child from its mother—both of which structure human alienation throughout life (*Écrits* 1–7; *Feminine* 167).

Artaud laments that the voyeuristic, yet castrated theater of his own day is abandoned by the elite and sends popular audiences to the movies (*Theater* 84). Today, one senses an even greater loss of theater along these lines. Despite the Artaudian ecstasies of the 1960s and 1970s, Broadway is now in decline (except for Disney's musicals), regional theaters struggle to survive, and audiences are captivated by the vast simulacrum of multiplex cinemas, video cassettes, and cable TV.[11] As Artaud (who had been a silent-screen actor and scriptwriter) stated in 1933: "Movies in their turn, murdering us with second-hand reproductions which, filtered through machines, cannot *unite with* our sensibility, have maintained us for ten years in an ineffectual torpor, in which our faculties appear to be foundering" (84). Like Eliot (in his jibes at poetry recital audiences and his critiques of irreligious culture), Artaud fears that such mechanized torpor will make the public more gullible for "war, plague, famine, and slaughter" (78). Thus, he proposes homeopathic doses of such terrors, uniting physically (as well as spiritually) with all the spectators' faculties, not just their castrated voyeurism.

Like Eliot, Artaud says: "Let the dead poets make way for others." But unlike Eliot, he would not uphold the official, literary tradition of masterpieces (even if readjusted for new, individual talent).[12] Artaud's view of the new in literature is more like Kristeva's theory of an abject chora, as the revolutionary power in poetic language. "Beneath the poetry of the texts, there is the actual poetry, without form and without text" (Artaud, *Theater* 78). Kristeva, in fact, cites Artaud many times as evidence for the actual, choral poetry (genotext), beneath form and text.[13] Artaud, who was three-quarters Greek by blood (Esslin 15), still respected ancient Greek drama, even while deconstructing the classical text. In *Oedipus Rex* Artaud values "the theme of incest and the idea that nature mocks at morality and that there are certain unspecified powers at large which we would do well to beware of, call them *destiny* or anything you choose" (*Theater* 74–75). He also likes "the presence of a plague epidemic" in Sophocles' play, but its cathartic power is not homeopathic enough for contemporary audiences. Its poison is too ameliorated by "a manner and language that have lost all touch with the rude and epileptic rhythm of our time" (75). In Aristotle's terms, the mythos (plot) rings true, but diction and song do not.[14] Thus (in Kristeva's terms), the genotext of ancient drama, and of *Oedipus* in particular, still bears a choral power. Though his writings have been taken by the influential poststructuralists Deleuze and Guattari as a revolt against the dominance of the Oedipus myth in psychoanalysis and Western culture, Artaud shows the perversity (and schizoanalysis) of anti-Oedipus lying within Oedipal dogma.[15]

Artaud also points outside the text, or rather to the outside within it, for the power that has been lost: "if we are so incapable today of giving an idea of Aeschylus, Sophocles, Shakespeare that is worthy of them, it is probably because we have lost the sense of their theater's physics. It is because . . . their whole scenic rhythm escapes us" (108). Perverting Aristotle's hierarchy and neoclassical laws, Artaud would reinvoke the true cathartic cruelty of classical myth and character through spectacle, song, diction, and thought. For it is the dominance of words over gesture, psychology over passion, that has ossified the dramatic text into a mere skeleton of its former living power.

> This obstinacy in making characters talk about feelings, passions, desires, and impulses of a strictly psychological order, in which a single word is to compensate for innumerable gestures, is the reason, since we are in the domain of precision, the theater has lost its true *raison d'être* and why we have come to long for a silence in it in which we could listen more closely to life. (*Theater* 118)

The loss of theater, in the skeleton of the text, is its potential for new life. Artaud's theatrical physics would open the corpus of Western drama (and Christianity) to hear, in its dead silences, life's pulse. He would thus amplify the rhythm and spectacle of that lost (m)other within the patriarchal specter, in order to stage the bloody show of being torn from the womb, of being born into the fate of life and death.

In an early essay on theater, "The Evolution of Decor" (1924), Artaud also desires to contact the author lost within the text: "We must reestablish a kind of magnetic intercommunication between the spirit of the author and the spirit of the director" (*SW* 53).[16] Despite his later cry of "no more masterpieces," Artaud here summons the "great dramatists, the genre dramatists, [who] thought outside the theatre." He says that Aeschylus, Sophocles, Shakespeare, Racine, Corneille, and Molière "are forever probing the inner scene changes, the sort of perpetual comings and goings of the protagonists' souls" (*CW* 1:152). At this point, Artaud does not attack the psychology of character in these playwrights' works; instead he focuses on the theater within the minds (and spirits) of protagonists—as revealed by the great artists' scripts.[17] Even with his later emphasis of stage effects over text in *The Theater and Its Double*, Artaud confesses that the written page will be his goal for historical transcendence: "all these gropings, researches, and shocks will culminate nevertheless in a work *written down* . . . by new means of notation" (111). So it is to Artaud's own dramatic texts that I now turn, via his ultimate, schizophrenic poetry (deconstructing in the hands of Derrida)—to disclose the postmodern sense of loss at the edges of his page and stage.

A Fatal *Soufflé*

Like Sartre's existentialist canonization of Genet (which I shall analyze in the next chapter), Derrida exalts Artaud as poststructuralist saint, as both actor and martyr. Allen Thiher has aptly summarized Derrida's antitheological hagiography:

> Artaud is a victim of the structuration of Western metaphysics. He is a martyr to its determination of language as a metaphysical sign as well as to its ontico-theology that has culminated in the Western theatrical stage and its practice of representation. (504)

I will examine Derrida's St. Artaud in order to look through that postmodern hero of metaphysical victimization for another Artaud, within his psychobiography and dramatic corpus. That other Artaud plays the villainous father and thus reincarnates a phallic mother's womb, ghosting both the modernist return to essential ritual truth and the postmodern pleasure in diverse interpretations, performance texts, and the Derridean scripture of infinitely deferring *écriture*.

In Derrida's essay "The Theater of Cruelty and the Closure of Representation" (1966), the practice of Artaudian cruelty is very much a hypothetical dream—a theoretical space—though its "present inexistence," along with its "implacable necessity," is also "historic in an absolute and radical sense" (*Writing and Difference* [*WD*] 233–34). Its potential (and prior) reality can be glimpsed only by deconstructing the theological space that has existed in Western theater throughout its history. Thus, Artaud's theater, in Derrida's view, mirrors his own critique of Western metaphysics and his desire to see beyond the closure of representation. Artaud's schizophrenic écriture becomes a choral genotext refocusing the postmodern character of Artaud, as played by Derrida, into a Samson-like martyr destroying the oppressive temple (and proscenium frame) of Cartesian philosophy. Ironically though, it is through Artaud's gnostic stress upon breath in the Jewish Cabala, and on the hieroglyphic logos of Balinese dance drama, that Derrida sees his way beyond "phono-phallogocentrism" to a postmodern clearing of "presence*less* presence"—as he puts it in a later essay ("Living On" 146).[18]

Using Artaud, Derrida redefines theater's persistent theological structure as its current and perennial "perversion" (*WD* 236–37). It is dominated
by speech, by the "phonic text," coming from an absent author as creator,
master, and god, who thus "governs" the theological stage "from afar"
through the logos of the Word (235). But Derrida then looks back, through
Artaud's words (and Nietzsche's), to a primordial point in time, before the
Word became flesh, "at the eve of theatrical representation, at the origin of
tragedy" (Derrida, *WD* 236). According to Derrida, Artaud would unmask
theater's theologically perverse "erasure of the stage" that began with
ancient classical drama, its Word-made-flesh masque hiding the original,
primal theater's mise-en-scène of "autopresentation" (236–38). Together
they would disclose a stage before theater history and its progressive stages
of "classical forgetting" (236)—at the edge of a ritual, preverbal womb,
"Representation, then, as the autopresentation of pure visibility and even
pure sensibility" (238).

Derrida directly borrows the theological terms of John 1:14, of the
Word become flesh, while seeking a preverbal immediacy instead. Artaud's
nontheological stage "lays bare the flesh of the word, lays bare the word's
sonority, intonation, intensity" (*WD* 240). Thus, Derrida is careful to note
that while the theater of cruelty "expulses God from the stage," it is not a
theater of atheism. Like Deleuze and Guattari, Derrida shows Artaud's
deconstruction of the modern sense of loss known as "the death of God"
(reviving Nietzsche's premodern revelation).[19] Artaud fights with the
absent, yet still governing from afar God, bringing Him down to the stage
to address His deadly erasure.[20] Like Jacob's struggle with his angel, the
theater of cruelty wrestles with the dead God, "whose death," says Derrida,
"as difference and repetition within life, has never ceased to menace life"
(235). Performing as well as interpreting Artaud, Derrida rechristens this
dead God to distinguish Him from another One: "not the living God, but
the Death-God." Who then is the Other, the living God? For Derrida and
his Artaud, as for Nietzsche, it is "Life" itself (*WD* 246).[21]

In Derrida's view, Artaud proposes a nontheological, yet also nonathe-
istic, "hieratic theatre." While producing a nontheological space, Artaud
still seeks the divine in that space. "The divine has been ruined by God,"
says Derrida. "That is to say, by man . . . permitting himself to be separated
from Life by God"—a deed that Artaud would undo. But he would undo it,
in my view, by returning to the lost mother's body (or its ghost) behind the
mirror stage. He thus desires the immediate (and perversely real) divinity of
Life, in an unnamed mother goddess beyond Christian theology and classi-

cal theater. But he must go through the latter to reach the former, reperverting the rigorous and violent erasure of many historical stages, personal and theatrical. As Derrida puts it (with no reference to the mother goddess): "The restoration of divine cruelty, hence, must traverse the murder of God, that is to say, primarily the murder of the man-God" (243).

This primary murder of the man-God masks the repressed power of a perverse mother goddess (or chora) buried beneath, yet still haunting, the successive layers of theological stages. Fortunately, Derrida's Artaudian project of traversing that repetitive murder and erasing its Oedipal guilt, unlike Deleuze and Guattari's, does not forget the womb behind it. Yet Derrida fails to recognize the uterine signifier (in the broadest sense) within Christian theology, Western stage space, and psychoanalytic myth: the mother at the foot of the cross, bearing an earlier nativity scene, and Jocasta hanging behind Oedipus's blinded eyes.[22]

There is an initial stage of cruelty for all of us in the trauma of birth (as Otto Rank argued): thrust and pulled from a warm, wet bed of flesh into the cold, blazing, empty air. But some continue to experience this pain intimately throughout their lives, as did Artaud. His desire for cruelty onstage shows not only the painful loss of (m)other earth religions, repressed by Western theology and imperialist technologies, but also the loss, repression, and yet infection of a maternal body that lingers perversely at the birth edge of our souls.

Perverse Mothering

Object-relations psychoanalyst Estela V. Welldon has recently pointed to an overidealization of the mother in Western culture and a symptomatic forgetting of her part in perverse relationships: "even in the original oedipal situation we fail to notice Jocasta's responsibility." Welldon remarks that "Jocasta was far better equipped, even consciously, to recognize Oedipus as her son than vice versa." Thus, Welldon pushes past Freud's focus on Oedipal desire (more like his contemporary, Melanie Klein), to the mother's shaping of the child's polymorphous perversity. According to Greek myth, Jocasta's husband, Laius,[23] was a pedophiliac. Welldon speculates that this was his reason for not wanting his wife to have a child (85). Jocasta's marriage to him shows her to be a "willing victim of a perverse relationship." But she also tricks him into impregnating her by getting him drunk. "In other words, she was already exercising her own power over her offspring, which was to lead her to give him away at birth." Welldon even surmises that Jocasta knew, at least unconsciously, that she "could pursue the lost relationship [with Oedipus], the power of motherhood later being replaced by that of incest, which would be more rewarding for her" (86).

Welldon reanalyzes the myth in this way, showing a side of it that Freud forgot,[24] not to blame mothers rather than sons, but to deconstruct the idealization of motherhood, which permits and even encourages maternal perversities (83). Indeed, she blames society for not recognizing women as responsible and not helping them with "the power of the womb" (as she titles one of her chapters). In case after case, in her own practice and others', she traces the symptoms of patients (male and female) back to the particular perversities of mothers and grandmothers, fatefully repeated in each generation, though with certain transformations depending upon outside events, such as the death of a close family member.[25] Such directness may open Welldon's theory to charges of essentialism, but she stresses the "inherent attributes" of the female body as a crucial difference in order to debunk the glorification of that body, and of motherhood, by Western society (10–11).[26] Thus, for my purposes, she not only provides psychoanalytic details on the force of the womb, but also checks the tendency to idealize that female organ.[27] Welldon helps to show how a perverse mother goddess persists in patriarchy, along with the desire to return to an idealized womb—which one can see in both modernist nostalgia and postmodern liberation.

Often maternal perversity occurs as a mother's revenge against her own abuse by one or both of her parents: thus the violence and incest continue as if through psychogenetics. But perverse mothering can also create a schizophrenic child, as Welldon shows by citing the studies of J. N. Rosen and C. W. Wahl (qtd. in Welldon 64, 103). In Artaud's case, there is some biographical evidence that suggests such perverse mothering as a source of his schizophrenia, along with other factors in his early childhood. (With such evidence, interpreted psychoanalytically, I do not mean to give a complete diagnosis of the historical Artaud, nor to blame his parents for child abuse. Rather, I want to analyze the significance of his character to postmodern theatricality.) His father, a shipping agent, was largely absent from home but did give him the double *Nom du Père*, though castrating the king: from Antoine-Roi Artaud to Antonin Artaud (Hayman 36–37). Both his mother and father were of Greek ancestry and were, in fact, cousins. His grandmothers were thus sisters, and were also close at hand.[28] Such details about Artaud's mother and grandmothers indicate a perversity different from the Jocasta myth, or rather its mirror image: "She overwhelmed him with affection and then, abruptly, withdrew it. Apparently he soon became as prone as she was to accesses of hysterical rage" (Hayman 37–38).

What Hayman describes as violent hysteria in both mother and son may actually have been a perverse relationship between them—leading to Artaud's role as postmodern prophet. For today, even under common patriarchal pressures, "women who feel in an inferior position try in a vicarious but vigorous way to achieve their own fantasies of power through their own reproductive organs, and furthermore to act them out." Welldon adds that "underlying motivations vary from the so-called normal to the very sadistic and cruel" (46). Indeed, Welldon sees sadism as the characteristic motivation for all perversion and connects this, in Kleinian fashion, to common childhood mourning (first for the womb and breast, but also for other objects) and the renewed threat of loss—especially loss of the mother as primary object (9, 17, 67). With Artaud's mother and childhood, specific incidents of loss and mourning can be found that illuminate his later belief in a theater of cruelty and its significance to postmodern identity.

Artaud's Jocasta-like mother stole him from his father (from the *Nom du Père*),[29] by giving him a nickname, *Nanaqui*. This was a diminutive for *Antonaki*, yet also similar to *Neneka*, the nickname of the mother of Antonin's mother (Hayman 38). Such symbolic control again suggests the possibility of a perverse mothering that was multigenerational (Welldon 53, 59). For Antonin was very close to his maternal grandmother and continued to use his childhood nickname well into adulthood, especially in relationships with women.[30] He also signed letters with it, such as this one, addressed to his mother, when he was fifteen years old.

> Forgive, I beg you to forgive a guilty son, a repentant heart. Oh! mama, I love you more than anything in the world, I love you, and I am tortured with remorse at what I did. I am mad. I am a monster but forgive me. What madness possesses me to do such things. Oh! I love you and I could never repeat it often enough, how enormous my sin is, but how good you are. . . . When I have deserved it, kiss me and may I then be forgiven for always, may I never fall back into the error. (Qtd. in Hayman 38)

This letter may indicate the guilt and self-disgust of an incest victim. It certainly shows the young Artaud's idolization of his mother, his belief in her redemptive kisses (though it seems he may never deserve them again),[31] and the consciousness of a certain "madness" already possessing him. After his father's death in 1924, when Artaud was twenty-seven, his mother came to live with him in Paris and did so for thirteen years, until his commitment to a series of asylums in France after his trips to Mexico and Ireland (Greene 22). Throughout the year 1943, while living at the Rodez asylum, Artaud signed his letters "Antonin Nalpas," using his mother's maiden name as his own (Esslin 54).[32] Perhaps he was actually signaling through the flames: the Jocasta figure(s) of his Oedipus complex.

While lecturing in Mexico, Artaud spoke of his "obscure hatred of the Father, and of my father in particular." But on the day "I saw him die," says Artaud, "that inhuman severity with which I accused him of treating me, suddenly ceased. Another being emerged from that body." This spectacle of the good double (as specter) emerging from the body of the cruel, inhuman father gave Artaud a cathartic vision, he claims. "And I, who suffer from unease in my body, understood that he had suffered unease in his body and that there is a lie in existence against which we are born to protest" (qtd. in Esslin 100). The "lie" refers, I think, to the painful human paradox of mortal body and immortal desire. But it also seems to connect Artaud's long history of psychosomatic illness to a parallel "unease" in at least one of his parents. Esslin ties it to the incest in Artaud's plays, *The Spurt of Blood* and *The Cenci,* as well as to his analysis (in *The Theater and Its Double*) of the brother-sister incest in John Ford's *'Tis Pity She's a Whore* (100). I will analyze Artaud's drama later in this chapter. But first I must mention certain tragic events in his early life that indicate another reason for his interest in the subject of incest and his extreme sensitivity to the uneasy lie of life. One can then see, through Artaud's vision of theater, the reincarnation of perverse cruelty at the heart of patriarchal/maternal orthodoxy—with violent, revolutionary consequences from generation to generation.

The Dead Rivals

Artaud had eight brothers and sisters, but only two survived infancy. A few months before Antonin's fifth birthday, his baby brother, Robert, died (after living only three days). Then Antonin himself seemed to become ill with meningitis, possibly terminal. At that time, shortly after the death of Robert, he was his mother's only surviving boy, and one of only two surviving children. Antonin and his sister (Marie-Ange), who survived infancy together despite the death of so many siblings, "developed close, affectionately protective instincts towards each other" (Hayman 36). But when he was eight years old, Antonin was again traumatized by the death of his baby sister, Germaine (at the age of seven months). She became a figure in his later writings, along with his grandmother-sisters and other women in his adult life, all of whom he sometimes referred to as his "daughters" (Hayman 37; Esslin 15; Artaud, CW 1:21).

Even without applying psychoanalytic terms, one can see that Artaud's childhood symptoms of terminal meningitis may have come from mental trauma as well as physical illness. He must have suffered some degree of "survivor's guilt" from a very early age (with so many dead siblings preceding him), confirmed and reconfirmed by the deaths of his brother and sister when he was five and eight. Maybe he was also caught in a spectral competition for his mourning mother's affection, fighting against long dead and recently dead baby brothers and sisters—as evidenced by his later concern with bringing the spirit world to the stage in all its cruel antagonism. Many other details of Artaud's biography evidence this as well: his mother's hot and cold treatment of him (and hysterical rages) early in his life, his own near death at age five and again at age ten while visiting his grandmother, and his mother's closeness to him as an adult, apparently using him as a substitute for the dead father. The specifics of Artaud's brushes with death as a child and of his incestuous relations (at least psychologically) with mother, sister, and grandmothers thus help to clarify his later theatrics: his dramas of incest, his theories of gnostic spectacle, and his own lifelong roles as martyr and shaman.

However accidental his near drowning at the age of ten, while his family was visiting the maternal grandmother in Smyrna (Hayman 38), the young Artaud was, at some level, touching the world of the dead inhabited by many sibling rivals and entered just two years earlier by his sister, Germaine. By virtue of the family's holiday geography, he was returning to the ancient Greek chora of grandmother and water, but he took that a step further—as he would often do in his theatrical career. Antonin was already performing then (as "Nanaqui") for an audience of multigenerational matriarchs, usually absent father, and sibling spirits. According to Melanie Klein, "the death instinct within" is, contrary to Freud's castration theory, "the primordial anxiety," which the ego must deflect outward (216). This necessitates, even in the supposedly normal infant, a "splitting process" that is both Manichaean and melodramatic: "during the first few months he predominantly keeps the good object apart from the bad one and thus, in a fundamental way, preserves it" (217). For Lacanians (and much of postmodern theory) the subject is not an ego; it is fundamentally split by the Father's Name/No and the Other's desire. For Kleinians (like Welldon) there is also a fundamental splitting process in the first months of life, which creates particular character traits and perhaps later symptoms, but this operates between the infantile ego and objects outside it, primarily the mother's body parts.[33] From either perspective, however, Artaud's near drowning at age ten not only reflects, in many later ripples, the gnostic doubles of his dramatic and theoretical corpus; it also refers back to the origin of his subjectivity in a fundamental split—through the torsions of incestuous, mournful, and fatal surroundings. The death instinct within the young Artaud, or the desire of the (m)Other within him, split his soul. So, he acted out the life/death, good/evil, love/hate womb within his own body by drowning (at grandmother's place), yet also living on.

Deleuze and Guattari found a universal schizophrenia in the paradigm of Artaud, through Lacan's theory of split subjectivity in relation to the Other.[34] Klein theorized an early (pre-Oedipal) "paranoid-schizoid position" for all infants,[35] "normally" extending through the first three to four months (216), which also illuminates Artaud's paradigmatic function in modern theater and postmodern theory. According to Klein, the earliest anxiety, arising from the death instinct within the infant, "is felt as fear of annihilation (death) and takes the form of fear of persecution" (179). She thus points behind the threatening father of Freud's castration complex to a phallic (m)Other figure, like the "papa-mama" that Artaud disbelieved yet feared in his final writings (*SW* 550).[36] Klein describes, even before the child's fear of castration, its paranoid fear of annihilation (with schizoid splitting) and its own epistemophilic attack upon the mother's womb: "the struggle with the father's penis in the mother" (88). Mirroring the infant's desire "to destroy the libidinal object by biting, devouring and cutting it," a perverse, phallic mother appears: "an unreal, phantastic image of parents who devour, cut and bite" (71). Because of the child's "early sadistic super-ego, which has already been set up, these united parents are extremely cruel and much dreaded assailants" (88).[37] In this view, we all experience the paranoid-schizoid position of the first quarter year of life. But it is the failure of some egos to "work through" this position (and the subsequent depressive position with its Oedipal complex) that leads to psychosis and schizophrenia (177).[38] Hence, Artaud's depictions of metaphysical incest in his drama and proposed theater of cruelty, like his later psychosis and schizophrenic writings, reflect not only his personal history, but also a profound perversity at the origin of theater inside and outside us.

Artaud's own body, from childhood on, was split into good and evil metaphysics. In a letter to a physician discussing his lifelong psychosomatic illness (initially thought to be meningitis), written when he was thirty-five, he described a sensation of physical remoteness from myself as if I were never again going to control my limbs, my reflexes, my most spontaneous mechanical reactions. Also another feeling of hardness and horrible physical fatigue in my tongue when I speak, *the effort of thought* always reverberating physically through all my muscles. My stammer is variable and sometimes it disappears altogether, but it is enormously exhausting. From my earliest childhood (6 to 8 years) I noticed that these periods of stammering and of horrible physical contractions of the facial nerves and the tongue alternated with periods of calm and perfect relaxation. (Qtd. in Hayman 36–37)[39]

Artaud performed this living martyrdom for his mother and others around him from his childhood onward.[40] He was also an awkward stage actor for the same physical reasons.[41] Through his dream of an impossible theater, he became a postmodern shaman, taking us back to the womb in a Kleinian sense: an internal world of new life and deadly power, fixed fate yet pre-Oedipal perversity, cruel persecution but cathartic hope. Despite the performative conceit of such schizoid paradoxes, I believe that this trickster figure's symptoms, his "physical remoteness" from himself, his periodic loss of bodily control, his stammer, and his "contractions," were as sincere as his theater—in its failure and its success(ion). Artaud's own body, rebelling all his life against him, ultimately realized his revolutionary dream of creating a theatrical womb. Through his progressive metaphysical madness, Artaud's effort of thought shaped a reverberative theater out of his contracting muscles and stammering tongue—distilled (ironically) into written words, which return us to our common birthplace and its unbearable paranoia.

Stage Blood

Many of us prefer to remember the womb as a tragically lost place of peace and contentment. But this is only one side of the Manichaean melodrama in early infancy—splitting the womb (and breast) into double metaphysical objects, good and evil, in order to preserve it as lost Eden and future heaven, despite its persecutory power (Klein 157–58). Artaud would return us to the evil womb as well, in all its monstrous cruelty, by making theater into both Madonna and whore, by converting stage space into a phallic mother, cathartically reenacting the warring good and evil forces there.

Toward the end of his life (in a letter of 1946), Artaud claimed to have a prenatal memory.

It smelt of shit on my heart, this cistern with the trunk of me inside it, but the excrement was my self. In fact the cistern was a bleeding trunk, but a man's, while the white hole offering me its soul, a woman, was for me no more than nothing. (Qtd. in Hayman 131)

Here Artaud describes the cruelty within the papa-mama, the phallic mother's womb, and a common infantile association of fetus (himself) with feces. He also suggests his own ultimate fate as male womb—and as stage mother to a lost, spiritual theater. Psychoanalyst Louise J. Kaplan has recently argued that the male child has an "inner genital world" like the female (108). She even offers physical evidence: "since 90 percent of all male children also have an inguinal ring that remains open until approximately age six, the testicles can temporarily retract into the inguinal canal and seemingly disappear" (109).[42] According to Kaplan, the boy associates this castration effect of the testicles with both feces and breasts. "The scrotal sacs are anatomically close to the anus and sometimes look to a child like his feces, which do break off and disappear. Males of all ages sometimes imagine their scrotal sacs as analogous to female breasts" (110). Thus, the boy fantasizes about having a body like his mother's, "a body with an inner cavity that can make and hold a baby," because he longs to merge with her (107). But his own body also contributes to this perverse illusion of becoming the phallic mother: "the wish to be a mommy, but a mommy with a penis" (108). At nearly fifty and two years before his death, Artaud shows the fetishist's infantile belief in the phallic mother, while also denying his desire to become her (which Kaplan relates more specifically to transvestism [108])—to become the "nothing" of the mother goddess, of the "white hole" he is still trapped in.

In the 1920s Klein theorized a "femininity phase" for infant boys as well as girls: "a very early identification with the mother" (72–73). Both the idealized Madonna and the cruel phallic mother are introjected by the child in this phase. For it is based in the "anal-sadistic stage," during which the child feels threatened by the persecutory womb and breast (73–74). At that time the mother cuts off the child's oral and anal desires through weaning and toilet training. She is thus the primary castrator according to Klein, since her breasts and its feces appear to the child as extensions of its own body (74). The vengeful infant, in turn, "desires to get possession of the mother's faeces, by penetrating into her body, cutting it to pieces, devouring and destroying it." And yet, at the same time, says Klein, "Under the influence of his genital impulses, the boy is beginning to turn to his mother as love-object" (73). I believe that Artaud's early dramatic works, his later plans for theater, personal letters throughout his life, and his final asylum writings all return us to this cruel femininity phase that Klein defines. There the infant introjects, imitates, and fights the metaphysical powers of its parents, combining their masculine and feminine body parts to make an adored, yet threatening phallic (m)Other, but also splitting Her into good and evil figures. Artaud displays such gods and monsters upon the stage, projecting the contents of a child's womb across the mirror of its—and our own—originary vulnerability. Thus, the oral and anal sadism that Klein theorized from her treatment of children and adults appears in Artaud's theater of cruelty through his own "fixation points" in the paranoid-schizoid position (190)—liminal to our current, social order.

Artaud's short play *The Spurt of Blood* was published in 1925, in the first collection of his works, *Umbilical Limbo*. It begins with the conventional romantic situation of a young man and woman professing love for each other. But a preexisting tenseness between them is indicated by the repetition of initial lines: "I love you and everything is fine. You love me and everything is fine." The similarity of these lines, especially when spoken again by each of them, sets up a mirroring gap between the boy and girl, which discloses an opposite meaning to that stated, that is, everything is not fine in our love. Artaud suggests this, too, with his stage directions for the Girl, who speaks "in a quickened, throbbing voice," and for the Young Man, "suddenly turning aside" (CW 1:62). This split between statement and mood, signifier and signified, may even imply, given the context of the rest of the play (and Artaud's biography), the perverse love of sibling incest.[43]

These perverse limned professions of love rise to an idealized, nearly parodic height—after the mirroring is made even more explicit with the young man's command: "Face me." She does, although first mirroring his business of turning aside, then announcing herself as reflective object before him: "There" (CW 1:63). Through this shadow play, the boy becomes melodramatically inflated with the imago double he sees in her, with his own ideal ego, like the infant in Lacan's mirror stage. Speaking "on an exalted, high-pitched tone," he pronounces, "I love you, I am great, I am lucid, I am full, I am dense" (63).

But this already betrays a perversely unstable "mirage"—like the infant's in the mirror of the (m)Other's eye: "in a contrasting size *(un relief de stature)* that fixes it and in a symmetry that inverts it, in contrast with the turbulent movements that the subject feels are animating him" (Lacan, *Écrits* 2). For just after the girl's choral transfiguration of his statement and her thereness into "We love each other" (echoing his "high-pitched tone") and after the young man's universalizing summary, "We are intense. Ah, what a well-made world," their world falls apart. The framework of Western history, from its classical sky gods to Christian Trinity to Enlightenment proscenium and oriental Other, comes crashing down and cuts through their love knot.

> A hurricane comes between them. At that moment two stars collide, and a succession of limbs of flesh fall. Then feet, hands, scalps, masks, colonnades, porticoes, temples and alembics, falling slower and slower as if through space, then three scorpions one after the other and finally a frog, and a scarab which lands with heart-breaking, nauseating slowness. (CW 1:63)

This metonymic storm described by Artaud (and prefiguring the work of Robert Wilson today)[44] forces the young man and his girl offstage, after he astutely shouts: "Heaven's gone crazy" (63). It had gone crazy for Artaud and increasingly did in his later years. Thus, the momentary glimpse here of a cosmic, chaotic chora reflects the cruel womb he carried within him and would return us to theatrically—through the perverse fineness of love.

Then, however, father and mother appear to restore Oedipal order, though again Artaud reveals their fundamental perversity. "A Mediaeval KNIGHT in enormous armour enters, followed by a WETNURSE holding her bosom up with her hands and panting because of her swollen breasts." She perceives the sibling incest (with a "shrill cry" of alarm): "Our girl there, with him. . . . I tell you they are fucking." But the father permits it, as long as he can get his "Gruyère cheese" from the mother's pockets—though eating it makes him "cough and choke." This shows an abject response of both parental figures at the primal scene of child incest. With the mother's hysterical alarm and the father's narcissistic apathy, they appear together as impotent spectators. Yet the mother's body will soon reveal a revolutionary power (Kristeva), through her own abjection and the children's pre-Oedipal perversity in a polymorphous cosmos—especially with the failure of the father's hermetic law, as could be seen in the knight's gagging on the breast by-product that had been wrapped in "his papers" (63).[45]

Artaud begins to show the abject revolution a few lines later, when the young man returns to the stage (sans parents), looking for his significant Other, whom he has "lost." A priest questions him, "as if confessing someone." He asks: "What part of her body did you refer to most?" And the young man replies: "To God." This lost God as female body part parallels the earth goddess subsumed by Christianity (or Catholicism in particular), which the young man seeks. For the "disconcerted" priest, pushed into a Protestant "Swiss accent,"[46] then replies: "But that's out of date. We don't look at it that way. You'll have to ask the volcanoes and earthquakes about that" (64). Here Artaud indicates his own desire for the mother earth goddess, buried under the Western stage that he wants to make erupt.

Then it happens: "the earth quakes." Amidst thunder and lightning and chaotic characters running about "like mad," bumping into one another, falling and rising again, a "huge" hand of God appears. It seizes a whore by her hair, which then "catches fire and swells up visibly." This phallic hand of the Father and swelling hair of the perverse mother catalyzes the many, ecstatic images of Artaud's short play into one dominant symbol—enunciated by "A GIGANTIC VOICE: Bitch! Look at your body!" (64). But she is not the only one to look. The voyeuristic audience (or reader) also sees the horror of the bitch body that God's hand holds: "The WHORE's body appears completely naked and hideous under her blouse and skirt which turn transparent" (65). Here Artaud reveals the traditional proscenium "apron" as the skirt of the mother goddess, showing her split onstage into bountiful Madonna (large-breasted wetnurse) and hideous whore. Thus, Artaud carves a choral lens at the stage's edge (as in Nietzsche's Dionysian nostalgia)—giving the spectator a child's view, perverse and paranoid, but also fundamental to the Oedipal theology of Western theater.

The exhibited horror then strikes back at the patriarchal proscenium hand, which has raised her by the roots and framed her nakedness. "God, let go of me," says the whore, reperverting the tableau of divine male exposing hideous female. "She bites God's wrist. A great spurt of blood slashes across the stage, while in the midst of the brightest lightning flash we see the PRIEST making the sign of the cross" (65). This perversion of Calvary shows the earth goddess biting the sky god's wrist, instead of a pure virgin mother (along with other Marys, including a prostitute) obediently supporting her Son's ecstasy at the foot of His cross.[47] The spurt of blood slashing the stage also prefigures Artaud's profoundly Oedipal perversion of theater in his subsequent theories. By rebelling against the father violently and desiring the mother incestuously, he turns stage space and its history upside down, desublimating the cruelty of the proscenium cross and making Golgotha a womb. "Thus, theater space will be utilized not only in its dimensions and volume but, so to speak, *in its undersides (dans ses dessous)*" (Artaud, *Theater* 124). The stage earth will not only massage the spectator snake (81), but also transport it to its primordial lair—the skull upon which patriarchy rests.

Indeed, the stage becomes a graveyard, right after the spurt of blood and the priest's sign of the cross in the lightning flash. "When the lights come up again, the characters are all dead and their corpses lie all over the ground" (*CW* 1:65). But the whore and young man remain alive onstage, "devouring each other with their eyes." Not only do they devour each other like the Kleinian mother and child, but she falls into his arms and sighs "as if in an orgiastic climax." However, the wetnurse Madonna then carries onstage the dead body of the girl, sacrificial victim to the incestuous orgy. (Perhaps she also reflects Artaud's continued mourning for his dead siblings, particularly Germaine.) As a corpse on the stage floor, she is "flat as a pancake." The wetnurse is also flat; her bountiful breasts have been castrated. But the knight, representing both primal scene father and oral-sadistic child, still tries to squeeze some Gruyère out of her, "shaking her violently." Transfigured thus into Madonna-cum-whore, she responds "brazenly," saying "Here!" and lifting her skirt. The young man, as good boy and shocked spectator of the primal scene, "wants to run off but he freezes like a paralyzed puppet." (Whether or not he still holds the whore in his arms is not clear.) Fixated before the cruel spectacle, he responds "in a ventriloquist's voice and as if hovering in midair." With just this disembodied voice, he tries to defend his mother and, like the whore earlier, to fend off the patriarchal hand: "Don't hurt Mummy." In this way he reminds the knight (as father and bad boy) of his original, Oedipal sin, now being repeated. "Damn her," says the knight. And he "hides his face in horror" (*CW* 1:65).

The final image and statement of this short play then reconfirms, yet also brings to a climax its revolutionary orgy. "A host of scorpions crawl out from under the WETNURSE's dress and start swarming in her vagina which swells and splits, becomes transparent and shimmers like the sun." While the whore and young man "fly off like mad," the dead girl rises and says: "The Virgin! Ah, that's what he was looking for" (65).[48] Thus, the trinity of scorpions, falling from the sky in the play's first shocking spectacle, returns as the perverse, multiplied divinity of the mother goddess, whose vulval signifier even outshines the sun. This also prefigures Artaud's later theories and his influence upon many other theorists and theater artists. Although Artaud did send a spurt of blood across the twentieth-century stage by biting its theological hand, he also looked for a Kleinian womb within its Christian, proscenium heritage. Thus, a cruel phallic mother, castrated by classical drama, yet alive beneath the stage, erupts in Artaud's theories and plays. Yet she also threatens to love us to death, to reengulf us with the horror of a spectral womb that still drives our theater, society, and individual psyches.

Pantheological Theater

Returning now to Derrida, one sees, even more dramatically, how Artaud's nontheological stage space is also theological—in the sense of other, repressed faiths, which I am characterizing, historically and psychoanalytically, but not homogeneously, as mother (and earth) goddess religions. Derrida himself does not play out the paradox in these terms. But he does discuss in his essay, "La parole soufflée," the exploration of non-Western theologies by Artaud: "outside Europe, in Balinese theater, in the ancient Mexican, Hindu, Iranian, Egyptian, etc., cosmogonies" (191). Derrida also looks at Artaud's investigation of the Jewish Cabala—a mystical tradition within, though repressed by, the theology of the Judeo-Christian West. Therefore, I would add to Derrida's description of Artaud's nontheological space, its pantheological drive—or at least its pantheism. For it is the logos of the "theological" that Derrida sees Artaud striving beyond, and the "monotheo" embedded in that logos, not the "theo-" itself.[49] It is through the nonlogocentric, "nonphonetic writing" of the Cabala's "laws of breath" within Judeo-Christianity that Artaud seeks to create the divinity of Life onstage. Thus, in order to deconstruct the Death-God, Derrida's Artaud must traverse the theological murder of the man-God, the double of man's true life divinity, to reconstitute a truly theistic space.

Pantheism is certainly an aspect of Artaud's theatrical drive, beyond the Death-God of monotheology, toward the "living God" of omnipresent Life. Lecturing in Mexico in 1936, Artaud expressed the desire of "reviving the old sacred idea, the great idea of pagan pantheism" (*SW* 373). At times Artaud even identified himself with the other, evil god of the Christian tradition, often represented in the image of the ancient Pan. Derrida notes this, quoting from a letter by Artaud from 1945: "Against the pact of fear which gives birth to man and to God must be restored the unity of evil and life, of the Satanic and the divine: 'I, M. Antonin Artaud, born in Marseilles 4 September 1896, I am Satan and I am god'" (*WD* 332 n. 11). However, Artaud's pantheistic drive, to transgress monotheology and shatter its phonic Word and Author-God ruling from afar, also reconstitutes a closed theological space, bringing the complete living God to the stage. For according to Derrida, there is yet again a "closure" to this more genuine, originary theater of autopresentation, even though it would (un)erase the closure of logocentric representation, as a "closed space . . . produced from within itself and no longer organized from the vantage of an other absent site" (238). In his final psychotic writings, Artaud brings the Other more and more into his own body (as autopresentation) rather than trying to excavate it on a stage governed by the absent site of proscenium theology. But he still desires a disclosure of the lost womb within his psyche—as pantheological chora, not patriarchal logos.

At the end of "The Theater of Cruelty and the Closure of Representation," Derrida displays an infinity within the finite space of Artaud's theater: its "fatal limit."

> Closure is the circular limit within which the repetition of difference infinitely repeats itself. That is to say, closure is its *playing* space. . . . To think the closure of representation is thus to think the cruel powers of death and play which permit presence to be born to itself, and pleasurably to consume itself. (250)

Artaud's nontheological, yet pantheological, theater is thus the impossible, finite/infinite asymptote of death and play, of mortality and immortality, of the divine in human "presence" onstage. Not simply in the traditional sense of an actor "having presence" onstage, but also not excluding that sense of theatrical presence. For it is through that tradition and theology of theater, of the actor incarnating the pneumatic Word, that Artaud must fight to find an originary sense of presence, at the birth, or before the birth of tragedy: the death-play of mortal immortality and human divinity in the omphalic womb of stage space. But this also reflects the tragedy of Artaud's life, as disclosed by his drama: the cruel powers of dead siblings playing within the maternal womb of mourning that enclosed him. Or, as Derrida concludes, "To think the closure of representation is to think the tragic: not as the representation of fate, but as the fate of representation" (250). The fate that bound Artaud was this tragic drive to represent the unpresentable: the never present reason for life and death—his own and the ghosts' within him.

The ending of Derrida's prior essay, "La parole soufflée," is more wary of Artaud's cruel *jouissance*. "The transgression of metaphysics through the 'thought' which, Artaud tells us, has not yet begun, always risks returning to metaphysics." It is also with this sense of risk (and intellectual drama) that I insist on calling Artaud's theater "pantheological" as well as non. The alchemically unstable paradox of Artaud's physically metaphysical theater conjures a structure with an imminent danger of collapse, of repeating the original sin and tragic fall from Eden—back again into monotheological metaphysics. For Artaud must traverse those same myths (psychologically and culturally) in order to reverse their theology. Derrida admits this danger in his own discourse also: "we could appear to be criticizing Artaud's metaphysics from the standpoint of metaphysics itself." But he then insists this is the vitality (and drama) of his grammatology: "we are actually delimiting a fatal complicity." The asymptotic "fatal limit" of Artaud's theater of cruelty is also that of Derridean deconstruction, "a necessary dependency of all destructive discourses: they must inhabit the structures they demolish, and within them they must shelter an indestructible desire for full presence, for nondifference: simultaneously life and death" (194).

Artaud (as Derrida performs him)[50] must inhabit the structure of the Oedipus myth in his attempt to reverse and demolish Western theological theater. Yet he also strives to go outside the logos-law of tragic stage space. He searches through religious cosmogonies from outside Europe for a way out. But is there any way to get "outside" one's own culture? Han-liang Chang has suggested that Derrida suffers from the same "European hallucination" that he criticizes Leibniz for: a vision of salvation in the oriental Other (Chang 8). Derrida looks to Chinese hieroglyphic writing as an outside to logocentrism; but that Other, says Chang, shares with Western metaphysics a "belief in an ultimate, transcendental . . . reality, be it Tao or nature" (7). Thus, while Derrida, like Artaud (and Nietzsche), "refuses to subsume Life to Being" (Derrida, WD 246), he also risks repeating Leibniz's failure to see the theological, logocentric, universalizing tendencies of the East as well as the West. Both Derrida and Artaud, in their "orientalist" moments (Said), desire the absent site of the Other's tradition, misreading it to the degree that they project their desires upon it. Yet they also show a potential for presenceless presence within their own tradition, at the staged edges of loss.

Onstage Womb and Surgical Trickster

Artaud's search for the Other within (through pantheological rebellion against) the Western phallogocentric stage appears in his plan for a play, *The Philosopher's Stone*, published in 1929. The set Artaud describes, out of conventional theatrical materials, presents a cavelike opening or vulva within the proscenium frame. "A great red curtain" fills the back of a "recess cut into a great black frame." The curtain is itself "cut down the middle; and when drawn aside a great red light can be seen: in there is the operating theatre" (CW 2:73). This is not just a theater within a theater, but a choral, uterine edge—a vulval signifier shaped out of the inner proscenium curtain. This (ideo)graphic set as womb comes ritually alive through a perverse Oedipal triangle that Artaud again creates in the plot development for this play. The father figure, Dr. Pale, cuts up mannequins in his operating theater, inside the red curtain. In Kleinian terms, he is the castrative penis inside the womb, which in the case of Artaud's mother also held many lost siblings. "Dr Pale is in the midst of a veritable massacre of dummies in one corner of the set, chopping them up with an axe, like a wood cutter or a butcher." The mother figure, Isabelle, "writhes and despairs" as he chops. "Each blow echoes deep in her nerves. Her convulsions and shudders occur in total silence: she opens her mouth as if to cry out but we hear nothing."

Here in this silence (though she does emit a "drawn out hoot" from time to time [74]) one can hear the primal nothingness that obsessed Artaud, the deep nervous echo of maternal mourning that shaped his psychosomatic martyrdom and theatrical shamanism, through guilt for and competition with the incestuous dead. As he stated toward the end of his life: "Those who are alive are living off the dead." Or, more specifically about the womb: "Each time a child is born, it takes blood from my heart" (qtd. in Hayman 4).

After his *sparagmos* of mannequins, the doctor comes downstage, outside his womblike operating theater, holding a castrated "stump," one of the dead contents of the womb. He "seems to test its non-existent pulse; then he tosses it aside, rubs his hands, shakes himself, snorts, dusts himself off, raises his head and sniffs." As in the opening of *The Spurt of Blood,* Isabelle mirrors Dr. Pale's phallic, bestial movements, though she matches them "like a vague, barely suggested, distant echo." She then begins a "long erotic labour." Artaud carefully describes how the actress should (almost in a Brechtian sense) show a personal conflict in her gestures of making love. "Having nothing else but the doctor to batten on, she draws on him for her happiness." And yet, she also exhibits to the audience, in this primal scene, "a mixture of disgust and resignation in the impulse of her movement towards him" (74). She even lets slip a "silent rage" from under the mask of "her coaxings, her flirtations. . . . her caresses end in slaps, in scratches. She pulls his moustache with sudden, unexpected movements—rains blows on his stomach, steps on his toes as she stands to kiss his lips" (74–75).

The covert revolt of mourning mother against murderous father in this "sadistic love scene," which parallels (in subtler form) the whore's biting of God's hand in the earlier play, prepares the stage for the third character,

Harlequin, to march on and take over for the young man paralyzed by that other primal scene. Harlequin is a double of himself—the split good and bad boy (young man and knight) recombined. He has the rebellious body of Artaud: "a sort of bandy-legged monster, a hunchback, squinting, one-eyed cripple, who trembles in all his limbs as he walks." Yet he is also "the other, Harlequin, a fine lad who straightens up from time to time and throws out his chest when Dr Pale is not looking" (75). This other Harlequin, like the sick Antonin, is able to woo the mother, Isabelle, by using the hunchback mask to deceive the doctor. However, in his essay on van Gogh of 1947, Artaud also showed the failure of such tactics, after spending much of his own life in sanatoria and asylums, and enduring years of electroshock treatment. It was not because of "madness" that van Gogh "abandoned himself," according to Artaud. It was rather "the pressure of the evil influence, two days before his death, of Dr. Gachet, a so-called psychiatrist" (*SW* 492). Thus, the Oedipal success of Harlequin and Isabelle (two decades earlier), in their revolution against the murderous father, marks a lost, choral ideal in the tragedy of Artaud's life.

Even so, Harlequin must suffer much Dionysian dismemberment,[51] having "his legs, arms and head [chopped off] with an axe," before he beats the paternal phallus within the womb (because the exhausted surgeon has fallen asleep) and makes covert love to Isabelle (*SW* 2:76). The doctor wakes while they are in the act, but Isabelle deceives him yet again by giving birth to a "dummy of himself" (76–77). However, the child is female (77), and thus reflects a possible Oedipal fantasy of the young Artaud: that he fathered his dead baby sister, Germaine. For he did call her his "daughter," as she increasingly haunted him toward the end of his life. He even mentions her in the brief introduction to his *Collected Works:* "Germaine Artaud strangled at seven months, watched me from St. Peter's cemetery in Marseilles, until the day in 1931 when, in the middle of the Dome in Montparnasse, I had the impression she was nearby, watching me" (*CW* 1:21). This spectral Other watching him, from Artaud's childhood illness to his drama to his theories and ultimate madness, drives his performance of the double—body and soul, hunchback and Harlequin, brother and father. Yet Artaud strives to undo such splitting by turning the castrative proscenium and its patriarchal surgeries into a unifying space of cruelty, a body without organs, as shown in the ecstatic union of Harlequin and Isabelle: "shaking themselves in the air like sieves in a gesture copied from the act of love" (78). Although the theater can only copy, Artaud tries to bring it to the edge of the reality, both horrible and beautiful, of the womb within him—to make spectators and performers one body, as spiritual sieve.

The Peyote D(ist)ance

Deleuze remarks that the schizophrenic body as sieve can be found not only in Artaud's writings, but also in Freud's (his essay "The Unconscious").

> Freud emphasized the schizophrenic aptitude for perceiving the surface and the skin as if each were pierced by an infinite number of little holes. As a result, the entire body is nothing but depth; it snatches and carries all things in this gaping depth, which represents a fundamental involution. ("Schizophrenic" 286)

Artaud's failure to transform the theater into a body-sieve led to the fundamental involution of his own schizophrenic body—after his failure, too, in transforming the European mind with the ancient rituals of Mexico, and in leading an Irish revolution with the magic cane of St. Patrick. But prior to those failed revolutions, Artaud planned to stage an Aztec revolution against Cortez in his notes for *The Conquest of Mexico* as the "first spectacle of the Theater of Cruelty" (*Theater* 126). Though he also failed to stage this play, his plans for it moved beyond personal, familial martyrdom, extending the whore's rebellion against God, and Harlequin's against Dr. Pale, to the history and religion of the colonial Other—and thus moved toward today's postcolonial theories. A decade later (in 1947), Artaud declared that "the pre-Columbian Indians were a strangely civilized people . . . [who] knew a form of civilization based exclusively on the principle of cruelty" (*SW* 568). For he had personally found, in his own trip to Mexico, behind both the Spanish conquest and the Aztec empire, a primitive, yet strangely civilized tribe called the Tarahumara.[52] They showed him a pantheological union of "the Male and Female principles of Nature" (*Peyote* 11), which he desired, but could not invoke on the European stage.

The fundamental involution that Artaud desired for theater appeared to him in mystical visions on the Mexican landscape. He "saw" there a Cabalic "music of Numbers" (*Peyote* 15), like the tempos of breath he had planned for the affective athleticism of actors in his theater of cruelty (*Theater* 134). But he also suffered from excruciating withdrawal symptoms as he traveled toward the Tarahumara, because he had thrown away his heroin in order to enter their peyote ritual with a purer mind and body (Hayman 108). Through this road to Calvary in the other's ritual, Artaud foresaw his own ultimate crucifixion in the pantheological theater of his later asylum writings. But he also saw the distance between himself and the (m)Other at the base of that cross—in the primitive, non-Western mirror.

Artaud concludes his description of the peyote ritual with a caveat: he is still blocked from its lost mystery by his own modern body and the culture it carries. Artaud realizes he cannot bring back to Europe anything more than relics of the Tarahumara: "a collection of outworn imageries from which the Age, true to its own system, would at most derive ideas for advertisements and models for clothing designers." And yet, through this despair of ever uniting ancient and modern, Male and Female cultures, Artaud prophesies his own sacrificial *sparagmos*. His schizophrenic body-sieve will become the male womb of a new stage of loss. "It is now necessary that what lay hidden behind this heavy grinding [of the modern age] which reduces dawn to darkness—that this thing be pulled out, and that it serve, that it serve precisely by my *crucifixion*" (*Peyote* 58).

Like Harlequin who, in order to trick the sadistic Father, comes to him (and Isabelle) "to have the philosopher's stone taken out of me" (*CW* 2:75), Artaud—through radical surgery as well as ecstatic love—must give birth to a new cross, as pre-Oedipal stone *lingam*. Out of his own martyred body-sieve as theatrical womb, a new *père*-version of "La Pierre philosophale," must be pulled out.[53] For it is not enough to return to ancient rituals and relics, or even to partake in communion with the drug of a primitive Other. Even then he "did not succeed in penetrating" the Mexican (m)Other's "mysterious tradition" (56). And it was not only Artaud who felt a "terrible sensation of loss, of a void to be filled, of an event that miscarries" as he anticipated the peyote rite (47). A priest of that rite tells him that the Ciguri (peyote root and god) has become for the Tarahumara themselves a lost ritual tool; it is now their "vice" (34).

With his theater of cruelty and *The Conquest of Mexico* Artaud wanted to cut through the vice of proscenium space, making the Western stage an open, bleeding birth-wound: "Montezuma cuts the living space, rips it open like the sex of a woman in order to cause the invisible to spring forth" (*Theater* 130). But he failed to realize this rebirth and bring Europe to it, despite his own trip to Mexico and ecstatic communion in the peyote rite. That mystical rapture remained trapped within his physical, drug-addicted experience, and in the loss of the peyote god within the other culture. Hence, Artaud's psychotic involution increased. He could no longer be saved by the absent site of a primordial people, "whose rites and culture are older than the Flood, [and who] actually possessed this [alchemical] science well before the appearance of the Legend of the Grail, or the founding of the Sect of the Rosicrucians" (*Peyote* 17). For it is not simply an orientalist's return to the lost rituals of Mexico that Artaud ultimately desires. It is the impossible return to the mother goddess buried within his own culture, beneath Judeo-Christian theology and European theater.[54] His highly personal dream of a new theater of autopresentation can only be born through loss—through the intimate cruelty of the (m)Other's womb within one's own body and its pantheon of ghosts.

The Spectator as Thief

Derrida professes to find, in the uniqueness of Artaud's theatrical madness, an "archaic ground" that is historical in a new way (*WD* 174). But this ground must be exhumed through deconstruction, according to Derrida (thus distinguishing his method from Michel Foucault's historical archaeology). The deconstructive Derrida "believe[s] in the necessity of reducing the unique, of analyzing it and decomposing it by shattering it even further." He also believes that his own text/performance about Artaud "destroys itself as commentary by exhuming the differences (of madness and the work, of the psyche and the text, of example and essence, etc.) which implicitly support both criticism and the clinic." Through this faith in a deconstructive madness, Derrida would unearth a primal, yet postmodern vortex: "The tumultuous presence of this archaic ground will thus magnetize the discourse which will be attracted into the resonance of the cries of Antonin Artaud."

Despite Artaud's failure to join Tarahumara ritual with his dream for European theater, Derrida finds an original sacred ground within Artaud's subsequent psychotic writings and cries: "Artaud promises the existence of a speech that is a body, of a body that is a theater, of a theater that is a text because it is no longer enslaved to a writing more ancient than itself, an ur-text or an ur-speech" (174–75). But like other poststructuralists (e.g. Deleuze and Guattari) Derrida makes Artaud into a martyred, evolutionary hero against clinical psychiatry and phallogocentrism—even suggesting a relation to the contemporaneous Jewish sacrifice of the Holocaust. "Beating his flesh in order to reawaken it at the eve prior to the deportation, Artaud attempted to forbid that his speech be spirited away *[soufflé]* from his body" (175). Thus, Derrida leads us to (and to a degree reenacts) the final performance of Artaud's theater of cruelty, where the birth cry of the zygote within the womb is held tightly inside Artaud's own body—kept from thieving doctors and spectators, but also released to us through his writings.[55]

Derrida follows Artaud's ghost, whose tragic cry suffuses the postmodern stage, into the womb within his corpus. There Derrida lets his own essay, "La parole soufflée," be prompted to such a degree that he plays

Artaud, borrowing the other's first-person presence and persona: "ever since my birth, I no longer am my body. . . . My body has thus always been stolen from me. Who could have stolen it from me, if not an Other, and how could he have gotten hold of it from the beginning unless he had slipped into my place inside my mother's belly, unless I had been *stolen from my birth. . . ?*" (Derrida, *WD* 180). In terms of the originary myths of Western theater, one can also see here—through Derrida's dream of the Other's presence at Artaud's birth—the Olympian sky god Zeus, in a death stroke of lightning, stealing Dionysus from the flames of the earth goddess Semele's womb. But Derrida pursues a womb prior to that plot, by chasing and deconstructing Artaud's Death-God thief in the theater of his double. "It is the history of the body / which *pursued* (and did not follow) mine / and which, in order to go first and be born, / projected itself across my body / and / was born / through the disemboweling of my body / of which he kept a piece / in order to pass himself off / as me" (Artaud, qtd. in Derrida, *WD* 181).

However, because Derrida, as theoretical chorus, elevates Artaud to heroic status as a rebel against psychiatry, he avoids hearing the resonance of this cry within Artaud's childhood psychobiography, as I have analyzed it earlier in this chapter. The answer to Artaud's Sphinx-like riddle of the history of a body that pursued, and yet did not follow him, is his own. But it is also the Other's, the spectator's. Behind the mirror stage of ego illusion, Artaud sees the ghost of each of his dead siblings, pursuing him like Furies. Yet each double also projects across his body, is born before him, as him, disemboweling him and stealing a piece of him, making him its (their) abject womb and impersonating him—like Derrida.

A cruel nostalgia for the womb (which is lost at birth, yet persists as a ghost within his body) lies at the heart of Artaud's Death-God murdering theater. Through it he echoes Dionysus's lament of the death-loss of his mother at his own birth, foreshadowing his furious reentry into the hysteria of the female Bacchae at the same death-place. "Look, those ruins, her house, smoking still, / alive still with a most unnatural flame" (Euripides 79). It is through the ruins of theological space in Western theater that Derrida's Artaud pursues the Death-God, the Father-Son-Ghost, and reenters the womb of death's immediacy. Artaud, as quoted by Derrida, even echoes Christian theology: "through dying / I have come to achieve real immortality" (Derrida 181). But Derrida sees Artaud pointing to the Christian God as the villain—as the mirror stage gap and sibling shadow: "God is thus the proper name of that which deprives us of our own nature, of our own birth; consequently he will always have spoken before us, on the sly." This Death-

God is the thief and lie of life. "He is the difference which insinuates itself between myself and myself as my death" (181). But what is the other side of that difference, the truth behind the mirror?

"God is false value," Derrida says, as if impersonating Artaud. "My truth, what I am worth, has been purloined from me by some One who in my stead became God at the exit from the Orifice, at birth" (181–82). What is this truth, this real, yet purloined, worth, that lies inside the Orifice (the vulval signifier)? In my view, Derrida plays Artaud all the way back to the anal-sadistic stage of Kleinian theory, discovering there that his stolen fetus is the feces:

> original value, the ur-value that I should have retained within myself, or rather should have retained as my self, . . . that which was stolen from me as soon as I fell far from the Orifice, and which is stolen from me again each time that a part of me falls far from myself—this is the work, excrement, dross, . . . which can become, as is well known, a persecuting arm, an arm eventually directed against myself. (182)

Derrida, through Artaud, seeks the immediate immortality of death-in-life (the womb within him), thus perverting "ontotheology" through his own shit—even though that originally valuable shit has become the persecutory arm attached to the hand of God.[56] Derrida maintains the villain as metaphysical and male, rather than showing the personal prehistory of God's persecutory power, as Kleinian theory suggests, in the infant's fantasy of the (phallic) mother as primary castrator: bountiful, yet devouring breasts; generous, but toilet-training womb; instilling superego guilt, along with the father (or Father) who steals certain pleasures by naming them perverse.

According to Derrida, the thieving eye/ear of the spectator, as Death-God, steals "all speech fallen from the body . . . offering itself as spectacle" (175). He, too, must be murdered, along with the Author. Artaud does this through encopresis: holding the art work (feces) within his body. The turd—the penis of Artaud as phallic mother—is kept within his body-womb, kept from the Thief of theological theater. Here is Derrida's wording for this, while wearing the mask of Artaud:

> My work, my trace, the excrement that robs *me of* my possessions after I have been *stolen from* my birth, must thus be rejected. But to reject it is not, here, to refuse it but to retain it. To keep myself, to keep my body and my speech, I must retain the work within me, conjoin myself with it so that there will be no opportunity for the Thief to

come between it and me: it must be kept from falling far from my body as writing. (182–83)

Derrida's Artaud would bring the spectators of his theater of cruelty into an originary, hieroglyphic theater of death-in-life within his own body. Yet, he does this by murdering them, or rather by exorcising the Death-God within them. He cuts into the scopic drive itself, motive power of their Death-God-like thievery. He holds the work, the shit, within him, to create an art without works,[57] thus denying the Father-God's castration of him—and of the phallic mother that he then becomes. He unites his own dream thallus (Weber) to the historical/mythical omphalos of the mother goddess in a pantheological stage space that does not exist theatrically.

This may seem a bit mad; and so it is. (It is also a fine reason for the ultimate impossibility of Artaud's theatrical dream.) According to Derrida, the point at which Artaud most profoundly inhabits and deconstructs Western metaphysics is in its "determination of madness as the disease of alienation." And yet, "Artaud still *summons* this metaphysics, draws upon its fund of values, and attempts to be more faithful to it than it is to itself by means of an absolute restoration of the proper to the eve prior to all dissociation" (183). Artaud's ghost, which I am chasing with the help of Derrida, appears to vanish into an impossible belief, into the locus of alienation before alienation, behind the mirror (stage). However, in that very moment of impossibility before birth, the ghost unveils itself, as a belief sustained by alienation[58]—a belief in the continuous reality of death and life within the human body, theatrically described.

Death-God in the House

The only production of Artaud's planned theater of cruelty, and his only surviving full-length drama, was a rewriting of Shelley's *The Cenci*.[59] In it Artaud depicts the absolute cruelty of a father's unholy spirit (whom he played), barring the way back to an ideal womb, and leaving only the persecutory one. But the cruelty of the Cenci, and the rebellion of his family against him, also reflects an appeal to the audience, which corresponds, in my view, to the Derridean delineation of Artaud's later view of the spectator as Death-God. Thus, this dramatic text about incest and patricide discloses, too, the performative incest and patricidal desire in Artaud's love/hate affair with the spectator watching it.[60] Like the Cenci family, Artaud desired the other side of the persecutory Other, the good breast and womb in the darkness beyond the footlights and stage apron. But the audiences of his play in May 1935, and the mostly hostile reviewers,[61] forced it to close after seventeen performances (Hayman 99). Ironically, by exposing the cruel vulnerability of his own paranoid-schizoid position onstage, Artaud asked his spectators to play the role of castrative Death-God and cruel Cenci. "I have made an immense effort, and here I am on the verge of the abyss. That is the result. From the theatrical point of view I believe the conception was good. . . . But I was betrayed by the realization" (Artaud, qtd. in Hayman 99).[62]

At the beginning of *The Cenci,* the real mother of Count Cenci's children, Beatrice and Bernardo, is already lost. According to Shelley's appendix to his drama, the historical Francesco Cenci's first wife "died after she had given birth to seven unfortunate children" (93). Artaud's play, like Shelley's, hardly mentions her, but her absence is palpable in Count Cenci's powerful rage against his other family members. She is, as lost Other, the fundamental alienation in which Cenci's perverse belief in his own cruel destiny is sustained[63]—and through which he converts his daughter to patricidal hatred: "I often dream that I am destiny itself. This is how my vices are best understood, and my natural bent for hatred and, above all, why I loathe most those who are closest to me in blood" (Artaud, CW 4:123).

Cenci rises above loss and mourning for his first wife through hatred of his sons and incest with his daughter. He triumphs over his own mortal vulnerability by negating all ideals and destroying his descendants. "I feel myself to be, I know I am one of the forces of nature." (This telling hesitation between feeling and knowing will grow as Artaud's play deconstructs Cartesian certainty.) "There is no life, no death, no God, no incest, no contrition, no crime in my existence. I obey my own law, of which I am my own master—and all the worse for those who are caught and sink without a trace in my inferno" (CW 4:123). As he assumes the stature of fate itself, of perverse patriarchal master, of evil force in nature, Cenci becomes Artaud's male embodiment of the persecutory phallic mother, fueled by the seductive fire of mournful rage for the lost mother/wife. "I cannot resist the forces burning with violence inside me." In order to avoid the threat of God—of society, family, and his first wife's ghost, as omnipresent, thieving audience—Cenci tries to become his own Other, an all-consuming (and suicidal) Death-God.

Even more than the sadistic Dr. Pale, the Cenci is a figure for Satan, as Camillo tells him: "Even Lucifer could not be more convincing." Count Cenci plays the position of that perverse god to the Christian order, thus incarnating its other pantheological heritage, "living proof of age-old Christian tradition" (123).[64] But Cenci also reveals how his children and second wife, Lucretia, are a threat to his godlike self-engendering identity: "My family poisons my existence" (134). So he raises his relations with them to a supernatural level of perversity, by celebrating the deaths of his sons and tightening his incestuous grip upon his daughter. "There can be no human relationships between those born only to replace their kin, between those thirsting to devour one another." Here one can see a Kleinian inversion of the child's oral- and anal-sadistic fantasies of the devouring breast and womb. The phallic mother now fears his/her own voracious, cannibalistic offspring.

Thus, Artaud displays his personal vision (and the Kleinian logic) of an originary war within the womb—whereby oral interpretation becomes fatal consumption. For the Cenci's self-fulfilling paranoia forces his remaining family members to destroy him, through his expression of fear that they will do so and his verbal counteroffensive against them. "It is your war against me," he says to his second wife, Lucretia. "I can return it in kind, you know. Dare you deny it was you who persuaded my daughter to turn last night's banquet into an assembly of murderers?" (134). His murderers were not there that night, but they soon will be—as the Other desires.

At that banquet (in the previous scene), the insecurely omnipotent Cenci exhibits textual proof that "the heavens" are on his side: letters telling of his sons' deaths, which he interprets as meaning "two less to plague me" (128). His daughter, Beatrice, disbelieves, though she holds the letters in her own hands. She interprets them differently, using the book of Nature: "The heavens would already have opened if it were not a lie. No one can defy God's justice with impunity."[65] But Cenci's response to her, as public speech to the "assembly of murderers" (his family and dinner guests), demonstrates that his own Sadean law of cruelty[66] is greater than God's, or rather part of the Death-God's rule: "may the wrath of God strike me dead if I am lying. You will see—the justice you invoked is on my side." He then worships his perverse Providence by consecrating a goblet of table wine into his own sons' blood. "The priest drinks God's blood at mass. Who can prevent me believing I am drinking the blood of my sons?"

This black mass is shocking enough to drive his guests toward the doors, but Cenci's further oral performance holds them in spellbound silence: "I drink to my family's destruction. If there is a God in heaven, may a father's curses take effect and tear them all from his throne" (128).[67] Cenci then attempts to consummate his perverse communion and implicate all present by passing the goblet around for them to drink. But one of the guests "sends the goblet flying with the back of his hand." The others again "rush about, panic-stricken," as Cenci threatens not to let them leave the

FIG. 1. Beatrice (Iya Abdy) with her father, the Cenci (Antonin Artaud), during the banquet scene, in Artaud's production of *The Cenci* in 1935. Note the woundlike openings in the chest and stomach areas of Artaud's costume. (Photograph copyright Lipnitzki-Viollet. Courtesy of Roger-Viollet.)

room alive. Yet they also, according to Artaud's stage directions,[68] "advance as if into battle, but a ghostly battle. They are about to attack ghosts, their arms raised as if they were holding pikes or shields." Beatrice then enters this battle, appealing to the fathers in Cenci's audience—and in the audience of the play: "Do not leave us alone with this wild beast or I will never be able to look on white hair again without cursing all fathers." But her prayer to patriarchal goodness fails.[69] The Death-God is in the audience, too. Cenci's phallic-maternal power controls the crowd of spectators onstage as if it were one choral organ.[70] "The crowd draws its breath as if it had received a violent punch in the stomach, belches it out in a great shout" (129).

The Cenci's oral control of the crowd onstage, and perhaps of the audience in the theater, reveals a seductive danger to the Dionysian liberation of Derridean deconstruction (and Kristevan *jouissance*). To the degree to which Derrida, in playing upon Artaud's final writings, identifies with his paranoid-schizoid psychosis (as in Deleuze and Guattari's "schizoanalysis"), there lies the ultimate narcissistic temptation of becoming the Other—as in Artaud's original performance of his cruel hero's familial and social violence. Artaud believed that by such cruel performance onstage, the spectator (and actor) might be relieved of the violence in society, which exists already within the body and psychic text of all human beings from a very early age. But Artaud also saw the risk in his proposed theater of cathartic cruelty and played that out through his own ultimate madness. Whether this catharsis is worth its profound side-effects, or rather, how the medicine might be purified to reduce the risk of backfire, is still being worked out today in theater, especially at its most perverse edges. Similar questions arise in mainstream debates about violence and sexuality in the mass-media theaters of film and television.

In the banquet scene's cruel finale (which Artaud added to Shelley's version), Cenci calmly seduces his daughter, Beatrice, after beating her at the games of oral interpretation, ritual display, and riot control. Again playing with orality and ritual, he persuades her to bring him "a huge goblet full of wine"—because he is "thirsty" (130–31). When she does this, he tries to caress her hair; but she "jerks it back violently." Count Cenci, clenching his teeth, calls her a "viper" and says: "I know a charm that will make you meek and tame." According to Artaud's stage directions, "she darts out, having fully understood." Cenci reiterates: "The spell is working. From now on she cannot escape me" (131). Thus, Cenci shows his own phallic power as snake charmer, somewhat like Artaud's theory of charming his spectators (*Theater* 81). Cenci forces his daughter into incest and into a knowing hatred of her father's unwavering perversity. He permanently takes away her hope to "forgive" him (*CW* 4:130); he steals the last, possible remnants of the good Father. This makes her meek and tame, as his hand reaches beyond her body to control her soul. Though she feels utter panic and runs from the room, he has cast his spell on her, like the metaphysical curse upon his sons. He has shaped her into the viper that will strike and kill him. But then he will continue to haunt her, even more incestuously, through an ineradicable, Oedipal guilt.

The evil Providence with which Cenci blankets his family shows how he has subsumed the loss of the mother—as good breast and womb—into his own perversity. He negates her loss by devouring her spirit, joining it with its opposite. He becomes the desired and feared phallic mother, a Dionysus wearing the patriarchal Apollonian mask. After the banquet seduction of guests and daughter, he secures his omnipotence as this Death-God figure by determining his own fate: forcing his family to make him its foremost ghost.

Artaud heightens the absent presence of this incestuous ghost by adding "a vast bed" to the set description in the next scene of Shelley's text (act 2, scene 1). This scene begins with Lucretia and Bernardo alone together, consoling each other intimately, perhaps while sitting on the bed. Artaud adds a suggestive stage direction for Lucretia: "Cradles BERNARDO in her arms" (131). As they share the burden of Cenci's oppression, Lucretia replaces Bernardo's real mother. "Do not cry. I am not your mother, yet I love you as though I were." She even suggests a rebirthing of him as her own possession. "I have suffered—All great sorrow is like childbirth, Bernardo, to every real woman." Lucretia thus mirrors the Cenci's seduction and spell upon Beatrice at the end of the previous scene. For in his overwhelming cruelty (deriving from a great, but repressed, sorrow for his dead wife), he also gives birth: converting his children to his perverse law and desire. Of course, the watching theater audience is also participating voyeuristically in this seductive scene.

Beatrice then bursts into the room, bearing the pervasive presence of the incestuous father, which has infected her mind with his paranoia. "Has he passed this way? Have you seen him, mother? *(Listens)* It is he. I hear his footstep on the stair. Isn't that his hand on the door? Since yesterday, he seems to be everywhere" (132). In this hypersensitive state, possessed by her father's omnipresent evil spirit, Beatrice also suggests the presence of the good Other, the dead mother, in the room. First, she says, "Have you seen him, mother?" Then she says, "I am exhausted, Lucretia. Help us, mother, help us"—as if praying to her real mother rather than referring to her stepmother, Lucretia. (In Shelley's text Beatrice speaks to her brother, then prays to her mother, as a "duteous child," and to "Thou, great God" [22].) Yet, instead of bringing back the good mother, Beatrice hallucinates the evil father: "I see him as if he were here—his dreadful face appears." This ghost blocks her appeal to the other one, just as he had disproved her appeal to heaven in the banquet scene. Beatrice then shows to what extent she has introjected, as well as projected, the Cenci figure. For she still loves the incestuous father, as well as the good mother behind him. "I ought to hate him, yet I cannot." And this is the way that he possesses her soul so incestuously. His perversity turns the goodness and desire within Beatrice into anticipatory guilt. "His living form is inside me like the guilt of a crime." (This line is not in Shelley's text.) Like the footsteps she now hears that "penetrate these walls" (132), Cenci will continue to rape her with guilt, even beyond his death and absence, as he forces her to murder him.

Count Cenci refers to this when he appears in the room a few moments later, corners the "trembling" Beatrice, seizes her arm as she "slide[s] along the wall," and asks: "Well, what are you waiting for?" (133). It is not just sex that he means, though she does report at the beginning of the next act that her father has raped her (138). At this point he also desires the greater incest of her murdering him. His "monstrous scheme," as she refers to it (132), which would actualize his paranoia and complete his fantasy of ultimate union in death—with Oedipal daughter and lost wife—is now a secret that he and Beatrice share.

After letting Bernardo and Beatrice leave, Cenci "stretches himself out comfortably on the bed" (133) and accuses Lucretia of plotting to murder him. Cenci's powerful death drive, mixed with eroticism, returns to the primary sadistic/masochistic drive within the Kleinian womb. It also reveals the self-de(con)structive urge of his omnipotent fantasies. "I am the only one who can free myself from this suffering." Regaining his heroic hubris, his phallacy above the abject chora, Cenci "takes a few steps towards the place where LUCRETIA exited" and intercourses with his loss—with the darkness and evil he sees in the mirror of night. "And you, O night, you who magnify everything, enter here (Strikes his chest) with every monstrous form of every conceivable crime. You cannot lighten my darkness. My actions will make me greater than you" (135).

This mirror-stage egoism in Cenci's speech to the night is even clearer in another draft by Artaud: "this Life like a glass eye, half-opened, half-closed, the sky where the shadows are enlarged, everything agrees with what I have become" (215 n. 52). In the (m)Other's glass eye, Cenci sees the cruel "dehiscence" of Life in human mortality (Lacan, *Écrits* 4). Perhaps the spectator as Death-God sees it, too, in the mirror of the stage—but with a cruelty beyond the Derridean ideal of sacred autopresentation. Despite our transcendent consciousness, civilization, artworks, and dreams, "Life" instrumentalizes us. Life uses us as its perverse objects (through our erotic and death drives) merely to perpetuate particular genes. Providence is evil. The heavens are bloodthirsty. And children are their parents' executioners. The Cenci's villainous heroism would display this truth for all to see—and thus rise fatally above his own fear. "My actions are now more afraid of me than I am of my actions" (215 n. 52).

Beatrice also expresses the lie of Life, after telling Lucretia that she has been raped by her father. "My only crime was being born. I am free to choose how I die, but I did not choose to be born. That was the fateful blow" (139). Here Artaud's stage direction also indicates that Beatrice, in her consciousness of fate, has found the mother goddess repressed by Christianity: "She clasps LUCRETIA's legs, like Mary Magdalen at the foot of the cross." Yet Beatrice has been irrevocably inseminated by the Father's perverse death drive, his insane immortality. "Madness is like death. I am dead, but my soul clings to life and cannot free itself." She thus converts to the Cenci's deadly faith, through (as Lucretia says) "the justice that permits such loathsome crimes" (139).

Beatrice then tells of a dream she had "every night" as a child, which shows that the incest is not new, only her awareness of its providence is. In the dream she was alone and naked with "a wild animal such as only exists in dreams" (139). She seemed to have a choice for a moment—indicating her later feelings of guilt. "I could escape but I had to hide my glaring nudity" (139–40). A door opened, but she felt hungry and thirsty. "Soon, I saw a horde of foul creatures swarming at my feet. And this horde was also thirsty." Because of her and their thirst, she searched for daylight: "For I felt that only daylight would satisfy me." But the wild beast followed her "from cave to cave. Feeling it near, I realised my thirst was not only stubbornness" (140). This remembered dream (added to Shelley's text) reflects Beatrice's current fear of, yet desire for, her incestuous father, and her guilt for their history together. It even parallels her panic in the earlier bedroom scene, as her father's footsteps penetrated the walls of that cave. Yet it also reflects Artaud's battle within the Kleinian womb: not only his own thirsty desire to devour the breast, and paranoiac fear that it would devour and castrate him, but also his fear of thirsty, dead siblings—the swarming horde of foul creatures surrounding him—through his mother's mourning.

The audience (and reader) of the play is thus cast in the role of lost, ideal mother—of good breast and womb—as well as thieving Death-God. For in watching Beatrice's struggle onstage and in hearing her dream story, the spectators mirror the foul, thirsty horde of ghosts, yet potentially unite into the communal good mother, at least in Artaud's dream. Hence, the anatomy of patriarchal paranoia in *The Cenci* is Artaud's own. He puts it onstage, in all its extreme cruelty, like Count Cenci with his guests and family, in order to evoke the Other to such evil—even if it is death. In the first assassination attempt upon the Cenci (act 3, scene 2), Artaud's stage directions indicate the supernatural force of his Kleinian paranoia: "merged with the wind, we hear voices repeating the name 'Cenci.' First on a high, drawn out tone, then like a pendulum: CENCI, CENCI, CENCI, CENCI." This chant recalls Cenci's speech to the night (and another at the outset of the play) in which he identifies himself with the force of nature. Yet, the voices also represent the forces of fear and hatred that Cenci has invoked from all persons around him, in order to become the Other—to become the perversity of Life instrumentalizing human beings. The choral storm of voices chanting his name raises him to a level of heroic courage, which mirrors his perverse fear: "(Faces the voices, shouts into the storm) WELL! WHAT?" (143). The assassins fire and miss.

But the Cenci's desire for death is still as great as his immortal luck. After the botched assassination, he passionately seeks his daughter, Beatrice, the substitute for his dead wife. "Desire, passion, love . . . I don't know which it is . . . but I am on fire" (143). Instead, he finds his second wife, Lucretia. Together they articulate the death-drive riddle of a pre-Oedipal Sphinx. For they both suffer from its mystery—in his cruelty and her failure to kill him. First, Lucretia tells him of this cruelty, from the victim's side: "I don't want to die. We were not born for this torture." However, Cenci is also a victim, tortured and dying inside: "What about me? Can you tell me why I was born?" (144). She cannot give him an answer. But he is enforcing the only answer he can find, by acting upon his desire for his daughter and for death.

After Lucretia leaves, Cenci "staggers" under the weight of his chosen fate (144). While he had at the beginning of the play, like Artaud in his last years, denied God and any other source of his existence, he now turns to that absence as his justification for cruelty, his reason for being born. Here Cenci no longer claims to be "destiny itself" (123). His soliloquy even implies an absent voice and divine hand. "Repent! Why? Repentance is in God's hands. It is up to him to rue my actions. Why did he make me the father of a being whom I desire so utterly?" Cenci blames God for his own desire. But he also introjects the cruel drive of the heavenly womb, of the divine papa-mama.[71] "I have opened the floodgates so as not to be engulfed." Hence, his theater of cruelty is a revolt against the creative hand of an evil God—the perverse Other whose womb encloses him, yet also quickens within him. "There is a devil within me destined to avenge the world's sins" (144). Cenci rebels against, yet mimics, his view of God's evil.

In the middle of this soliloquy, Cenci (played originally by Artaud) asks for company from any sympathetic spectators: "Are we free? Who can maintain we are free when the heavens are ready to fall on us?" In this way, too, the response he gives to begin the speech alone onstage ("Repent! Why?") is directed to the Death-God, as thief and judge, in the audience.

Artaud thus brings God and the heavens into the theater, by wrestling with tragic fate, through a supremely perverse hero, who tries to seduce his audience into cosmic battle—as he has his own daughter.

When the mute and mummified assassins fail again to kill Count Cenci (144–45), Beatrice's vengeance ignites, though in sympathetic guilt with her father. "You claim to be killers. Yet you were frightened of an old man whose conscience troubled him in his dreams. Go up there and smash his skull open. Or I will kill him with whatever weapon comes to hand and accuse you of his death" (146). With this command the assassins at last consummate the death-drive union of father and daughter: "A loud cry is heard" offstage. Beatrice rewards her surrogates with a stolen symbol of patriarchy, a "priest's chasuble glittering with gold." And then, Count Cenci, a perverse double of Hamlet's father's ghost, "appears high up at the back of the stage, his fist clutching his right eye, as if he were holding something." That something which Artaud does not specify corresponds historically to the nail driven into Cenci's eye (and into his throat) at his murder, as Shelley's appendix mentions (97). Shelley alters this cruel detail in his play. Instead, the assassins report that they "strangled him" (61). Artaud makes the assassins mute and shows Cenci at his historical moment of transcendent, immortal pain. Cenci holds in his hand the answer to the riddle of life: the nail driven into his eye, completing his vision of divine evil, though the Death-God spectators steal the (in)sight.

When the dead body is discovered, Beatrice shows her virgin hands as proof of her innocence. "They are spotlessly clean." Yet the patriarchal Camillo sees both her innocence and guilt: "There is a secret here and I mean to penetrate it." He penetrates her virgin mask by pulling Bernardo away from her (and Lucretia), out of a womblike circle of guards surrounding them. He pulls Bernardo by the head out of that circle, like a doctor separating Madonna and child at its birth. Bernardo flails his arms: "*(Hysterically)* No, no, no. I will follow her, wherever she goes." Lucretia recognizes this incestuous passion: "My God! It is old Cenci himself. Cenci, be still." Here and in the subsequent, final scene, the perverse father's ghost possesses his children. But (with an expressionist twist) their torture chamber also reflects the perversity of modern patriarchy and its industrial life: "The prison is as noisy as a factory at full production" (150). Beatrice is forced to walk in an endless circle, hanging by her hair from a suspended horizontal wheel (149–50). This evokes Bernardo's incestuous idolization of her pain, "drunk with admiration for her." The martyred virgin responds in kind: "be faithful to the love you have vowed for me." She then gives him a song "as a cure for the evils of living" (150).

In a long variation of this song elsewhere in Artaud's manuscript, Beatrice makes the sibling union overt: "Brother lie down on the wheel beside me, / each of its turning spokes / is like a century in the closed tomb" (218 n. 58). She also shows the Father's perverse ghost as omnipresent, both on earth and in the afterlife. Before being "swallowed by the nether world," she sings, "Will we not first have to pass through my father / like the spirit of the wind." It is thus that Beatrice and Bernardo are cut off from the good in mother nature by their cruel Father, even more so after his death. "In fact, I am now aware / he alone existed on earth for me. His spirit is in every living thing" (220 n. 58). In the shorter version of the song, Beatrice gives a succinct formula for Artaudian catharsis.

> So my soul is disfigured
> by life,
> I return it to God
> like a conflagration,
> to cure him of all creation.
>
> (150)

Artaud would also return his own disfigured soul, embodied by this character, to the Death-God of the audience, curing it and himself of the cruel, creative womb—through theatrical conflagration.

Bernardo responds to his sister's song like an ideal incestuous audience, uniting with the death-in-life passion of the actor onstage, signaling through the flames.

> They are coming.
> Let me kiss your warm lips
> before the all-consuming fire
> destroys their smooth petals.
> Before all that was Beatrice
> ends
> like a great wind.

Bernardo kisses the chora of maternal passion, mourning, and wisdom. Through his choral admiration of her martyrdom, Beatrice attains a Joan of Arc–like courage, though admitting her deed. "I am not guilty of the crime I committed." She rises above patriarchal justice, familial and religious: "The Pope's cruelty is as great as old Cenci's" (151). And yet, she also despairs at her ultimate submission to mother earth and maternal loss: "To be swallowed by the mournful earth, endlessly cursing oneself." Beatrice does not end the play as a revolutionary saint. She joins her father in an eternal curse, in the theatrical womb of cruelty's afterlife. "Oh, in dying what horrible visions will appear before my eyes. Who can assure me I will not meet my father after life? The thought makes my dying most bitter. In the end, I fear it will teach me I am not unlike him after all" (153). Beatrice has not yet reached her end in these, her final lines. But she is at the threshold of the Other, joining his villainy and her heroism in one fearful desire.[72]

Moral Effect?

As Derrida and Artaud offer us the forbidden fruit from a cruelly perverse tree of knowledge, they raise profound implications about the relations between author, actor, spectator, and reader. Derrida's Artaud wrestles with the Death-God as spectator/reader of his final writings, like Beatrice with the Cenci. But Artaud also became the Death-God (like the Cenci he played) when he turned his body into a phallic womb—through the psychotic texts that were his ultimate performance. Derrida (dis)misses the metaphysical twist in this postmodern martyrdom: the delusion of immortality in Artaud's écriture (and the Cenci's speeches). Derrida also fails to consider the absent mother, though he does describe the womb, as "auto-presentation" and "Orifice," of Artaud's final corpus. Hence my recourse, through a lack in Artaud's Derridean rebirth, to the cruel/ideal Kleinian womb and Kristevan chora.[73] In *The Cenci* the lost mother, as repressed choral power (which is not simply her), returns with a vengeance through both father and daughter. Loss structures his evil: from mournful rage to transcendent egotism, incestuous greed, and infectious mimetic violence. Yet Beatrice's words and actions against her father force him to remove his mask of immor(t)ality—like Artaud's final murder of the Death-God spectator.

And thus, Artaud's failed plan for a theater of cruelty, resonating through most, if not all, stage experimentation since his death, contains an Oedipal desire for and against the spectator-Other, expressed as revolutionary defiance.

> Whatever the conflicts that haunt the mind of a given period, I defy any spectator to whom such violent scenes will have transferred their blood, who will have felt in himself the transit of a superior action, who will have seen the extraordinary and essential movements of his thought illuminated in extraordinary deeds—the violence and blood

having been placed at the service of the violence of the thought—I defy
that spectator to give himself up, once outside the theater, to ideas of
war, riot, and blatant murder. (*Theater* 82)

Is he right? Would *The Cenci,* if performed perfectly onstage, have this
effect? Would there be a transfusion of blood between performers and spectators, an incestuous communion of superior action and thought, cathartically curing us of violence through violence? Perhaps theater can someday
be a meta-physical rite that will exorcise our familial ghosts and "make our
demons FLOW" (60). It does seem that in our day, even more than in
Artaud's, there is an "implacable necessity," as Derrida put it (*WD* 233), for
this impossible seduction of spectators, "through the skin" (Artaud 79),
toward metaphysical "temptations" (90). And yet, if Artaud ended up with
his shit as his salvation (Derrida 183), we seem no closer to that kind
of "severe moral purity, which is not afraid to pay life the price it must be
paid" (Artaud 122)—despite our plethora of seductive violence in movies
and television, surrounding us like a cruel womb.[74]

The problem is, as Artaud mentions: a theater of cruelty is quite dangerous.

Everything depends upon the manner and the purity with which the
thing is done. There is a risk. But let it not be forgotten that though a
theatrical gesture is violent, it is disinterested; and that the theater
teaches precisely the uselessness of the action which, once done, is not
to be done, and the superior use of the state unused by the action and
which, *restored,* produces a purification. (82)

Unfortunately, film and TV do not often give us the disinterested violence
of a theatrical gesture. They are too caught up in the endless mimesis of life
and art in the postmodern simulacrum,[75] making money out of seductive
violence and admirable villains onscreen, and perhaps inspiring real-life
violence, which will soon be made again into a moving picture. Serial killers
(male and female) and other violent sociopaths become our metaparental
gods. Most of us worship them merely monetarily, but some of us go farther. Artaud would have us go so far, through art, that we could not act out
such violence in life. His theatrical cruelty would teach us the vast uselessness of Cenci's curse, perpetuated through his incest and revenge upon his
own blood—without any justice, heroic or poetic, at the end of each suffering generation. How could we repeat this violence in our own family life
after seeing him and his family torturing themselves onstage?

Perhaps we are still seeking a superior, unacted state, restorative, and purifying—through our replication of blood and gore in popular drama. But we also seem to have fallen into an endless perversion through that safety valve of collective violence. We have merely surrounded ourselves with a cruel, imprisoning womb of fatal representation.[76] Theater, cinema, and TV have become what Artaud complained of—concerning his origin in the (m)Other:

> a uterus I had nothing to do with then or even before I was born, because that is not how one is born, being copulated and masturbated nine months by the membrane, that shining membrane that devours without teeth, as it says in the UPANISHADS, and I know that I was born otherwise, out of my works and not out of a mother, but the MOTHER wanted to take me and you see the result in my life.—I was born only out of my own pain. . . . And it would seem that the uterus found this pain good, 49 years ago, since it chose to take it for its own and to take nourishment from it with no pretense of maternity. (*SW* 442–43)

Despite the postmodern delight in mass-mediated surfaces and textual/bodily *différance,* we still seem to long for the ideal, lost womb, like the modernist Artaud, to counter the cruel "hyperreal" (Baudrillard)[77] of our cultural uterus and its devouring membrane.

My final two chapters find playwrights who also react in distinctly prophetic ways to the lost womb of theater and its cruel power. While Genet transforms abject criminality into revolutionary art, Brecht fights alienation with alienation in order to free us from our perpetual re-presentations of fate. For patriarchy's phallic mother is both lost and found, cruel and ideal, repressed and powerfully present—in the hypertheatricality of mind, art, and mass media today.

Chapter 5

Genet's Dismemberment through Lacan's Orders and Irigaray's Cave

Of all the dramatists in my study, Jean Genet is closest historically to the postmodern period—usually viewed as the latter half or third of the twentieth century. Yet his work first received praise through the modernist desire to recover a lost universal order, albeit existential rather than religious. Also, like his predecessor Artaud, Genet's power as a revolutionary writer derives from his own sense of childhood loss. But whereas Artaud's incestuous competition with dead siblings produced his psychic martyrdom, Genet became an existentialist saint through orphanhood and thievery. Thus, his originary loss of both mother and father developed into a distinctly playful violence, as well as profoundly painful alienation.

Already in 1952, before most of Genet's plays were written, he was canonized by Jean-Paul Sartre as a perverse reincarnation of St. Genet, third-century martyr and patron of actors.[1] Sartre begins his book on Genet the novelist and playwright by marking a "sacred" theater of mythical loss. "In his early childhood, a liturgical drama was performed, a drama of which he was the officiant: he knew paradise and lost it, he was a child and was driven from his childhood" (1). Sartre then describes the ritual drama of Genet's childhood as a fall from paradise into the lie of innocence (5–6), through abandonment by his original mother—whom he worshiped and hated like a "Mother Goddess" (7–8)—and through identification as thief by the peasant society that adopted him (10, 23, 51–53).

Jacques Derrida has found a different significance to Genet's identity—through a reference in his autobiography, *The Thief's Journal* (1949), to the broom flower, *genêt* (44; Derrida, *Glas* 182). Genet's father was never known to him; he received the *Nom du Père* of his mother as his own. According to biographer Edmund White, this was due to the fact that Camille Genet kept her baby for seven months, for whatever reason (perhaps in order to wean him), before giving him up (9–10). "So this flower name would be a cryptogram or a cryptonym," says Derrida (183). He deconstructs Genet's nom de plume, and the lost mother at its thalloid roots. All that remains of her is the (s)crypt of her name, her signature on Genet's birth certificate. Here Derrida discerns, according to Jane Marie Todd, "a figure for the author/text/signature relationship" (4–5), entombing and enwombing one another through mournful creativity. As with Artaud's schizophrenic body becoming the womb of his final encopretic writings, Derrida's Genet "becomes a mother, the mother of his own life, in taking on the name of his mother" (Todd 5). He thus becomes his own perverse mother goddess, "creating a religion of abjection" (10). In becoming the mother of his text, Genet, like Artaud, "keeps it to himself, devotes himself to it, and finally kills it off, keeps it away from 'the world,' from the reader" (11). However, as I will show in this chapter, Genet goes farther than Artaud in sacrificing his playwriting womb to the actual *sparagmos* of theater.

In 1962, Robert Brustein identified St. Genet as the direct descendant of St. Artaud. In the concluding chapter of *The Theatre of Revolt*, Brustein shows how "Genet inherits Artaud's radical messianism" (379). He even states, in direct disagreement with Roger Blin (who worked theatrically with both men), that "Genet, the dramatist, in short, is largely created by Artaud" (378). Brustein returns to Sartre's vision in order to target his own Artaud/Genet double, who "creates a drama of appearances through which a deeper reality is evoked" (387–88). And yet Brustein also indicates that Genet's revolt moves beyond the earlier artist of cruelty. "He not only dreams, like Artaud, but like Pirandello, analyzes his dreams" (393).[2]

Subsequent analysis of Genet in the 1970s has gone in both the Brustein and Blin directions: for[3] or against[4] the close relation between Artaud and Genet. I shall not claim to resolve this debate about authorial parenting,[5] as I move from the preceding chapter on Artaud to the current one on Genet. But I hope to shed some light on it by a close examination of the Lacanian orders (Imaginary, Symbolic, and Real) in Genet's dramatic texts. For his exaltation of rehearsal disguises, of antitheological ritual, of deeper realities within appearances and analyzed dreams, points not only to Genet's inheritance of Artaudian desires. These characteristics of Genet's plays also project toward the present and future, through multiple refractions and intersections of the mirror stage, from the author's psyche and biography to the reader's—or director's, actors', and spectators'. It is this dispersal of Genet's onanistic writings that I hope to trace, in order to show the personal dismemberment in his perverse passage from criminal to saint. Here Genet's texts tempt us, too, toward the "impossible nothing" that he desired as (m)Other—the abyss at the stage edge where mirrors are formed, cutting through our dramatic, communal corpus.

The Whirligig of a Broom Flower's Womb

Derrida's *Glas* (1974) points to the loss of Genet, as self-deconstructing broom flower,[6] in Sartre's idolization. "In *Saint Genet,* the question of the flower, the anthological question, is, among others, infallibly avoided" (*Glas* 13). In 1973 Georges Bataille also criticized Sartre's vision as losing the reality of Genet's "shame" (151). But other scholars in the 1970s (in France and the United States) adhered to Sartre's focus on the "whirligig" of reality and imagination in Genet's plays (611).[7] More recently, Una Chaudhuri has disputed Sartre's "metaphysical whirligig of illusion and reality . . . [which] freezes into a static and impotent image: consciousness as the mutual reflection of two empty mirrors, endlessly reflecting each other's reflections" (6).[8] My own argument in the current chapter is not directly opposed to any of these views. But I would shift the focus, unlike Chaudhuri, to the Lacanian terms of Real, Imaginary, and Symbolic. This will open Sartre's whirligig of reality and imagination,[9] now frozen in the mirrors of critical fixation, to a newly dynamic analysis of Genet. First, though, I will dwell briefly on Genet's childhood (but not on the complex issue of his developing homosexuality) to refine the edges of maternal loss at the heart of his texts. I will also conclude this chapter with psychoanalytic feminist Luce Irigaray's redefinition of Plato's cave, to further unearth the *hystera* in Genet's stage edge.

Recently, American feminists, spurred by Derrida's analysis of the broom flower signature and Hélène Cixous's further name play,[10] have turned to an excavation of the mother goddess within Genet's life and drama. Mary Ann Frese Witt summarizes such inspiration: "Derrida, like Cixous, identifies the double-edged nourishing space and phallic, castrating mother as the motivating force behind Genet's writing" (173). Witt then proposes her own reading, which "sees a female (primarily matriarchal) principle as the unacknowledged power behind, and ultimate destroyer of, what appears to be a male-ordered world in each of Genet's texts." Against Sartre's argument that Genet wrote himself out of prison, Witt finds "imprisoning spaces, often signs of an absent, desired maternal space" in his work. Thus, the mother goddess in Genet is not only subversive and liberating, but also imprisoning—at least for males. "The female presence not only stands in dialogical opposition to the male world, but ultimately undermines and engulfs it" (174). In my view, this marks the kairological revenge of a Medean (or Cixous's laughing Medusan) earth mother, as womb and tomb, reengulfing the male order of sky god religions and patriarchal empires, which have violently repressed her throughout chronological history.

Witt also refers to Kristeva's theory of "woman's time" and to Mircea Eliade's of mythological time. Both, according to Witt, relate to "the space-time configuration" in Genet's works, which is "originally the time of prison, the prison that figures as a maternal breast or womb, that resembles Kristeva's sense of Plato's *chora*" (180). I have used this term recurrently in preceding chapters, but here I shall reserve my explicit discussion of Genet's chora for the end of the chapter, and view it then in terms of Irigaray's rebellion within the philosophical prison of Plato's cave (as false *hystera*). Witt does not refer to Irigaray's poststructuralist theory of the womb, but rather looks back to the structuralism of J. J. Bachofen's *Mutterrecht*.[11] The significance of Bachofen's theory, in Witt's view, is that it describes "man's nostalgia for a 'rule by mothers'" in the evolution of the Western social order from prehistory through various stages of patriarchy (Witt 176). Witt's own nostalgia for the Great Mother focuses upon Her subversive, liberating power as primordial feminist and postcolonialist.[12]

However, Witt (like Cixous) tends to idealize the liberative space-time of Genet's female characters without acknowledging the regressive, mournful illusion in the lost utopia of the womb. Madame Irma, for example, attains "complete control" at the end of *The Balcony* (184). Here Witt actively forgets the reality/imagination dynamic that Sartre elucidated in Genet, to which Irma also submits, like her audience, at the play's end: "I'm going to prepare my costumes and studios for tomorrow. You must now go home, where everything—you can be quite sure—will be falser than here" (96).

I would argue that Irma and other female figures are as much trapped in the choral, space-time womb of Genet's plays as liberated by it. They do not take complete control over male figures or a male world but rather reveal a dangerous hypocrisy behind the masks and mirrors of revolutionary dreams. Patriarchal desire persists in Genet's plays—along with Symbolic, Imaginary, and Real orders—despite being turned inside out by the ideal (and horrible) phallic mother, whose Medusan laugh is idolized by Cixous and her American disciples.[13]

Harry E. Stewart has tried to overturn the Sartrean vision of Genet's childhood martyrdom by the symbolic order that named him orphan and thief. Stewart claims that the "facts concerning Genet's early life have been obscured by Sartre"—and also by Genet himself "as a means to embellish his [own] legend" ("Genet's Childhood" 107). Stewart interviewed Genet's foster sister, Mme. Lucie Girard, who "maintains that Genet had a happy, normal childhood." She also told Stewart that Genet's foster mother, Mme.

Charles Régnier, "absolutely adored the child." Stewart explains, too, that Genet's foster father was a carpenter, not a peasant farmer as Sartre indicates. According to Stewart, Mme. Régnier "was an extremely pious woman" (108). She spoiled the young Genet and dreamed that he would become a priest someday (108–9). For already, at an early age, "his favorite game was playing at being a priest."[14] Stewart focuses on the death of this foster mother in 1922, when Genet was almost twelve, as the turning point in his life (109)—as opposed to the mythical thievery, at about the same age, which Sartre fetishizes as determinant of the saint's fate.[15]

But such details, in my view, support a broader vision of Genet's current significance to both modern existentialism and postmodern feminism—both as thief/martyr fated by the Symbolic order and as rebelling whirligig, bearing Imaginary potential along with Real loss. Genet suffered a double betrayal of the maternal within patriarchy: he was the child of an unwed mother who abandoned him, except in name; he was then assigned to a foster mother who adored and spoiled him yet died. This double-deep (s)crypt would eventually bloom in the broom flower's perverse power as theatrical priest of violent, criminal rituals—raising the mother goddess buried beneath the Western stage. But unlike Artaud's evocation of that primordial womb in theory and body, and unlike Eliot's or Nietzsche's differential desires for a lost choral edge, Genet displays the hollowness of the Magna Mater's mask: the imprisoning illusions of transcendence in the ghost of the stage "apron."

Onanistic Escape

In his brief book on Proust, Samuel Beckett states,

> The laws of memory are subject to the more general laws of habit. Habit is a compromise effected between the individual and his environment, or between the individual and his own organic eccentricities, the guarantee of a dull inviolability, the lightning conductor of his existence. Habit is the ballast that chains the dog to his vomit. (7–8)

But in Proustian fictional memory, according to Beckett, there are breaks in the rule of Habit, "when for a moment the boredom of living is replaced by the suffering of being" (8). In such moments, existential Suffering pierces the "screen" of habitual memory and "opens a window on the real" (16). These observations can also be applied to the writings of Genet, particularly through the primal scene of his remembered rebirth as an author, although Genet's writings involve fantasy more than memory—in vomitory self-recreation.

Genet wrote his first novels in a prison cell, in an onanistic compromise with his environment. Through the Habit of his writing instrument, Genet disseminated his Suffering and sexual eccentricities onto paper, opening an imaginary window onto the real within him (in the Lacanian sense of Imaginary and Real orders as well). Even if this onanism, which Genet remembers as the origin for his novels, is merely an invented memory or a metaphor, the onanistic narcissism of his writing style remains apparent. Did he write to be read by anyone other than himself? Bataille, disagreeing with Sartre's consecration of St. Genet, says: "In fact there is no communication between Genet and the reader—and yet Sartre assumes that his work is valid. . . . [T]he consecrational operation, or poetry, is communication or nothing" (161).

If Genet wrote only for himself originally, he still imagined at least one reader. Indeed, the sole purpose of his writing would then have been to read it himself, to reread himself and his imaginings, and to reimagine himself through his written fantasies. He was at least communicating (and desiring communication) with himself. But then that "self" was an outside, future Genet-reader, whom Genet the writer was courting for potential communication/communion. This split between writing and reading moments, and between writing and reading Genets, reveals further splits between those moments (momentary selves) and the moment of the fantasizing self. All three of these Genets and the splits between them reside within the moment when "the suffering of being" breaks through "the boredom of living" and prison habitation. The tripartite subjectivity of Genet, as writer, reader, and daydreamer, illustrates both his imprisoned consciousness and its alienation from itself—in the desire for/of the Other (Lacan, *Four* 38).

This situation is not so different from any unknown writer, dreamer, and self-critic trying to be read by others—except that Genet was imprisoned by harder walls than Habit and the writer's desire to communicate. And yet, we are all (writers and nonwriters) constituted as split subjects, according to Lacan, as he builds on Freud's *Ich-spaltung*. "[T]he subject always realizes himself more in the Other, but he is already pursuing there more than half of himself. . . . [T]he subject is subject only from being subjected to the field of the Other. . . . That is why he must get out, get himself out" (*Four* 188). Genet did get himself out—if only out of prison—by writing novels in it and being read by the Other outside of it, particularly by Sartre and Cocteau. His pursuit of more than half of himself in his disseminated characters (his imaginary others) gave birth eventually to a real audience, larger perhaps than he ever dreamed. And when Genet turned to writing for the theater, real actors embodied his imaginary character-others, seen by real spectator-others. Genet's split subjectivity as dreamer, writer, and reader was then extended even farther in subjection to the field of the Other. Directors, actors, costume, lighting, and set designers and technicians, as well as the nightly audience, to some extent did then, and still do, reimagine and rewrite his plays onto the "live," public stage, as the real readers of his novels had been doing privately. The vomitoria of theaters thus led into Genet-the-playwright's new, expanded (yet still onanistic?) vomitorium.

According to Herbert Blau, one of the earliest directors of *The Balcony:* "Genet's drama courts the actor's suspicion and makes the experience of violation the main action of the drama. . . . The actor resists his scenario, and he should. The drama gains intensity of meaning from encouragement of the actor's natural grievances" (*Impossible* 268). In Blau's production (when Genet was relatively unknown and uncanonized), the play's sense of violation and resistance was played out between actors and script, between the actors and their characters, and between actors/characters and the theater audience. "Their task was to find the Self in the unison of their dependency. . . . As actors they would use the voyeuristic expectancies they could feel in the audience" (272). Actors of Genet's plays (of any play) must find a self, a character they portray onstage—though their idea of who they are at any moment and the audience's are not identical, are always in dialogical flux in performance.

The actor-audience relationship of theater mirrors Genet's tripartite, onanistic, prison subjectivity in both directions across the stage edge: the spectator reads, dreams, and (re)writes the character onstage as the actor is reading, imagining, and responding to the voyeuristic expectancies of the audience. The actors, especially in Genet's plays, imagine their characters and continually rewrite (react) them onstage by reading their audience's and fellow actors' reactions. And the audience of spectators is dreaming the play (like Genet, the onanist) as they perceive the performance—actually changing it within themselves and in their effect on the actors (like Genet, the writer). This interactive gap between stage and seats mirrors the gap between Genet and his written characters. It also illustrates the splits within Genet, projected through his imaginary Others, reflecting and subjecting him as he dreams, writes, and rereads them (and himself). Thus, his writing for the theater both realized and extended his split subjectivity.[16]

Outcast(e) in the Mirror

Genet began life as the fatherless child of a prostitute or "maidservant" (White 8), as an outcast from society. His idea of "self" came through crime—through a violent self-engendering, as Ihab Hassan explains. "The outcast rebuffs not only society but also the very order of things. He works against nature, invents his sex and self, in order to sever all ties with creation" (*Dismemberment* 180). Yet this rebuff is a way of using the rejected laws of society and order of nature to buff up the outcast's own identity. The ties are never really severed; they are indeed tightened. The criminal supposedly builds his own scaffolding of identity as "outlaw" and temporarily escapes the law to prove it, but this status eventually brings him even more under the eyes and hand of the law—as prisoner. His self-scaffolding seeks the cell bars. He needs the being caught to prove he is an outlaw.

At the conclusion of Genet's first written play, *Deathwatch,* a murder is committed in a prison cell by Lefranc for the sake of the watching Other, Green Eyes (and the theater audience). The act is a gift of love: to the "ego ideal" of murderer that Green Eyes represents. Yet the act fails to unify Lefranc's ideal ego with his ego ideal;[17] it does not return him to the symbiosis behind the mirror-stage (which is impossible, yet yearned for). On the contrary, the act proves that Lefranc is a "fraud," as Green Eyes tells him. That is still his identity in spite of, and still more because of, his new deed. When the guard arrives, he "leers at Green Eyes" (163), implying that only the known "Murderer" will be believed as the current murderer. Even if Lefranc were to claim the killing, he would only be seen as a fraud.

The silent spectators of the theater audience are thus placed in an ultimate, though impotent, juridical position. They have seen the truth that the guard has missed. Yet they also see the criminals' identities locked into the performance of their own character roles.[18] If Green Eyes had committed the murder, it would have been natural and magnificent as in the mythical past; but Lefranc, trying to imitate Green Eyes's greatness, commits a fraudulent murder, for he is not a Murderer. The killing of Maurice both succeeds and fails as a Symbolic act: it fails to secure Lefranc a new, transcendent identity, but it succeeds in proving the greatness of the Other, in whom his subjectivity is constituted, the gazing mirror of Green Eyes.

The outcast is also cast in the role (and caste) of outcast. Genet's onanistic rebellion of writing gained him a new identity as novelist/playwright and freed him from prison walls, but it also further subjected him to the Law of the Father. Unlike Lefranc, Genet changes his way of being in the world (to a degree), but he never escapes the scaffolding of language. He must continue to vomit, to hang himself on his onanisticly created characters, to prove his new identity by being caught onstage and in print. He must, that is, until he stops. Only thirteen years after his release from prison, Genet's last play is published. One reason might have been that the extension of his split subjectivity increased with each successive play. From *Deathwatch* through *The Maids* to *The Balcony*, Genet expands his setting and subject; and even further with *The Blacks* and *The Screens*, Genet's imaginary reflections of himself take on black faces (wearing white masks) and Arab identities, with their own colonial histories, rebellions, and fates.

Real Lost

In an interview with Ruediger Wischenbart in 1984, Genet was asked about his involvement with the Black Panthers and the PLO,[19] about his "attraction to such groups." He responded (after referring to Proust),

> I was thirty when I started to write. I was thirty-four or thirty-five when I stopped writing. It was a dream, a day-dream at least. I wrote in prison. When I came out, I was lost. I really found myself—my way around the real world—only in those two revolutionary movements: the Black Panthers and the Palestinians. That's when I submitted to the real world. . . . I acted under the conditions of the real world and not in the world of syntax.

Yet, two sentences later Genet also admits: "Dreams are real." In Lacanian terms the outer world of objects and experiences is inevitably screened by the inner, Imaginary world, which creates the personal/collective fantasy called "reality" (and daydream) through the Symbolic, the social world of syntax.[20] But there is also a Real within the unconscious. Dreams, like plays, seem real, or sometimes too real, because they bear an uncanny, excess meaning, only partially interpretable through the Imaginary and Symbolic, pointing to the unconscious, inaccessible Real. Genet's Imaginary "dream world" of writing (42) linked the Real within him to the world outside him through the Symbolic: through his writings being published and performed onstage.[21]

However, in becoming Real outside him, Genet's plays also became more and more lost to him. Genet's tragic journey from onanistic writer, through gradually more social dramas, to the ideal ego of "intellectual guerrilla" (as the title of the Wischenbart interview refers to him) displays a continual, inevitable failure to reach the Real—to directly connect the Real within to the Real outside. For the Real, in Lacanian terms, is always mediated by the Symbolic and the Imaginary; it is always beyond reach.[22] Genet seems to suggest this himself (indirectly) at the end of the Wischenbart interview. He says that he will "betray" the Palestinians as soon as they "establish themselves," that is, when they become more Real than Symbolic (45–46). Wischenbart asks if this statement isn't "just an ironic gesture." Genet insists it was an "honest" statement, but adds: "I am honest only with myself. As soon as I start talking I am already betrayed by the situation. I am betrayed by the person who listens to me. . . . My choice of words betrays me" (46).[23] Genet's extreme sensitivity to the split in human subjectivity, to the gaps between the personal Imaginary, the Symbolic of verbal expression (and of "self" constitution), and the Real outside/within yet always at a distance, indicates a reason for his greatness as a writer, but also for the painful brevity of his writing career.

Genet's second play, *The Maids,* again concludes with a murder, but this time it is the ritual playing out of a murder of the master (Madame) by the slaves (maids). It is not only a matter of the slaves' *ressentiment* overcoming their master's power, as in the Hegelian typology of Nietzsche and Marx,[24] but also of a self-deconstructing ritual in which the maids take turns replaying and repaying their murderous *ressentiment* toward each other. Madame herself apparently escapes.[25] But the maids are trapped in their roles as much as the prisoners of *Deathwatch.* They play out their Imaginary and Symbolic murder of Madame (the subjecting Other) in each other. That is their only triumph.

Here, as in his later plays, Genet deconstructs the Marxist dream of proletarian revolution.[26] Genet's maids displace their common superego by ritually murdering Madame and dividing it (her) between them. But they also repeat—with every Real performance of the play and with the Imaginary ritual performed within the play—a resurrection of her as the "Madame" within each of them.[27] Their revolution returns the Real of utopia to its no place: out of reach within.

The Gaping I

According to Ellie Ragland-Sullivan's reading of Lacan, "the residue of a child's development is the Imaginary as it asserts itself in adult life in relation to Symbolic order contracts, pacts, and laws. But the Imaginary tends to subvert these laws, whether through innocuous irony or criminal acts" (*Lacan* 179). The Imaginary play of children likewise develops into adult theater's assertive, "serious" Imaginary, often trying to subvert society's Symbolic laws and representations. Yet Genet's plays rebel against their own rebellions, subvert their own subversions, and so approach (but never reach) the Real.

The childish clients of Madame Irma's brothel in *The Balcony* play out their Imaginary fantasies onstage, in the various "rooms" that the set turns to view, while offstage noises of a supposedly Real rebellion are occasionally heard. Is that rebellion outside the brothel going to subvert its perverted Imaginary? Or is the violence within the brothel (with its own illusions of reality) itself a rebellion against the reality outside? The Imaginary order of the brothel onstage and the machine-gun sounds of a Real order offstage approach a violent meeting as the play proceeds. But the walls of the Grand Balcony brothel also involve the Real in the eyes of the audience, watching from the darkness—from the Other side of the "fourth wall," at the mirror stage edge between seats and show.

The Imaginary/Symbolic perversions of *The Balcony* take place in front of multiple mirrors: the literal, onstage mirrors described in Genet's stage directions, the mirrors of other characters' eyes, and the mirror-eyes of Real theater spectators, reflected by certain props or set points onstage. For example, the "bishop" (the brothel client in bishop's vestments) verges on a mirror-stage-like *jouissance* of costumed identity: first in the eyes of the "confessing" woman (his whore) and then in the real mirror onstage (10–12). Finally, disrobed at the end of scene 1, he looks down upon his Imaginary/Symbolic in-vestments, "which are heaped on the floor," and tries again to join his outward, social "I" *(je)* with his inner sense of "myself" *(moi)*—even though the gap between them is now clear:

> Ornaments, laces, through you I re-enter myself *[je rentre en moi-meme]*. I reconquer a domain. . . . I install myself in a clearing where suicide at last becomes possible . . . and here I stand, face to face with my death. (*Balcony* 13; *Balcon* 51)

In the mirror of his fallen vestments on the floor, the "bishop"—or rather, the *moi* inside the costume—glimpses the gap between Imaginary and Symbolic. He faces an image of self as death, ultimately uniting *moi* and *je* as fallen figure.[28]

The "judge" also verges on *jouissance* in the mirror image of his "executioner" (the pimp, Arthur, who beats the thief/whore at the judge's command). Thus, the judge glimpses the gaps between Imaginary, Real, and Symbolic "word."

FIG. 2. *The Balcony*, by Jean Genet. The bishop and a crucifix. Actor's Workshop of San Francisco production, directed by Herbert Blau, 1960. (Photograph by Hank Kranzler. All rights reserved.)

JUDGE: I'm pleased with you. Executioner! Masterly mountain of meat, hunk of beef that's set in motion at a word from me! *(He pretends to look at himself in the Executioner.)* Mirror that glorifies me! Image that I can touch, I love you. . . . *(He touches him.)* Are you there?

(18–19)

The client playing "general" in the brothel is also phallically aroused, like the bishop and judge, by the potential of pure, hollow, Symbolic Being. In his brothel room, he "rides" an Imaginary horse (his whore) into death, whereupon, in the whore/horse's words: "The nation weeps for that splendid hero who died in battle" (27).

However, the real "hero" of the play is the chief of police, realizing his heroism by "putting down" the supposedly Real rebellion outside the brothel (49). But even the heroic chief of police needs a further revolution, a new brothel perversion of his own, to create his Symbolic place within the brothel—to bridge the gap between its Imaginary and the Real outside. After quashing the outside rebellion, the chief of police watches the former rebel leader, Roger, play an Imaginary "chief of police" in one of the brothel rooms. The real chief hopes this new brothel scene will give him (or rather, his image) a permanent, Symbolic status as one of the brothel roles, replayed over and over again. But Roger, still the rebel, perverts the perversion by castrating himself while playing the chief of police. And yet, the supposedly Real violence of Roger's further rebellion plays into the chief's Imaginary/Symbolic intention, stated earlier in the play: "to appear in the form of a gigantic phallus, a prick of great status" (78). As predicted by the judge, though, the chief may have to wait "two thousand years" for Roger's castrated penis to give birth to a new Symbolic hero in the chief's image. So, in the end, the chief of police exits into the brothel's Imaginary mausoleum to await his *jouissance* of Symbolic resurrection.

Madame Irma experiences a double *jouissance* in *The Balcony:* first as Madame of the "Grand Balcony" brothel—through her assistant Carmen's mirror-eyes (37)—then later as the new queen, when the Grand Balcony extends and swallows the Real outside after the offstage rebellion is put down. This extension of the Grand Balcony's Imaginary/Symbolic realm is depicted in the stage directions of scene 8, moving the setting to the outside of the building: "The scene is the balcony itself, which projects beyond the facade of the brothel" (70). In the next scene (9, the last of the play), the newly empowered figures from the brothel, bishop, judge, and general, think they must create a new social order, "invent an entire life" (71 [general]). But they actually restore and embody the old Symbolic order, which

FIG. 3. *The Balcony,* by Jean Genet. The judge looking down upon his thief/whore. Actor's Workshop of San Francisco production, directed by Herbert Blau, 1960. (Photograph by Hank Kranzler. All rights reserved.)

they had merely perverted in their Imaginary brothel scenes. Now their public, Symbolic images are confirmed by photographers, who insist on "the classical pose. A return to order, a return to classicism" (73).

However, the job of being a public symbol ruins the former, perverse pleasure of those same imaginary roles. The bishop, judge, and general threaten to rebel against the chief of police (79–80). Then the greater, outside threat of rebellion returns, overshadowing their little uprising. The chief of police and Queen Irma realize that the bishop's assassination of Chantal—Irma's former whore who was hired by the rebels to be their "singer" and "sign" of heroism (56)—has failed to make Chantal a safe symbol, a "saint" for the renewed order (81). Even so, this new threat of violence becomes the chief's hope for symbol-dom (prior to Roger's castration). For, according to the bishop and general, the "people" have "trembled so violently" that they are losing all hope and will "collapse": fall like Narcissus into the pool of the chief's reflection of the Symbolic order and fill him with their "drowned bodies" (85–86).

FIG. 4. *The Balcony,* by Jean Genet. The general and his horse/whore. Actor's Workshop of San Francisco production, directed by Herbert Blau, 1960. (Photograph by Hank Kranzler. All rights reserved.)

Roger's eventual castration also serves to detach the phallic symbol and reified image of the chief—as he himself had predicted: "I'll make my image detach itself from me. I'll make it penetrate into your studios, force its way in, reflect and multiply itself" (48). Madame/Queen Irma's brothel order is thus reconfirmed in power—through the revolutionary violence supposedly attempting to overthrow it. The ostensible reality of the revolution outside is itself perverted by the power of the brothel/theater mirrors. And yet, the desire for revolution is revealed as a demand of the overall social order, as just another room of that Other brothel, which supersedes Irma's little place.

The primary perversion in the Grand Balcony brothel, presented onstage in the play, *The Balcony,* is the voyeurism of the real theater audience. In the middle of the final scene, the chief of police turns to Irma's panoptic "mechanism" for viewing all the brothel studios and (according to Genet's stage directions) "the two panels of the double mirror forming the back of the stage silently draw apart, revealing the interior of the Special [Mausoleum] Studio" (87). That "double mirror" not only reflects the onstage action, but also the sea of spectators' eyes and faces watching. The drawing apart of the backstage mirrors at this moment, showing the characters of symbolic authority watching the scene in the Mausoleum Studio, also shows the watching audience an image of themselves splitting open, revealing the Imaginary/Symbolic "Mausoleum Studio" within them. The Real within the audience is reflected onstage, though still out of reach, lost to the scene: viewing, imagining, and mirroring *The Balcony.*[29]

Edges of Violent Re-Creation

The return of the Real becomes racial in the next play written by Genet, *The Blacks: A Clown Show.* As Hassan has noted, "Genet now reverses himself: the rebels . . . win" (*Dismemberment* 202). But in their gradual overthrowing of white colonial power, the rebel blacks must pervert themselves with white masks and their slave performance before a specifically white (or symbolically white) audience, according to Genet's demands.[30] As the chief of police waits two thousand years in a brothel tomb to alter the Symbolic order of *The Balcony,* so the blacks masquerade for whites in order to someday create a black Symbolic order.

The foolish "court" of blacks with white masks, watching from the balcony over the stage, reflect the watching white theater audience. They represent the oppression of the old Symbolic yet also act to subvert it. Change comes through the supposedly Real rebel violence offstage and also onstage through the Imaginary/Symbolic violence of a ritually reenacted murder. These two, elaborate, deceitful mechanisms combine, intersect, and copulate to finally create the possibility for new "gestures of love" by the murderer Village and the whore Virtue at the end of the play (128).

The blacks' Real offstage rebellion, as reported during the play to the leader of the masquerade, Archibald, by the character Newport News (running on- and offstage again and again), inseminates the onstage play with a violent purpose. But the onstage masquerade, masking the offstage violence, is also a revolution. The funeral rite and reenacted murder around the absent, Imaginary body and Symbolic mask of a white girl (worn by a black male) ignites a further ritual revolution onstage: the violent perversion of white symbols of authority through their imaginary replaying. The blacks impersonate whites in order to kill and overthrow them, in order to kill and overthrow the white Symbolic and Imaginary of their own consciousness (and unconscious). They hope to reinvent their own blackness by overturning that which Virtue describes as "what I see and what goes on in my own soul and what I call the temptation of the Whites" (24).[31]

Early in the play, Archibald mockingly reassures the real theater audience that a safe, comfortable distance will be maintained between the stage and seats: "We shall increase the distance that separates us—a distance that is basic—by our pomp, our manners, our insolence—for we are also actors" (12). This increase of distance is also (in a Brechtian sense)[32] basic to the re-creation of black identity, Imaginary and Symbolic, throughout the play. The pomp, manners, and insolence of blacks playing whites and of blacks playing blacks draws out the strands of Symbolic order from Imaginary representation, creating a potential for re-presentation beyond the masquerade.

And yet the basic distance, or Lacanian gap, between this Imaginary/Symbolic representation and the Real social world beyond the theater's masquerade (and within it, in its Real audience) remains present in the play. The gap is, in fact, increasingly revealed, deferring the climax and success of black revolution into the realm of the dead. In the play's face-off between black and white matriarchs, for example, Felicity (the black queen) calls forth the "beauty" and tragic perpetuity of black, criminal violence.[33]

> FELICITY *(with her hands on her hips; exploding)*: . . . Negroes, come back me up! And don't let the crime be glossed over. *(to the Queen)*: No one could possibly deny it, it's sprouting, sprouting, my beauty, it's growing, bright and green, it's bursting into bloom, into perfume, and that lovely tree, that crime of mine, is all Africa! . . .

THE [White Masked] QUEEN: And if I'm dead, why do you go on and on killing me, murdering me over and over in my color? . . .
FELICITY: I shall have the corpse of your corpse's ghost.

(102–3)

The violence and criminal transgression essential to Genet's writing bothers critics, such as Harry E. Stewart, who details "those real criminals and their crimes which are the object of Genet's . . . real, horrifying adoration" ("Genet's Favorite Murderers" 635). Stewart connects the actual "Lilac Murder," the rape and dismemberment of a four-year-old girl by one Louis Menesclou, who is mentioned by name in the dedication of Genet's novel, *Querelle,* to the allusions of Genet's first play, *Deathwatch.* Also, according to Stewart: "Genet's fascination with Gilles de Rais . . . reveals additional aspects of his attraction to vicious psychopaths—in particular his deeprooted desire to 'become' them" (637). Stewart lists several other "vicious psychopaths" attractive to Genet and "misused" (i.e., reinvented) in his literary adoration of them as characters in his novels and plays. I appreciate the evidence of Stewart's research but take a different view: Genet's attraction to "real" criminals reveals not only a deep-rooted desire to become (or play) them, but also a genuine violence in such desire, which is not his alone.

Several of Lacan's early psychoanalytic writings also concerned the subject of criminal violence, according to Carolyn Dean ("Law" 43, 51, 53).[34] One of the crimes Lacan analyzed was the celebrated Papin case of 1931 (which also inspired Genet's play, *The Maids*): the sudden, brutal murder of their mistress and her daughter by two maids, Christine and Lea von Papin, who then displayed an inexplicable tranquillity concerning their gruesome deed. In 1933 Lacan gave an explanation for the maids' strange reaction to their own crime through the Freudian concept of self-punishment, "necessitated by the irrepressible guilt feelings attached to their latent homosexuality" (Dean, "Law" 51).[35] Lacan also extended Freud's concept of self-punishment (characterized by a conflict between id and superego) into a description of the crime itself as a "cure" in the von Papin case and others.

Madness seeks an impossible reconciliation between the real and the ideal. It is this attempted reconciliation that constitutes the motive behind "unmotivated" or "inexplicable" crime, one that liberates the criminal from his madness at the same time as it perpetuates the discrepancy between who he is and who he wants to be that is the origin of his folie in the first place. For the crime, in fact, marks what Lacan calls . . . the limits of signification: it is the *passage à l'acte* by which the criminal moves from pathology to "cure"—from delirium . . . to the relief effected by the self-punishment the crime permits. The crime represents as well a movement from the symbolic to the unrepresentable [the Real] because it designates the limits of the symbolic. (Dean, "Law" 54–55)

Genet, the criminal, moved from onanistic prison writing to the temporary "cure" of his novelistic and theatrical legitimacy, to the self-punishment of his subjective split through the orders of theater. But he never lost his pathological sense of violence. In fact, his writings illustrate how essential violence is to the creative act of those novels and plays that approach the void between real and ideal, which touch the razor edge of the Symbolic at the limit of signification and the unrepresentable Real. Such writing demonstrates the intrinsic gaps in being between Imaginary, Symbolic, and Real: the lack and want-to-be (Lacan's *manque-à-être*) of being human. Violent, psychopathic criminals—and violent, criminal writers like Genet—show us our human edges.

Particularly in Genet's plays, theater audiences watch and contribute their own voyeuristic desires to those of the actors, director, and other theater artists: to see, hear, and touch the limit edges of being human. Though touching goes beyond voyeurism and is usually forbidden to the audience, the desire to experience with senses more intimate than sight and hearing, and to experience more intimate sights and sounds, is always a part of the theater's Real-ity: the ever-present gap between stage and seats (even in environmental staging). The gap is accentuated in Genet's plays between stage and seats, between spectators and actors (and their characters), as Archibald tells the audience in *The Blacks*. But it is also mirrored onstage in accentuated gaps between characters watching and performing for each other, often involving the erotic titillation and teasing (out) of the Other's voyeurism.

According to Lacan, "man's desire is the desire of the Other"—even in defiance of the Other (*Four* 38).[36] Genet's murderous martyrs demonstrate not only a desire *for* the Other, but also—in their subversive defiance—the desire *of* the Other's Symbolic order and power. The Other wants their rebellion. Their violence and criminal "madness" liberates them yet also perpetuates their roles as revolutionary subjects of the Other: lacking, wanting, finding, and losing Being *(manque-à-être)*. But the Other is also represented in the seats of the theater. The Other that must be attacked, shocked, seduced, idolized, and loved. The mirror of the gaze between stage and seats, along with the many mirrors onstage in the revolutionary rituals of Genet's plays, both reflect and are seen through, redoubling images and symbols of the Real in violent juxtaposition.[37]

Laughter after Life's Void

The desire for and demands of violent criminal beauty continue from the rebels of *The Balcony* and *The Blacks* to the Arabs of *The Screens*. But the gaps between Symbolic, Imaginary, and Real gape even wider, as the rebellion (the Algerian War) moves onstage. In the first scene, an old Arab woman borrows her European Other's symbol of erotic beauty and feminine power, high-heeled shoes, and dances "beautiful and proud" before her son; yet, as they both "burst out laughing," the valise full of imaginary wedding presents "falls to the ground and opens . . . empty" (14–16). Like Felicity in *The Blacks,* this old Arab woman ("The Mother" is her title) comes to personify the perverse beauty of revolution: "I'll compel you to steal cutlets and chickens in your dreams every night. I'll recite a hundred and twenty-seven insults a hundred and twenty-seven times, and each insult will be so beautiful, ladies, that it'll make you gleam" (44).

Yet the ultimate force she eventually embodies is the cynical, reckless, omnirebellious power of laughter,[38] as she tells the audience: "I'm Laughter—not just any laughter, but the kind that appears when all goes wrong" (112). When her son, Said, a traitor to the Arab cause, ends up as the martyred antihero of the play, she tells him to escape from both sides—and from his own legend in the making.

> THE MOTHER: . . . Make a getaway. Don't let yourself be conned by either the old [Arab] girl or the soldiers. Don't serve either of them, don't serve any purpose whatever. I think they're going to make up a song about you. The words have been written. People are humming it. It's in the air. *(She screams.)* Said, squelch the inspiration, shit on them!
>
> (199)

As *The Screens* plays itself out onstage, the world of the dead grows in relation to the conflicts of the living. Genet represents this unrepresentable Real world of death as Being-in-Laughter. The dead on a higher level (or balcony) of the stage watch and laugh at the absurd struggles on lower levels of living rebels and their enemies, the colonists and soldiers. As representatives from both sides meet in death, they laugh together at the folly and madness of living (169). Sergeant Gadget, for example, who died while shitting, laughs with the Arab women and explains the emptiness of "the uniform, the stripes, the decorations," an emptiness he had seen in his superior officers' (mirror) eyes—which "emptied" while they shitted, too (169–70). Said's mother is there with him, laughing in the world of the dead. Even Kadidja is there: the vehement rebel matriarch who in life (in scene 12) called upon "evil" to "impregnate" her people and called forth the bloody gifts of revolution, which various Arab rebels drew upon the screens (97–101). Now in the world of the dead, she and the mother "writhe on the ground with laughter until they have hiccups" (155).

According to Ragland-Sullivan's view of Lacanian theory, "the Imaginary and the Symbolic place themselves as screens over the Real and prevent it from ever actually 'thinking' itself. In this sense the Real of psychic experience lies beyond the dream" (*Lacan* 192). The Real of Genet's psychic experience (like that of his actors and audiences) lies beyond the hypertheatrical, Imaginary/Symbolic dreams and screens of his plays. And yet the gaps between these Lacanian dimensions are realized onstage in the sharp-edged mirrors of Genet's plays. This theatrical realization, like the limit edge of actual criminal violence, is to some degree a *passage à l'acte,* a "cure" for the pathological split between ideal and real.[39] Genet finds his final play-cure *(sinthome)* in the dream of death as Laughing-Being realized in *The Screens.* There the combined chorus of specters and spectators, laughing together in an outdoor theater, climaxes the playwright's extending, split subjectivity: from solipsistic, onanistic, prison writer to a tentative connection with the Other of theater—and the split subjects in the seats. Then, however, Genet stopped writing for the theater, "cured" by the self-punishment of that crime.

Living/Dead Wings

The outside (offstage) rebellion of *The Balcony* and *The Blacks* moves inside the stage space in *The Screens,* but the stage itself is turned inside out, into an "open-air theater," according to Genet's demand (9). In his notes to director Roger Blin, during rehearsals for that play's premiere in 1966, Genet tolls the death knell for theater's proscenium history—in his own desire to overcome such metaphysics: "I feel it dying together with the society which came to see itself mirrored on-stage." He then describes the "fundamental immorality" of proscenium space, with the audience screening itself from the real performance. For those spectators, "the 'house'—dress circle, orchestra, boxes—was an initial spectacle, which in essence formed a screen—or a prism—which their gaze had to pass through before perceiving the spectacle on-stage" (*Letters* 25). In order to move beyond this screen and return to a communal space, Genet desires a Greek theater for his play, *The Screens:* "in which tiers of seats, carved out of a hill, would be mere earthen benches." He also imagines allowing the spectators to "walk up to the stage if one feels like it, the way one approaches a painting, or steps back away from it." He thus suggests something like postmodern environmental staging: "a certain space . . . reserved directly on-stage for a certain number of walk-ons—silent and motionless—who would be part of the audience," though he would have them wear "costumes designed by the costume designer" (27).

But here Genet betrays the lie of environmental as well as proscenium staging. For he has merely moved the fundamental immorality of the spectators, as spectacle and screen, onto the stage. The stage edge taboo, traditionally dividing performers from audience, is compressed, but not erased. In his published version of *The Screens,* Genet also asks for tiered seats as *theatron,* but not for a reserved spectator space onstage. Yet he maintains the sense of paintings with the onstage screens and other props: "One or more real objects must always be on the stage, in contrast with the objects drawn in *trompe-l'oeil* on each screen" (9). He also demands proscenium-like wings, despite the open-air environment: "The back and sides of the stage are to be formed by high, uneven boards, painted black." This allows for entrances and exits of actors (and white screens) to be made "through spaces between the boards, right and left"—as in theater's historical development from Greek *skene* toward Renaissance proscenium.

In 1969 psychoanalyst André Green examined elements of proscenium space as paralleling the Freudian unconscious. Freud himself called the unconscious the "other scene"; but Green looks to the stage edge and proscenium wings as thresholds within the mind. He compares "the line of separation" at the stage edge, holding the audience in place, to the stillness of the dreamer's body: "the cessation of motility [that] is a precondition for the deployment of the dream" (1–2). He sees the dream spectacle as occurring on a stagelike space. "So much so that, in the dream, when the dreamer's representation becomes overloaded, the dreamer splits it into two and sets up another character to represent, separately, one or more of his characteristics or affects" (2).[40]

Taking a cue from Derrida's essay on the "'enclosure' of representation" in Artaud, Green describes a "double reversal" at the stage edge and proscenium wings, correlative to the lure of the unconscious (3). The first reversal occurs at the stage edge, "the invisible frontier where the spectator's gaze meets a barrier that stops it and sends it back . . . to the onlooker, that is, to himself as source of the gaze." The mirror of the stage edge thus entices the spectators to look beyond the scene onstage—at what cannot be seen in the audience, behind each spectator's own eyes, though reflected back to them by the performers being watched. As I have argued, environmental staging "may try to eliminate this edge; it is only reconstituted elsewhere." For this edge and its reversal of perception (even in the environmental mixing of stage and audience spaces) involves the dynamics of a psychic barrier, repression, which places the Real of stage objects beyond reach, yet "will not allow the perceiver ever to escape them."

In preceding chapters I analyzed the belief/perversion dialectic at the stage edge of Eliot's drama and Nietzsche's dream of a prehistoric theatrical womb. This can also be seen in what Green describes as the "fundamental otherness of the spectacle for the spectator," which, though inevitably distant, "solicits him" toward the edge of the stage (4). Artaud's impossible desire to join seats and stage through ritual communion corresponds, too, to Green's analysis of the spectator's gaze and its stage edge reversal: "the gaze detaches itself to some extent from its object, otherwise the total participation of the spectator with the forces of the spectacle would merge them beneath the eye of a God bringing about from on high the coalescence of auditorium and stage."[41] But with Genet's drama, and particularly *The Screens,* Green's second reversal becomes especially pertinent. "The boundary between auditorium and stage is duplicated by the boundary between the stage as visible space and the invisible space off-stage." This other stage edge, traditionally marked by proscenium wings, is redefined by Genet's high, uneven, black boards—and by white screens brought through those boards into playing areas on various platform levels. As with Genet's other revolutionary plays in more conventional staging, these barriers hide what Green describes as the offstage space(s) "of manipulation, suspicion, plotting."

Because of a third barrier, at the edge of an outside world separate from theater, Green sees offstage space as limited, as "confined within the walls of the great chamber," unlike cinema (4).[42] Yet this tie to the outside world, through the limits of offstage space, stimulates the lure of loss at the stage/offstage edge: "offering itself as one to be transgressed, passed beyond." Here the gaze of the spectator is again reversed, affecting, too, "the unsaid, the unspoken element, of the stage space" (5). The elusive illusion of the heard, as well as the seen, bearing the unheard and unseen, "will be caught in the movement of return into its opposite, joining itself to the first reversal [at the audience edge], which consists of a turning round upon oneself." With this seductive spin of representation and its perceptual limits, round the spectator's eye/ear, Green reveals in conventional, proscenium staging what Artaud wanted to manifest experimentally by putting the spectators at the center of the space with the performance encircling them. However, Green's theoretical demonstration avoids the danger of fetishizing the spectator as central presence, by showing the Lacanian *aphanisis* (fading) of the spectator in the mirror stage of performance, "like the negative hallucination in which the subject looks at himself in the mirror and sees all the elements of the setting around him, but not his own image."

Genet's *The Screens* reveals a further degree of reflective fading in the onstage opposition of living and dead worlds. Borrowing from the traditional onstage/offstage border, Genet shows the parallel threshold between mortal/immortal realms when Kadidja "breaks through the paper of the screen" to join the dead in laughter (143). This also reflects the dead world in the unconscious of each spectator, whose gaze cannot penetrate the seductively unseen and unheard beyond the edges of the stage. For the Medusan laughter of the dead is not only directed at the living world of rebels and enemies; it is also aimed at the spectators, living and dead. The dead onstage laugh at the living, onstage and off. But they also laugh with the dead in the audience, with the lost ones born by each spectator, especially if the audience laughs out loud. "No one must be turned away from or deprived of the spectacle: it must be so beautiful that the dead are made beautiful too, and blush because of it" (Genet, *Letters* 11).

What Witt sees as the "apotheosis of the Mothers" at the end of *The Screens,* in an underworld "ruled by Warda (in her eternal form), Kadidja and the Mother" (184),[43] was, in Genet's own terms, an attempt "to break down whatever separates us from the dead" (11). He makes explicit to Blin the conventional oppositions being evoked and challenged:[44] "If we maintain that life and the stage are opposites, it is because we strongly suspect that the stage is a site closely akin to death, a place where all liberties are possible" (12). In the ultimate laughter of the dead there is freedom from colonial oppression, poverty, revolutionary heroism, and tragedy—even from the horrible beauty of the *sparagmos* painted onto the screens by the Arab rebels under the command of Kadidja. At first when she is dead, she wants to continue the fight and "still help those up above." But soon she learns: "That would mean trying to die less. And one must die more and more" (*Screens* 145). Likewise, another rebel figure "slowly goes through all the screens, ripping them; it grows bigger and bigger as it draws near. Finally, it is behind the last screen, that is, the one nearest the audience, and, tearing this last sheet of paper, appears: it is THE MOTHER" (147).

The World as Phallic Womb

Genet lost his original mother to the world of prostitution (which he also entered), and his foster mother to the world of the dead. His lifelong rebellion, breaking through Imaginary and Symbolic screens to reach the void of the Real, resulted in his temporary cure through those realms of theater. But after the suicide of his funambulist lover, Abdallah Bentaga, in 1964, Genet destroyed the manuscripts of two plays that he had written after *The Screens*—and later attempted suicide himself (White 472, 477, 496). He also became involved with certain terrorist groups: the Black Panthers, Baader-Meinhof, and PLO. This was another way for him to continue as outlaw and rebel, after breaking through the screens of theater. He identified with such groups, despite his skin color, because he was still fundamentally an outcast, even as famous author and existentialist saint. "Perhaps I'm a black with white or pink skin, but I'm black. I don't know my family" ("Hubert Fichte" 75). Genet carefully distinguished the real revolution of his terrorist friends from that of his own former art: "you risk your body with a revolutionary action, but by creating a work of art you may risk your reputation, but you don't endanger your body" (73). However, he continued as outlaw and rebel, in body as well as art, through the symptomatic cure *(sinthome)* of his homosexuality, which he called "the solution to a neurosis" (92).[45]

In the 1970s Luce Irigaray struggled to find a theoretical cure for the systematic neurosis (and *père-version*) of patriarchy's heterosexual demands. She rebelled against the phallocentrism of Lacanian psychoanalysis,[46] and against the entire history of Western philosophy, by returning to the origin of both in Plato's cave. The publication of her challenge to those orders, *Speculum of the Other Woman,* made her an outcast; she was dismissed from the department of psychoanalysis at the University of Paris VIII (Jacqueline Rose 54n). But a comparison of her struggle within Plato's cave to Genet's within proscenium theater shows that her desire for an impossible cure yields, like his, an acute sense of our common social disease.

In her examination of the theatrics of Plato's parable for Western education (from *The Republic,* book VII), Irigaray finds seductive barriers similar (though without reference) to André Green's stage edge and proscenium wings. Plato's spectators, as prisoners, are chained in place, facing away from the source of light inside the cave, seeing only shadows on a wall. Although Green's spectators sit unchained and face the stage, their gaze is barred by the double reversal of stage edge mirror and offstage space.

Irigaray notices that Plato's spectator-prisoners "are forbidden not only to look at it [the stage action behind them] but to move toward it" (249). She also reviews what the omniscient Plato (Socrates) sees behind them: a "wallcurtain or restraining wall," reminiscent of both stage edge and wings, "the backcloth of representation." Irigaray finds in this *teikhion* the "reenactment, reprise, representation of a *hymen that has elsewhere been stealthily taken away.*" But this screen "is never, ever, crossed, opened, penetrated, pierced, or torn." While the audience is chained facing away from it, the actors move freely behind the wall-curtain, raising objects over it, thus casting shadows on the cave wall opposite, which the spectators can see. Irigaray highlights the phallic as well as hymenal dynamics here. The actors' bodies remain behind the screen. "But by thrusting their bodies *high enough,* the men will succeed in getting across the screen some symbol, reproduction, fetish of their 'bodies' or those of other living animals" (250). Through this Platonic shadow puppetry, within a womblike cave, Irigaray reveals not only the tricks of patriarchal representation, but also the cruelty of its phallic hierarchy. The theatrical fetishism of Plato's cave, like Lacanian psychoanalysis, tames the (m)Other's power by phallicizing the womb, artfully distancing the mysterious source of life.

Yet, Irigaray finds in this lost originary space—like the Kleinian violence which Artaud desired onstage—a revolutionary potential for truth to be dis-played. In her subsequent, more optimistic book, *This Sex Which Is Not One* (1977), Irigaray reveals an ecstatic force in the multiple organs and fluids of the female body, somewhat like the Being-in-Laughter of Genet's underworld mothers. "Isn't laughter the first form of liberation from secular oppression? *Isn't the phallic tantamount to the seriousness of meaning?* Perhaps woman, and the sexual relation, transcend it 'first' in laughter?" (163). In a Lacanian view, Irigaray's transcendence is also tantamount to psychosis (as was Artaud's): a foreclosure of the Name and Law of the Father. Be that as it may, I now return to her fight within Plato's cave, to show how hard-won her feminist, hom(m)osexual[47] liberation is, like that of Genet.

In Genet's stage directions for *The Screens,* the dead characters in the underworld look down in order to watch live characters on platforms above them (145). To them the living are ludicrous shades, as opposed to their own true nothingness, like the shadows removed from ideal reality in the theater of Plato's cave. Irigaray moves about that cave and puppet theater, unlike the spectators chained to face the wall. She becomes a fluid, metaphysical spectator, ghosting Plato's tale, yet detecting a further, repressed presence. Irigaray's reverse or para-Platonism (à la Deleuze and

Foucault) shows that "the cave is made in the image of the world," but that it is also "always already an attempt to re-present another cave, the *hystera*, the mold which silently dictates all replicas, all possible forms, all possible relation of forms and between forms, of any replica" (*Speculum* 246).

Thus, Irigaray tries to raise the womb, lost within Western history, philosophy, and psychoanalysis, as originary signifier—against the phallus. She carefully analyzes the traces of an erased vagina in Plato's description of the passageway out of the cave. But whereas Plato shows the true light of the sun as being outside the cave, Irigaray reveals both the sun outside and the fire within the cave (causing the shadow play) as false images of the true (m)Other deeper in the earth—volcanic source of light and life within the maternal body repressed by patriarchy.

Unlike the spectator-prisoners, chained in "a phallic line, a phallic time, backs turned on origin" (245), Irigaray moves about the cave-womb to excavate it as tomb of lost maternal power. She "transgresses these established borders" in Plato's inverted proscenium, bringing body to the "ghosts" she finds there (282)—like Genet's incarnation of the Real dead onstage, through Imaginary and Symbolic screens of revolution. Breaking through the mirrors of Plato's dismembering "speculum" (254–55), Irigaray, as ghostly body, explores the "*silent virginity* of the back of the cave" (263). She crosses the reversals of stage edge and proscenium wings—the divisions and multiplications of illusion in Plato's theater. She perceives that the wall-curtain is merely a

> *screen that sets men gazing in different directions*—some gazing "off," into the wings / some gazing in fascination—preventing them from glimpsing each other, from mingling, taking each other's measure, except by means of the *interposed object-fetish* that captures and hides the light. (265–66)

Irigaray then follows Plato's escape from the cave into the sunlight's ostensible "Truth." Yet, in the surface shadows of that outdoor theater, she again finds the trace of loss—at the stage edge of mother earth: "the nostalgia we feel for something even more true" (269).

So, Irigaray returns to the cave, mirroring and perverting Plato's escape from it with her Nietzschean lantern: "it is necessary *to forget in order to remember what is truer*" (273). She unforgets the Platonic passage away from a lost maternal body and instead leads us back to it—to what is truer in the underworld of our living bodies and unconscious memories. Yet she also shines her lantern on the Platonic warnings not to return this way.

For the patriarchal passage is "a one-way trip" toward the sun and Father. "It will take the life of anyone who dares to move through in reverse." Like Genet, Irigaray takes the risk and breaks through the screens. She discloses the falseness of the cave's re-presented, inside-out womb (284), and of the entire, patriarchal world outside, which is merely a representational caul of sky and frozen water, mirroring the lie of the cave (285, 289). Irigaray would show us a true passageway within the tomb of the mother—through the choral pit and castrative wings of an Other theater.

"The mother is in this *death therefore,* crossed and re-marked by the impression that is still rooted in the senses" (318). Yet the excess *jouissance* of her corpse gives life and hope to Irigaray's revolutionary desires: "The Vengeance of Children Freed from Their Chains" (364). Although according to Plato's parable any rebellious philosopher who might rouse the chained spectators from their shadow trance would certainly be put to death, Irigaray dares to awaken us to the world's theatrical deception. For we, the imprisoned spectators and rebellious philosopher—like the laughing martyrs of *The Screens*—are "already dead: the poor present of an effigied copula." And yet, the Father's law that catches, punishes, and kills such already dead rebels makes "blood flow from their wounds, blood that still recalls a very ancient relationship with the mother" (Irigaray 364). Thus, the omnipresent violence of Imaginary/Symbolic representation begins to return us to the lost Real, recalling her whom we mourn and cannot reach.

In my final chapter, I shall move to the opposite end of modern theater's spectrum of loss as power. With Brecht, unlike Artaud and Genet, the ritual return to the lost stage mother is emphatically rejected. But like them, Brecht would rescue theater's effective truth. Thus, his theories and plays mirror the mourning of Artaud's and Genet's—yet create a different revolutionary perversion, through the homeopathic dis-ease of alienation rather than the beauty of cruelty.

Chapter 6

Brecht's Repression of the Kristevan *Chora*

If loss is at the heart of theater, then the difference between specific modern artists (or theorists) might be measured in the distance that each attains from the ritual abyss at the stage's edge. Nietzsche desired a choral communion with tragedy's prehistoric womb yet described separate orders of audience, chorus, and actor. Eliot tried to revive a choral poetics by returning to the transcendent sacrifice of medieval mystery and morality plays, or by bringing ancient Greek passions and plots into modern British families and drawing rooms. He thus moved from a small, parochial, but participative audience to a larger, popular, observing one, more distanced from the rite. Artaud suffered the loss of ritual more intensely. His dream of cruel, cathartic communion turned inward, after public theatrical failures, to meet the Other audience of ghosts within his own body. Hence, he increased his distance from the institutional stage edge but approached and expressed an internal abyss—turning that edge (and theater's history) inside out for future generations of revolutionaries. Genet, as rebel, martyr, and outlaw, revealed the perversities within the social order and its conventional beliefs, through the mirrors of theater's ritual edge, at a violently beautiful and tragically comic distance.

But the modern dramatist and theorist who most explicitly made distance into a virtue, by converting the symptomatic loss of ritual into the cure of alienated actors and spectators, was Bertolt Brecht. He turned theater inside out in the opposite direction from Artaud, through a belief in its revolutionary effect beyond Genet's mirrors, and a perversion of its choral womb that transcended Nietzsche's dreams and Eliot's sacrifices. Brecht's theater has profoundly altered the role of the spectator, as well as the performer's role in society and history, yet at a certain affective cost—which I mean to excavate in this final chapter.

Brecht's theater has also had a pervasive influence upon postmodern theory, not only for Marxists like Jameson and Eagleton, but also for radical feminists. Sue-Ellen Case celebrates the homosexual sadomasochism of Brecht's early plays, in which she sees the role of the mother as pointing to "the new discourse of desire and corporeality, called for by such feminist writers as Cixous, Irigaray, and Kristeva" (69). Elin Diamond proposes a "gestic feminist criticism" that would be both "a recovery of the radical potential of the Brechtian critique and a discovery, for feminist theory, of the specificity of theater" (82). But Brecht's own radical shift, from the Dionysian perversions of his early drama to the Apollonian unmasking in his later theory of *Gestus,* is too quickly dismissed by Case and overidealized by Diamond.[1] Neither feminist considers the contradictory desires behind Brecht's virile, modernist, demystifying confidence nor analyzes the repression of bodily affect that his protestant faith in alienation demands.

However, John Fuegi's recent biography, *Brecht and Company,* does challenge the status of Brecht's plays and theories in relation to his repression of feminine labor. With a feminist's sensitivity to the lives of actual women who worked (and slept) with Brecht, Fuegi accuses the great playwright of abusing his collaborators by presenting much of their work as solely his own—and thus denying them royalty returns as well. According to Fuegi, "huge sections of some of the most famous 'Brecht' plays and large sections of new dramaturgical theories are clearly written by [Elisabeth] Hauptmann," including the *Lehrstücke* (learning plays) and *Saint Joan of the Stockyards* (145). Fuegi also states that *The Mother* "borrows heavily from the stage devices Hauptmann had introduced to the [Brecht] collective from her work with Japanese medieval drama" (261). Even some of Brecht's later plays, such as *Mother Courage* and *Good Person of Szechwan,* were partly created by another lover, Margarete Steffin (380, 388), as well as by Hauptmann (431)—says Fuegi. He thus characterizes the works written solely by Brecht as having "a central and often violent, misogynist male figure," while those by the collective have stronger female characters, "at a level well above that of Brecht working alone" (144).

These allegations have drawn many countercharges against Fuegi's scholarship (and perversity), even from colleagues in the International Brecht Society, which he founded.[2] In the midst of such a battle over the name of "Brecht" and the true authorship of his works, my own view lies close to that of Danish journalist Jan Andersen: "in a collaborative process it is almost impossible to identify who got which idea and who wrote which passage in a play, a song, or a poem" (17). Yet I admit that my use of the name "Brecht" (in analyzing the works Fuegi lists) should be taken as referring also to his coworkers in the Brecht Collective, particularly to the chora of women playwrights repressed by the name and personality of Bertolt

Brecht. As Gay Gibson Cima points out: "Part of the reason why the members of the Collective stayed with Brecht was that they were able to contribute in a substantive way to the joint projects despite his cruelty" (101). Fuegi's shocking disclosures, however debatable, provide biographical evidence for my analysis of repression and expression in Brecht's work—even though this Author's name may also mask the edges of maternal loss in other (mostly female) contributors.

In order to examine the shift from Brecht's early Dionysian plays to his later collaborative and more Apollonian works, I shall use Julia Kristeva's theory of the abject, semiotic chora (as womb of language, art, and personal/social psyche). Brecht's repression of the chora in his plays and theories involves both personal and communal loss: from the refusal to mourn the death of his mother to the distancing of abject emotions in his work and his masking of female coauthors.[3] Yet such choral repression also involves the loss—and further distancing—of a ritual womb at the modern stage edge (as explored in the first half of this book). So, I turn next to the views of Brecht's friend and Marxist colleague Walter Benjamin, on the ritual origins of theater, suppressed by Brecht's epic stage.

The Epic/Ritual Edge

In 1939, despite his enthusiasm for Brecht's work, Benjamin described a ritual stickiness at the edge of the epic stage. On the one hand, he praised Brecht's "filling in of the orchestra pit," so that the stage "no longer rises from an unfathomable depth; it has become a dais." Yet Benjamin also remarked that the orchestra pit is "of all the elements of theater the one that bears the most indelible traces of its ritual origin" (*Illuminations* 154). While Brecht had admitted that theater "may be said to be derived from ritual" *(aus dem Kultischen),* he insisted, apparently without Benjamin's sacral nostalgia, that it only "becomes theater once the two have separated" (*Theatre* 181; GW 16:664). For Brecht, theater must continue to separate itself from ritual in order to realize the dream of his distancing effect.

What theater "brought over from the mysteries," according to Brecht, "was not its former ritual function, but purely and simply the pleasure which accompanied this." He points as evidence to Aristotle's theory of catharsis: "a purification which is performed not only in a pleasurable way, but precisely for the purpose of pleasure" (*Theatre* 181).[4] In my view, however, Brechtian purification bears the ritual purposes of both pleasure and instruction, as it censors and redirects tragic affect. His moral apparatus would manipulate empathic identification away from the metaphysical illusions of character, toward the better memory and historical consciousness of the self-alienated actor. But there remains a self-deceptive trap in this optimistic power of purposeful loss. As Herbert Blau has indicated, a "conflict between pleasure and instruction" persists at the heart of Brechtian entertainment, which relies on its own "illusion of alienation" (*Audience* 264).[5]

Such conflict and illusion continues to play a strong role in current theater and performance theory. For the critical pleasure that Benjamin found as spectator, "attempt[ing] to sit down" on the epic stage (*Illuminations* 154), has become in recent decades a characteristic perversity of "environmental theater"—though with a different type of stage and a more prominent hieratic resonance, through Grotowski's roots in both Brecht and Artaud (Wiles 106–7). Yet, as Richard Schechner explains, Brecht's alienation effect also "worked to keep alive the tensions" between ritual efficacy and theatrical entertainment, between spectator participation and separation (*Performance* 120–42). Brecht, however, insisted, unlike Schechner, that theatrical efficacy arises not in ritual participation, but through a critical separation of spectators from the stage (and from each other), which effects a future participation in political action outside the theater's walls.

In effect, Brecht's social dream turns theater inside out (stretching it outward, rather than inward like Artaud's mystical dream). Epic theater not only converts attitudes and structures of society into hieroglyphic gests,[6] making a manifest stage language out of the political unconscious. It would also move spectators to act upon the stage of the world, by separating them from the narcissism of symbiotic illusion. The actor leads them in this, through a sharpened consciousness of mirror stage alienation: the split subject playing character, caught in plot, and yet showing the potential for change.[7] Brecht himself seems to have had a somewhat Lacanian conception of subjectivity in a 1926 interview,[8] even before his turn toward Marx (though, as Willett notes, the interviewer may have altered these words): "The continuity of ego is a myth. A man is an atom that perpetually breaks up and forms anew. We have to show things as they are" (*Theatre* 15–16).

Brecht distilled his proto-postmodern, ego-deconstructing A-effect, at least in part, from ritual Chinese acting. He wanted to extract from that traditional, oriental wine a contemporary, Marxist brandy—without sacred magic and communal metaphysics. For he saw the ritual *Verfremdungseffekt* of the Chinese actor as already transcending Stanislavsky's dependence upon subconscious memory (*Theatre* 93–94). And yet, there is a return of the repressed in Brecht's borrowing from the East over the body of Stanislavsky. Brecht believes he can alienate the oriental A-effect, bringing it out of its spirit world, in order to then demystify his own. He thus reritualizes its ritual, for the sake of occidental enlightenment.[9] Rejecting the collective memory of the Other's religious tradition of theater, Brecht would still transform it toward his own collective purposes, by affecting the subconscious future of his audience.

This helps to explain Benjamin's paradoxical description of the Brechtian distancing effect, as bringing the audience closer to, or even onto, the stage. Indeed, Brecht's (or the Brecht Collective's) *Lehrstücke* were designed to be performed without an audience (*Theatre* 33; Wiles 73), all spectators being also performers. In *The Measures Taken* they form a "Control Chorus" that oversees the ritual reenactment of a young comrade's rebellion against the Party and his death at its hands. They then measure the reasons for making this martyr, as an expedient sacrifice to the Party's "thousand eyes" and immortal Revolution (29).[10]

For Benjamin, who saw the coming of the Revolution as messianic, Brecht's epic drama, as well as his didactic *Lehrstücke*, decreased the theater's abysmal, orchestral distance, "which separates the players from the audience as it does the dead from the living" (*Illuminations* 154). This parallels the desire expressed by Karl Marx in his *Eighteenth Brumaire* to, as Terry Eagleton puts it, "summon the dead to the aid of the present, drawing from them something of their dangerous power" (*Ideology* 213). But Benjamin's statement refers implicitly to his own pre-Brechtian study of the baroque mourning-play. There he had carefully distinguished ancient tragedy from baroque *Trauerspiel* through the latter's allegorical melancholia—deriving from medieval mystery plays and Platonic metaphysics, rather than from Greek drama (*Origin* 113). With Brecht's epic theater, Benjamin now discovers another paradigm shift. The Brechtian stage as dais is a revolutionary departure, not only from the fatalistic empathy of tragedy and its neo-Aristotelian imitations, but also from the paralyzing melancholia of the mourning-play, which Benjamin had earlier seen as a persistent modern form. His description of this new stage also suggests a revolutionary relationship to the dead—even though Brecht represses (and sublimates) that dangerous power as he takes techniques from Chinese acting and plots from the ghost drama of Japanese No.

Brecht's epic drama focuses upon historical victimization, rather than tragic fate. It takes the allegorical ruin that fascinated Benjamin in baroque drama and makes a modern questioning fetish, cut out of social attitudes and gestures, to stimulate revolutionary passions.[11] But it thus finds its roots in the perennial theatrical perversity of empathic identification,[12] invoking a ritual stage that it then abjects as a melancholic base for its new moral vision of theater's purpose. Brecht himself suggests this (without diagnosing the melancholia) when he defends his theater against charges of "moralizing too much." He cites Nietzsche's criticism of the moralizing institution desired by the neoclassical Schiller and insists that his epic theater ought to "observe" the victims of history, thus transforming mournfulness into analysis and action. Such observation cuts through the melancholia of tragic loss, "and then the thick end of the wedge follow[s]: the story's moral" (*Theatre* 75).

But this observing wedge also serves the dead (and future) victims of history in a new ritual way. At certain points in Brecht's plays, despite the nihilistic perversity of Baal or alienating antiheroines like Mother Courage, one finds great sacrificial respect for the sufferings and losses of the dead (as I shall indicate with *Drums in the Night,* the *Lehrstücke,* and *The Mother*). This sustains the melancholic sense of historical debt, while emphasizing current social injustice—within ostensibly moral systems. "We are not in fact speaking in the name of morality but in that of the victims. These truly are two distinct matters, for the victims are often told that they ought to be contented with their lot, for moral reasons" (75). And yet, Brecht creates his theater of radical, ethical discontent by drawing (not completely unlike Artaud and Eliot) from older, overtly metaphysical forms—both East and West.

> Stylistically speaking, there is nothing all that new about the epic theater. Its expository character and its emphasis on virtuosity bring it close to the old Asiatic theater. Didactic tendencies are to be found in the medieval mystery plays and the classical Spanish theater, and also in the theater of the Jesuits. (75–76)

Here Brecht's rhetoric shows a Benjaminian influence of messianic desire and historical faith, despite his own atheistic confidence and iconoclastic purposes. This ritual/epic double bind also affects Brecht's conception of his audience—theoretically, historically, and sexually.

Beyond Mourning and Melancholia

Unlike the communal desires of Eliot and Artaud, in their response to the modern loss of theater, Brecht insisted upon a divided audience for his epic drama. He directly opposed plays "of the aristotelian type . . . [through which a] collective entity is created in the auditorium for *the duration of the entertainment,* on the basis of the 'common humanity' shared by all spectators alike" (*Theatre* 60).[13] He thus suggests another type of tentative collectivity produced by his plays and A-effect, one more conscientious of historical and social differences, which would not "flatten out class conflicts" (60). Even so, Brecht's more overtly ideological *Lehrstücke* would seem to force the audience into just two collective divisions—with and against each didactic point in the play.

This manipulative tendency continues into Brecht's later drama and sometimes shows a gendered spin (especially given Fuegi's evidence of Brecht's manipulation of female coauthors in his collective). A note about the original (1932) production of *The Mother* describes that play as having owed much to agitprop theater, except that it "was meant to go further and teach the tactics of the class war" (61–62). Exploiting the didactic techniques of older, metaphysical forms of theater, Brecht takes the feminine side of the proletariat and invests her semiotic *ressentiment* with his Marxist libido. For, according to another note attributed to Brecht, *The Mother* "was addressed mainly to women. About 15,000 Berlin working-class women saw the play, which was a demonstration of methods of illegal revolutionary struggle" (62).

In his first (pre-1939) version of "What Is Epic Theatre?" Benjamin echoes Brecht's desire for a divided audience. Benjamin describes the undermining of the "false and deceptive totality called 'audience' . . . [by] the formation of separate parties within it . . . corresponding to conditions as they really are" (*Understanding* 10). But rather than speculate as to why this concept was cut from the essay, let us turn to contemporaneous journal entries by Benjamin. For these help to historicize the paradox of a theatrically divisive, yet politically uniting, alienation effect—in relation to Brecht's own feelings of personal loss and national danger. In his entry of August 3, 1938, Benjamin recounts two conversations in which Brecht had described his "manic" battle for the German audience against Hitler's cruel actors and vast historical script.

> They're planning for thirty thousand years ahead. Colossal things. Colossal crimes. They stop at nothing. They're out to destroy everything. . . . That is why we too must think of everything. They cripple the baby in the mother's womb.

There is a sense of premonitory mourning here for the future victims of Nazism, which surfaces in Brecht as an affect that Benjamin calls "a vehemence he rarely shows" (120).

This mourning becomes expressed in a seductive, Hitler-like rage, through which Brecht taps a messianic force. "While he was speaking like this I felt a power being exercised over me which was equal in strength to the power of fascism—I mean a power that sprang from the depths of history no less deep than the power of the fascists." Benjamin thus depicts Brecht as bearing a totemic energy, comparable to Hitler's, in their epic fight over the "womb" of German identity. But Brecht's words (as reported by Benjamin) also suggest personal loss and mourning. "It isn't just that they've taken my house, my fish-pound and my car from me; they've also robbed me of my stage and my audience" (120). After the war (in 1949), with part of his homeland and national audience returned to him, Brecht still insisted that his epic theater ought to arouse "righteous anger" and a "passionate" critical attitude (*Theatre* 227). This was in response to an interviewer relating the "avalanche of perverted emotions" in the Hitler period to the emotional effect of Schiller's historical drama. Brecht's A-effect, while wary of theatrical indulgence in emotion (onstage or in Nazi rallies), would thus whet the affect of mourning to expose the wrong reasons for further sacrifice.

In a section of *Black Sun: Depression and Melancholia* entitled "The Western Fate of Conveyance," Kristeva describes a "wager of conveyability . . . [that] is an attempt to fight depression (due to an intrusive preobject that I cannot give up) by means of a torrent of signs, which aims precisely at capturing the object of joy, fear, or pain" (67). Brecht also wagers an affective currency, although by a "literarization" of theater that distances emotion. His use of "screens on which the titles of each scene are projected" (*Theatre* 43), as well as placards, songs, and gestic acting, shows the audience a torrent of signs that aims to capture lost objects, but at a certain critical distance.[14]

Brecht fought the manic-depressiveness of Germany's social psyche with a materialist metaphysics. But he lost to the social theater of Hitlerism (and later submitted to the theater of Stalinism as well). Race war and heroic empathy beat Brecht's class war and A-effect. His home and audience were lost not only to the individual perversity of the Führer, but even more to the street scene of national socialist fetishism, as Brecht himself indicated in his early years of exile. "Not even Hitler's personal passions; that's not what has brought Germany to her present condition, worse luck. Far more than he himself imagines he is the tool and not the guiding hand" (*Theatre* 66–67). While Brecht wished to make his self-alienated actor, qua street demonstrator, into the audience's guiding gestic hand, this tool would not be enough to lift the socioeconomic depression of Germany after World War I, as she mourned the futility of so many dead. "You have become the carrion pit of Europe" (Brecht, *Poems* 57). Despite Brecht's alienation effects, this pit would grow to horribly monumental proportions, through the Nazi's response to national loss—repeating and multiplying the sacrifice, not only of their own, but also of the Jewish Other.

Freud recognized in both mourning and melancholia a "reaction to the loss of a loved object" (*SE* 14: 245). But whereas mourning is "for the most part occasioned only by a real loss of the object, by its death" (256), melancholia "is a loss of a more ideal kind . . . which is withdrawn from consciousness" (245). There is an identification of the melancholic ego with this unconscious, lost object, as though "the shadow of the object fell upon the ego" (249). One can see in Brecht's theater, through Benjamin's study of the German baroque, an attempt to distance both actor and spectator from the deadly shadow of character, and particularly from the temptation to tragic identification and heroic idealism—whether in theater or in government. Thus the epic stage would, in Freud's terms, turn the unconscious object loss of melancholia into the conscious work of mourning, in which "the world . . . has become poor and empty . . . [rather than] the ego itself" (*SE* 14:246). Brecht would also go beyond mourning, however, by not only focusing on the external world's poverty and emptiness, but also on conscious efforts to change it. This must occur not by an illusory filling in of the hollow ego, but by realizing, in a sharpened split of actor/character, spectator/activist, and stage/auditorium, that the irrevocable fact of human alienation nevertheless has alterable social consequences.

Kristeva describes a positive sense of melancholy, which is "affirmed in religious doubt." While she distinguishes "the clinical stupor of melancholia"[15] from the productive melancholy of art, she finds that "loss, mourning, absence set the imaginary act in motion and permanently fuel it as much as they menace and undermine it." She then points to "the fetish of the work of art [as being] erected in disavowal of this mobilizing affliction" ("Melancholic" 105). Brecht disavows the immobilizing affliction of Aristotelian pity and fear; yet his epic theater is both menaced and fueled by a certain, sympathetic melancholy, affirmed in his own religious skepticism. He reerects as well as analyzes social fetishes in his artworks, not only of commodities, but also of heroic saints and Führer-figures. Brecht's reconfigured fetishes, even when taking female form (and even more so if coauthored by women), abject yet mobilize the ritual womb of the stage's edge—its feminine, semiotic chora.[16]

Kristeva adapts Plato's myth of the cosmic space of the chora, as receptacle of becoming (*Timaeus* 67–70), to designate a preverbal semiotic space that persists within language: "the place where the subject is both generated and negated." Following Plato, she associates this chora with the maternal body, from which the infant must separate in order to enter the symbolic (*Revolution* 25–28). Like Brecht's separation of theater from primal ritual pleasures through his alienation effect, "the subject," according to Kristeva, "finding his identity in the symbolic, *separates* from his fusion with the mother, *confines* his jouissance to the genital, and transfers semiotic motility onto the symbolic order" (47). However, despite a similar transfer in Brecht's filling of the orchestra pit, Nietzsche's Dionysian chorus haunts the epic dais—as its displaced chora. While Kristeva finds a revolutionary potential in the chora, through the abject horrors of poetic language, Brecht disavows the sympathetic abjection of the Aristotelian spectator. Yet he also cuts and holds out fetishes to the audience as social keys, through the actor's uncanny *Gestus*.[17]

As Shuli Barzilai has remarked, Kristeva's critique of the Lacanian symbolic focuses on the borderline patient, whose exile from the symbolic means a diaspora at its edges. "This absence of identity—a psychic wandering or loss of place—is congruent with a discourse produced on the borders of language: 'what is *abject* draws me toward the place where meaning collapses'" (Barzilai 295; Kristeva, *Powers* 2). Brecht's own abject diaspora from a lost homeland, captured by the theater of Hitlerism, contributes to his A-effect coining, produced at the borders of stage language. His alienation effect *(Verfremdungseffekt)* also involves the affect of alienation *(Entfremdung)*. Thus, a remnant of the ritual chorus, with its loss of individual identity, persists in the gestic fetishes at Brecht's stage edge. The multiple meanings and identities of epic theater—with actor playing actor as well as character, and audience observing both through its own redoubling identifications—nevertheless hinge upon a place, the ritual abyss, where meaning collapses. In short, something in Brecht's drama, despite his theory of alienation, points beyond Freud (through Benjamin) to Kristeva and an abject womb.

The Chora in Brecht's Early Drama

Kristeva has declared that modern theater "does not exist—it does not take (a) place—and consequently, its semiology is a mirage."[18] Not only are God and the Author dead, so is theater. "As its only remaining locus of interplay is the space of language, modern theatre no longer exists outside the text." Kristeva relates this death of theater to the loss of sacred community: "a failure of de-monstration . . . a failure to constitute a communal discourse of play (interplay)." She points beyond Nietzsche to Mallarmé, who first asserted "the absence of a sacred locus that is always the locus, the place, of theater." How then could Brecht's theater bear a chora, as I have been arguing? Who is his audience, the Other of his theatrical desire, if "the post-Mallarméan survivors of the modern theatre are fantasies deprived of a public" ("Modern" 131)?[19]

Kristeva admits that a few instances of "interplay" do continue to take place, but they undergo either of two fates: Artaudian (without language) or Beckettian (a discourse of stereotypes "edged with debility") (131). She refers in the latter category to Brecht's theory (without naming it as such) of "putting the text in quotes" (132). With these two types of (post)modern theater, Kristeva finds that "the stage/audience separation . . . is merely a superficial problem." And yet, she concludes her essay (from the 1970s) with a hopeful twist that relies upon the stage/audience separation of "Brechtian distance," as it appears in American theatrical and cinematic experimentation. "Thus, it is within this overwhelmingly protestant society that the necessarily instinctual and maternal 'repressed' makes it return"—analogous, she says, to the Jesuit baroque (134). This reference to Brechtian theory in her hopes for a return of the maternal chora ("to develop a technical arsenal of 'alienation' . . . while waiting for the coming of a 'place': the remaking of language") parallels, in the opposite direction, Benjamin's praise for the epic stage edge, as a repression of ritual returns. Brecht's own protestant turn toward the pseudoscience of Marxism, while borrowing Jesuit (and oriental) didacticism, also rests upon a repression/return of the maternal—shaped by a specific religious background.

Brecht's mother (Sophie) was Protestant, his father (Berthold) a Catholic. The young Brecht attended a Protestant kindergarten and elementary school,[20] though his home city of Augsburg was 75 percent Catholic, and his father worked in "the Haindl paper factory, a Catholic family business" (Hayman 5). Brecht had to spend extra time at kindergarten because of his mother's illness. As a child he was also sick, suffering from cardiac trouble—perhaps like Artaud (though to a lesser degree) mirroring his mother's pain. Twice, before the age of nine, Brecht went to "a sanitorium in the Black Forest" (Hayman 6–7). Brecht's mother doted on him, yet she recoiled from his boyish sexuality, giving him the Bible to read medicinally (Hayman 10).[21] When her illness was diagnosed as breast cancer, she underwent a series of unsuccessful operations. Because of this, an additional servant was hired for household work. To make room for her, the twelve-year-old Brecht moved upstairs, where "he had all the benefits of home but little supervision" (Fuegi, *Brecht* 10). This, according to Fuegi, became a pattern of purposeful alienation in Brecht's life: "being part of a family and yet having a physically separate place proved to be so congenial to him that it was one he would seek to duplicate for the rest of his life" (71).[22] Even when his mother died and her corpse lay in an open coffin downstairs, the twenty-two-year-old Brecht was having a "raucous party" in his room above, according to his brother, Walter. This early repression of the chora—a distancing of the family and suffering/dead mother downstairs—parallels the A-effect in Brecht's later work. Such female and familial sacrifice also appears in his first play through an explicitly religious dilemma.

Brecht's first published drama takes place in the historical context of religious warfare (like the later *Mother Courage*). Written when he was not yet sixteen, Brecht's brief (three-scene) play, *The Bible,* reflects the split in his own inheritance of parental faith. But it also shows Brecht's sympathetic yet distanced reaction to his pious mother's breast cancer, since it presents a young woman's choice of physical sacrifice—for family or faith. *The Bible* takes place inside a Protestant city under siege. The Catholic field marshal will spare the city from further destruction on two conditions: all the citizens convert, and the mayor's daughter is offered to him for one night. In the first scene of the play, this young woman had rejected her grandfather's Bible as "cold" (*Werke* 1:10);[23] but now she takes courage in his faith and refuses to sell her soul for the safety of the city. As her grandfather says, "a soul is worth more than a thousand bodies" (12; my translation). Then her more practical brother gives her a Christian sounding argument in the opposite direction: "Isn't it beautiful to suffer for thousands of others? Hurry up!" (13). Thus, the Protestant heroine is forced to choose between a violation of her own body or that of her city by the Catholic other. Either way the chora (of heroine or city) will be sacrificed to a certain patriarchal ideal. As it happens, she takes the pious route, and the city is destroyed.[24]

Brecht published this play in 1914, six years before the death of his mother. In another six years, Brecht began reading *Das Kapital.* Then Karl Marx became the patriarch and "only spectator" for his plays (Brecht, *Theatre* 24). Thus, Brecht's dramatic wager on the faith of Marxism developed, at least in part, through his closeness to his mother (and the absence or distance of his father),[25] her religious influence, and her death. Horst Jesse has pointed out that Brecht's own physical weakness as a child "enhanced the closeness to his mother, also of delicate health" (19). In fact, he suffered a "heart shock," with palpitations and sweats, a couple years after his mother's diagnosis of breast cancer (Fuegi, *Brecht* 10). Yet, with such closeness also came criticism, both of her and of the Lutheran catechism that she had "urged him to learn" (Jesse 19). Even in the last year of her life, when

Brecht was twenty-two, his mother initiated a Bible reading regimen with him (21). She died soon thereafter. "Now my mother has died, yesterday towards evening, on the First of May. One won't be able to claw her up out again with one's fingernails" (Brecht, *Poems* 41).[26]

And yet, Brecht may have been able to reencrypt her in the bisexuality of his early plays and in his own escapades with his friend Caspar Neher,[27] who played Ekart to his Baal, along with the series of women that they shared.[28] Such reencrypting of the dead mother reaches a climax toward the end of *Baal* (Brecht's first full-length play) as the hero's body becomes more and more bloated with decay, pregnant with death. Through such abjection, however, Baal's bloated body raises an early A-effect.[29] For another character says of it: "there's something about that pale lump of fat that makes a man think" (*CP* 1:56). This line appears in the 1922 version of *Baal*, but not in the 1919 text (*Werke* 1:80, 136). Also, between these two versions, Baal's mother is cut from the play. Brecht eliminates one scene where she reprimands her son for his drunkenness and another showing her on her deathbed (*CP* 1:356). These revisions, along with the death of Brecht's own mother in 1920,[30] indicate an alienation effect developing through mourning and melancholia, with an abject encrypting of the lost maternal body in the unconscious of his drama.

According to the "Chorale of the Great Baal," Brecht's polymorphously perverse man-god has "survived" the ecstasy of intercourse with "that lusty woman Earth."

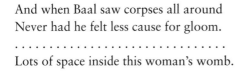

And when Baal saw corpses all around
Never had he felt less cause for gloom.
. . . .
Lots of space inside this woman's womb.

This distancing of mourning through Oedipal desire shows a playful perversion of affect that will, as Benjamin later observed, fill in the ritual chasm of the stage edge to create an epic dais. And yet, the conquered chora still threatens to erupt; for it still bears a horrible Real. "Even Baal is scared of babies, though" (*CP* 1:3–4).[31]

Baal refuses any guilt or mourning for Johanna, who has drowned herself after making love to him. And he tells his next lover, Sophie: "Throw your swollen body in the river! You disgust me" (39). But even as his passion for females dissolves, he sings to his male lover, Ekart, of a drowned woman. "As her pale body decayed in the water there / It happened (very slowly) that God forgot it" (46). Brecht's *Baal*, as antimourning play, tries to forget, yet reveals the trace of that which it puts under erasure: death, maternal body, and God.[32] For between its 1919 and 1922 versions, Brecht also eradicates five invocations of "God" among Baal's dying words, replacing them with three of "Dear Baal" (354).

However, this god of Brecht's own creation, whom he later imitates as a tavern singer as well as seducer of young women, will ultimately bow, in a displacement of his mother's religious desire, to the other Father, Karl Marx.[33] Not only will he call Marx his only spectator, but even describe him as if yet alive. "For a man with interests like his must of necessity be interested in my plays" (*Theatre* 24). Furthermore, according to Bernhard Reich, Brecht in the 1920s "believed that he would have to create for himself a network of followers and believers that would cover the whole of Germany" (qtd. in Esslin 21). Martin Esslin calls the Marxist Brecht "an idealist of truly religious fervour behind the mask of cynicism" (153).[34] And yet, to whatever degree Brecht made a religion of his scientific belief in Marxism, his drama continued to evoke, though also mock, a mourning for dead characters.

Begun shortly after Brecht's own wartime experience in an Augsburg military hospital, *Drums in the Night* is a comedy (set in Africa) about a soldier returning home, where he is thought to be dead. He finds that his sweetheart has a new fiancé. In this antimourning comedy, the sweetheart's father has had to fight to convince her, and her mother, to stop "Pining away for a corpse!" (*CP* 1:69). Her new fiancé also tells her: "I'm not putting up with a stiff between us in bed" (65). When the "ghost" actually appears (after four years as a prisoner of war), the fiancé yells, "Throw him out!" (75). The mother tells him to "suffer in silence." The father says (to her), "Let's not have any more sentimentality" (71). Andreas Kragler, the returning corpse, tries to express his sufferings to Anna, his former beloved. But his mind has alienated him, too, from his own mourning and loss: "It's as if everything in my head had been wiped away, there's nothing but sweat left in it." Anna calmly describes how the illusion of his presence gradually dissolved over time. He responds with a telling, abject remark: "I can't talk to you properly any more, I've got some nigger language in my throat" (77).

The choral language caught in Kragler's throat, like the pregnant abjection of Baal, reveals an infant A-effect (to distance such affect) in Brecht's dramatic corpus. In *Drums* the impossible demand of this Other, that the dead be redeemed through further sacrifice, erupts (as in Genet's *The Balcony* and *The Blacks*) with revolutionary violence just offstage. Kragler, however, refuses to join the Spartacists (unlike Brecht who participated in the brief revolution of 1918, while still an orderly in Augsburg). At the end of the play, Kragler throws the martial drum "at the moon which turns out to be a Japanese lantern. Drum and moon fall in the river, which has no water in it" (106). The hollowness of this gest (showing the emptiness of the signifier),[35] borrows oriental artifice like Brecht's later theory of an A-effect, and displays at a comic distance Kragler's crisis of speech[36] and Anna's of mourning. It still bears a critical mass of passionate sympathy even as it provokes analysis by semiotic shock.

So, too, does Brecht's earlier poem, "Legend of a Dead Soldier," which seems (as Esslin notes) to derive from his own wartime experience,[37] and is incorporated into this comedy as a ballad sung by the owner of a gin mill (CP 1:93, 369–71; Esslin 7–8). In it a dead soldier, dug up to be "put on parade," is given schnapps, nurses, his "half-naked wife," incense by a priest to repress the stink of his decay, paint over his bloody uniform, and finally "a hero's death / just like the handbook said." Brecht dedicates this song (in an appendix to the play) to a particular infantryman, Christian Grumbeis, who "died in Holy Week 1918" (CP 1:369–71).[38] Thus, repressed mourning propels the early A-effect of Brechtian satire toward the agitprop earnestness of his subsequent, Marxist plays—and the desire for/of an Other audience, representing future historical change.

A New Stage Mother

The plot of a No play, *Taniko*, formed the basis of Brecht's 1930 *Lehrstücke*, *He Who Says Yes* and *He Who Says No* (*Measures* 61 and 71). It also led, through the failure of these plays, to *The Measures Taken* (Esslin 142). Brecht (and Hauptmann),[39] following Arthur Waley's English version of this fifteenth-century drama by Zenchiku, omits its conclusion, in which a boy, sacrificed by his peers, is brought back to life by their teacher, a monk who turns out to be the reincarnation of his sect's founder (Hayman 150). At the end of the play, as Waley indicates in a footnote, the resurrected boy is carried onstage by a Spirit (235 n. 1). But Waley's translation and Brecht's initial adaptation both end with the boy's death. He is thrown off a cliff by his comrades because he has fallen ill during a journey through the mountains led by the teacher. In addition, Brecht changes the "ritual mountain-climbing" into a relief expedition "to get medicine and instructions" (Waley 231; Brecht, *Measures* 64). Yet the purpose of the boy joining the group is still to get help for his sick mother—through medicine rather than prayer. This recalls the fatal illness of Brecht's own mother a decade earlier, and his subsequent turn away from her religious piety toward the science of Marx. At the beginning of the play (Zenchiku's and Brecht's) the boy's father is already dead (230; 63). But in Brecht's version there is a distinct refusal to mourn not only the dead father (whom the boy has replaced), but also the mother, lost to the boy as he meets his death. Nor is the martyred boy mourned by his peers and teacher; for his sacrifice to the community redeems such loss and guilt.

The ritual fatalism of No drama suited Brecht's desire to show (and teach) faith in the Party. However, he eliminated the obvious spiritual elements of the No, such as the resurrection scene of *Taniko*. Yet, there is more than a trace of the ritual and spiritual remaining in Brecht's version.[40] As in his later adoption of Chinese acting for the A-effective *Gestus*,[40] Brecht used the chorus from the No play to demonstrate a communal body with united voice. This reflects a metaphysical audience (in the materialist sense) of Party and proletariat—with a future, revolutionary aura.[41]

After initial productions of *He Who Says Yes* at two Berlin schools, Brecht asked the boys who performed the character roles and the role of "Great Chorus" (as sole audience) about the appropriateness of the play to their own lives. Their answers were so negative that Brecht revised his play, making the boy's mission and his otherwise futile sacrifice more heroic by extending the mother's illness to an epidemic of the entire city. He thus returned to the dilemma of his first drama, written during his own boyhood, *The Bible* (Hayman 151–52). When this, too, failed to please as well as instruct, Brecht wrote *Der Neinsager* (*He Who Says No*), a further revised form of *Der Jasager*. In this version there is again no epidemic. But "Great Custom" demands that the boy be sacrificed (because he has fallen ill on the journey), as it does in Waley's translation of *Taniko*. This time, however, the boy says, "No." Here Brecht perverts the logic of his own initial *Lehrstück*, repudiating the symbolic order of the Party's choral wisdom, as he had the spiritual order of the Japanese myth.[42] He then returns the death-drive oracle to its original mask of ancient custom, to which guilt is assigned. But at the heart of this drive for further sacrifice remains an ill mother (and city), reflecting both the social disease Brecht's theater would ostensibly cure and his own sick mother whom he could not—despite his medical training and wartime experience.

"So far there is no known medicine for this disease," says the mother at the beginning of *Der Jasager* (*Measures* 63). In *Der Neinsager* this line is changed back to what it had been in *Taniko*: "Don't worry about my illness. It is of no consequence" (*Measures* 73; Waley 231). But the mother still desires that her son go with the teacher on the dangerous journey across the mountains to "the city beyond" in which there are "great doctors" (64, 74). In both plays (as in *Taniko*), the teacher checks the boy's mimicry of the (m)Other's desire by pressing a point of potential guilt (similar to that of Joyce's alter ego in *Portrait of the Artist*). "How can you leave your mother / When she is not well?" (*Measures* 64, 74; Waley 232). Brecht has the mother (in both versions, as in *Taniko*) perversely hold onto the boy, against her own material interests. She pressures him to stay, stimulating his Oedipal desire through the memory of an absent father. "Since the day / Your father left me / I have had none / But you at my side" (65, 75; Waley 232). The boy, however, insists on separating from her, not only for the sake of saving her life, but also to find a new, communal womb and symbolic order with the chorus and teacher.

In fact, in the *Yes* play (unlike the original No drama) it is the boy's own request that he be hurled into the valley to his death, rather than be left behind in his sickness, "for I am afraid to die alone." His answer thus goes beyond "accordance with necessity" (68): from faith in an alienated fate, though part of a larger purpose, to an abject fear like his mother's and the desire to consummate his sacrifice in the hands of the other boys. "Support your head on our arms," they say to him. "Don't exert yourself. / We will carry you gently." In acting together to sacrifice one bodily member, each in the community avoids guilt: "None guiltier than his neighbour." (The same words are given in Waley's translation of *Taniko* [235].) Yet it is a "bitter law" that they thus obey together, drawn to the mountain's ritual stage: "At the edge of the abyss." The martyr's final act is to hand over the empty jar for his mother's medicine, while he is "invisible," hidden by the bodies of the other boys "at the rear edge of the dais." With this gest—"Take my jar / fill it with medicine / And bring it to my mother / When you return" (69)— paralleling the Christian ritual of communion ("Take my body . . . take my blood"), the empty jar becomes a hollow fetish for the boy's sacrificial body, which is raised as invisible maternal phallus over the chora of communal cure.

In *Der Neinsager* the boy's unheroic refusal to obey the old symbolic order convinces the community to institute a new Great Custom, that of "rethinking every new situation." The other boys handle him with the same ritual gentleness, but instead of hurling him into the abyss, they carry him back to his mother. This time, acting communally, they avoid cowardice rather than heroic guilt: "None more cowardly than his neighbour." They even pervert the boy's cowardice into heroic success—as he changes the "law" (79). Yet a trace of the old law lingers in the birth of the new. For the teacher had used it as a basis for giving the boy a choice: "the Custom also prescribes that the one who has fallen ill should be asked whether the expedition should turn back on his account." Custom prescribes an answer, however, that the boy then repudiates (78). He both believes and perverts the old law.

Brecht returns to the more obedient choice and extends the question of communal guilt further in revising the same No material for *The Measures Taken*. He also makes the characters and chorus explicitly communist. Here the sacrifice has already occurred and, more like the No custom, the dead character returns, though as depicted by each of the killers in turn (like the A-effect of the street demonstrator [*Theatre* 121–29]) rather than as a ghost. Recent critics have tended to note a certain historical premonition in this *Lehrstück*. The desire it demonstrates for individual sacrifice to communal meaning parallels the acceptance of guilt and punishment by innocent victims in later Stalinist show trials.[43] Darko Suvin also calls *The Measures Taken* "a kind of Mystery play," in which the individual "should disappear into a collective *ad maiorem Dei gloriam*." This is characteristic, says Suvin, of the second phase of Brecht's drama, in direct contrast to his initial, almost absurdist individualism. "Such a play is a poetical expression of a lay faith whose aims are of this world but whose methodology is fundamentally religious, even though not theistic but political" (126–27). To this I would add that the "Control Chorus," while voicing Brecht's conversion to the faith of Marxism, also provides a meaning beyond, yet based upon, mourning.

The symbolic justification given by this new, choral mask for the measures and masses taken by communism—at the edge of Brecht's epic stage—bears the cost of an apparent erasure of the abject Other. As the young comrade, or rather his ghostlike character, is told during the demonstration of his previous sacrifice: "Therefore we must be the ones to shoot you and cast you into the lime-pit, so that the lime will burn away all traces of you" (*Measures* 33). But in this sacrifice of the ghost for the sake of one communal body (as in eucharistic mass-taking), the pain of burning lime is also transferred, leaving the trace of its erasure of all traces—in perverse, excessive pleasure and violence.

More than a trace of the maternal chora returns in Brecht's 1932 play, *The Mother*,[44] though again with a Marxist vengeance. It takes five scenes before Pelagea Vlasova can wear the Marxist mask firmly. At the end of scene 4 she still says, "You know I believe in a God in heaven. I don't want anything to do with violence" (23). But by scene 10 she is arguing theology with other women, trying to convert them to socialism and revolution through the death of God. They respond by reminding her of her own son's death because of such conversion: "If you'd read to your son from the bible more, he'd still be living today" (53–54). Yet Brecht's righteously perverse Vlasova transcends the melancholy of her poverty and the mourning for her son.

Writing shortly after *The Mother*'s premiere, Benjamin sees its heroine as both the ideal mother and ultimate Party member. "If the mothers are revolutionized, there is nothing left to revolutionize." Representing all motherhood, she bears the essence of the revolution's pragmatic force. "This unique attitude of the mother, this useful helpfulness which, as it were, resides in the folds of any mother's skirt, acquires now the social dimension (as solidarity of the oppressed) which it only possessed before in an animal sense" (*Understanding* 34). The animal sense of feminine abjection thus fuels heroic alienation in Benjamin's view of Brecht's dialectical drama. "Epic theatre, therefore, is the theatre of the hero who is beaten. A hero who is not beaten never makes a thinker." In the epic antimourning play, *The Mother,* Benjamin finds a portrait of Madonna and child: the mother goddess of praxis, who adopts Communism as the newborn messiah.

> And she sings these songs as a mother. For they are lullabies. Lullabies for Communism, which is small and weak but irresistibly growing. This Communism she has taken unto herself as a mother. It becomes clear too that she is loved by Communism as only a mother is loved: she is loved . . . as the inexhaustible source of help . . . where it is still pure-flowing. . . . The mother is praxis incarnate. (35)

Through her belief in the death of God, and yet also in the providential value of her son's death, Palegea Vlasova incarnates the Marxist chora, as antimourning heroine, nurturing revolutionary violence.

Nearly thirty years later, writing about the Berliner Ensemble's performance of *The Mother* in Paris, Roland Barthes claims that Vlasova "fulfills no stereotype: . . . her being is not on the level of her womb." Barthes sees her as an antiheroine, undermining the "stock images" of both Marxism and motherhood ("On Brecht's *Mother*" 139). Yet he also describes her spiritual character, perversely born out of her own son's death. "In Brecht's *The Mother,* the relation [of Christian mother directing, praying, or weeping for her child, as Monica does for Augustine] is inverted: it is the son who gives birth, spiritually, to the mother" (140–41). Barthes notes, too, that she is reborn through the son's "*praxis* and not through speech." Here the martyred son becomes the abject root (or Freudian dream stem and myceleum). "In the Brechtian order there is no inheritance unless it is inverted: once the son is dead, it is the mother who continues him, as if she were the new growth, the leaf now unfolding" (141).

This is also highly significant in relation to Barthes's later theoretical turn toward mourning, after the death of his own mother. At this point, though, he keeps her at a Brechtian distance. He thus demonstrates the abject bed of the A-effect.

> Her consciousness truly blooms only when her son is dead: she is never united with him. Thus, through this ripening, a distance separates mother from son, reminding us that this correct itinerary is a cruel one: love is not, here, an effusion, it is that force which transforms fact into consciousness, then into action: it is love which opens our eyes. (142)

This cruel force of love that buries mourning blooms, however, into the revolutionary rage that turns our eyes away from the son's corpse and mother's womb—toward a new, yet vengeful order.

The Hollow Pietà

Vlasova in *The Mother* becomes a Marxist goddess of consciousness and praxis—at first abject, but then transcendently alienated through heroic antimourning. She blossoms, too, from the mother of *Der Jasager*, left behind by the play's ending, still ill and medicine-less, after the sacrificial death of her son. Brecht's (or the Brecht Collective's) *Saint Joan of the Stockyards* further develops this heroine toward a much more ambiguous sacrifice.[45] Her maternity is erased, however, at least explicitly. Joan Dark appears more like the fiery daughter of Shaw's *Major Barbara*,[46] battling the Oedipal, capitalist father, "Meat King Pierpont Mauler," with her Salvation Army drums (*Saint Joan* 27). Yet she might also be seen, initially, as a Christian mother goddess of praxis (i.e., Virgin Mother). "We are the Soldiers of the Lord. . . . We march with drums beating and flags flying wherever unrest prevails and acts of violence threaten, to remind men of the Lord . . ." (33). Joan is thus, at the beginning, a stronger missionary force than Vlasova—particularly in fighting against violence with the absent Father's phallic Law: "summoned by rumored threats of violence . . . we wish to bring back / God. / Of little fame these days / almost disreputable. . . . A last attempt / to set Him upright [*aufzurichten*] in a crumbling [*zerfallender*] world" (31; *Werke* 3:133).

The twenty-some-year-old Joan metaphysically seduces Mauler into donating money.[47] "I feel as if a breath from another world were wafting toward me," he says (43). But she is eventually converted by him (like Major Barbara by Undershaft) to believe in the metaphysical materialism of economic law, "the not-to-be-known" (58). Yet this leads her (unlike Barbara) to believe in violence against Mauler and other capitalist gods as a just response to their fateful control.[48] For Joan then realizes how these gods of the commodities exchange have exploited her work, too. They have benefited directly from her pacifying of the proletariat through faith's opium. She had been a saint for the wrong side. Subsequently, however, she becomes a Vlasova-like force for violent change, marching beyond any mourning for a dead God, to kill the capitalist Father. "Only force helps where force rules, and / only men help where men are" (122).

Joan's remedy for still-drugged Christians is reminiscent of Marx's materialist inversion of Hegelian *Geist*. "So anyone down here who says there is a God / although there's none to be seen . . . should have his head banged on the pavement / until he croaks" (122). But the chorus of pious capitalists drowns out the heroine's cure with hosannas (122–23). Joan's sacrificial death is perverted;[49] her martyred body becomes a fetish object for the paradoxical, paralytic mourning of the chorus, with its "two souls." Thus, a double bind of belief in both capitalism and Christian charity is reconfirmed in the Faustian "breast" of the chorus, manipulated by Mauler, but mocked by Brecht's play (124–25).[50]

This Faustian chora gives birth, nearly a decade later, to Brecht's twin goddesses of capitalist praxis: Mother Courage and the Good Person of Szechwan. Each combines in one character the ruthless allegiance to economic law with the maternal instinct to save others, which distinguish Mauler and Joan. But this double bind in Mother Courage results in repeated failure, the loss of each of her children, one by one. Her daughter, Kattrin, is a more successful and ideal maternal figure.[51] She risks her life to save a baby in scene 5, while her mother does nothing, torn between helping her and saving some shirts (*CP* 5:176, 363). In scene 11 Kattrin again risks her life out of pity for others' children (333). She rises sacrificially, like and unlike Joan (for Kattrin's death does save the city), above the prayerful paralysis of the peasants. Yet they also play a choral role, evoking her heroism on the barn-roof stage, by beseeching "Our Father" so pitifully (205). Ironically, the peasants then reverse their prayers (after Kattrin has begun beating her drum), asking for pity from her—to stop saving the city, because they fear for their own lives. They thus demonstrate the ruthlessness of her altruistic heroism (206). And yet, as surrogate sacrificial mother, Kattrin becomes the most genuine martyr in all of Brecht's (or the Brecht Collective's) drama.[52]

Her mother's survival as a businesswoman, however, beyond any paralytic mourning for the deaths of her own children, also becomes temptingly heroic. But Brecht insisted that Courage be played antiheroically and antitragically. In his "Model" for the play, Brecht demanded that her lullaby of denial while holding Kattrin's dead body in the final scene "be sung without any sentimentality or desire to provoke sentimentality." For the lyrics in this Pietà tableau are "murderous: this mother's child must fare better than other children of other mothers" (CP 5:383). The murderous businesswoman's survival beyond mourning is then further critiqued in the play's final, A-effective gest. The solitary mother pushes her wagon onward to again supply a war that has taken away all her children. The mother goddess of praxis, now wearing a capitalist mask, is mocked. Yet this hollow fetish[53] (like Joan's martyrdom) raises an earnest, Brechtian question: how might tragic fate be altered?

In contrast, the Good Person of Szechwan (more like Joan Dark) converts from an initial altruism to cruel collusion, in fighting for her own and others' survival, particularly that of her unborn child. Yet, she continues to bear both souls, like a schizophrenic combination of Joan and the Mauler chorus, or Kattrin and Mother Courage. Hence, her Shen Teh/Shui Ta split extends the good mother (but bad provider) versus bad mother (yet good patriarchal capitalist) bind of Courage, and intensifies it in the conceit of the double persona. Brecht wrote of Weigel's performance of Courage that the "merchant mother became a great living contradiction, and it was this contradiction which utterly disfigured and transformed her" (387). In Shen Teh/Shui Ta Brecht (with the help of his female collaborators)[54] brings such disfigurement and transformation into the script. He also points to the social system and its economic metaphysics, represented by the three bumbling gods, rather than to the good/bad mother herself—as responsible for the tragic suffering.

The audiences of Mother Courage did not understand, according to Brecht, that the play was meant to reveal "the connection between war and commerce: the proletarian class can do away with war by doing away with capitalism" (386). (Whatever the credence of this statement economically or politically, it says a great deal about the play, and particularly about the battle between Kattrin and her mother.) Some audience members did see "that Mother Courage learns nothing from her misery," but even they did not understand the larger picture. "They did not see what the playwright was driving at: that war teaches people nothing" (388–89). In Brecht's own view, the play failed to teach the audience what the plot could not teach Courage; it failed to make the spectators learn through her failure to learn. Audiences in the postwar years did not analyze the mother's desire as their own. Instead, "they saw only her failure, her sufferings"—despite her "participation" in the military campaign, "her desire to share in the profits of the war business" (389). Thus, in *Good Person* Brecht displaces such capitalistic desire of the mother, making it that of the Other—of the gods (as audience) looking for goods in persons, and of the character, Shui Ta, whom they help create.

Lacking Gods and the Feminist Double

The good prostitute Shen Teh begins the play as altruistic and generous as Kattrin. But through the gods' desire to see her goodness (with their seed money), she must become cruel like Mother Courage. The voyeuristic desire of the gods for the whore's sacrificial goodness reflects, of course, that of the audience of paying customers across the edge of the stage. As the gods themselves tell Wang: "We can do nothing.—We are only observers" (*CP* 6:68). And yet, in the play's epilogue, one of the players turns to the audience for a better ending and answer. The plot's ending, with the perverse (or reverse) *dei ex machina* of the gods vacating their role as judges and "flying / Homeward to our nothingness," has left the audience, too, in a "void," the player admits apologetically. He (or she) also gives the audience a Derridean disclosure: "All questions [are] open though we've closed our play" (103). Or, more literally and scopophilicly, "The curtain closed *[Den Vorhang zu]* and all questions open" (*Werke* 6:278; my translation). The epilogue then shows, like Prospero's at the end of *The Tempest,* that the audience as Other is both feared and desired by the performers. "Especially since we live by your enjoyment. / Disgruntled spectators mean unemployment" (*CP* 6:103). To paraphrase Lacan's formula: the actor's desire is the desire of the audience—faithfully and perversely as well as economically.

However, in this epilogue, unlike Prospero's, the prayer is for release through thought, not just magical applause (or others' prayers)—though it also reflects the magical appeal of today's critical thought and theory. For the prayer of Brecht's player is directed totally to the human (and future) audience, rejecting higher forms of the Other,[55] and even questioning Marxist answers.

For love nor money we could find no out:
Refashion man? Or change the world about?
Or turn to different gods? Or don't we need
Any? Our bewilderment is great indeed.
There's only one solution comes to mind:
That you yourselves should ponder. . . .

(CP 6:103–4)

This echoes Shen Teh's plea to the gods (as judges) that their desire might be less painful. "Your order long ago / To be good and yet to live / Tore me like lightning into two halves" (100). She thus asks them to repudiate their already perverse law. She cannot bear to continue the sacrifice, to become a martyr and tragic heroine like Joan or Kattrin.

Yet, as the gods leave, Shen Teh clings to her split subjectivity, and barters for its continuance.

SHEN TEH: But I need my cousin!
THE FIRST GOD: Not too often!
SHEN TEH: At least once a week!
THE FIRST GOD: Once a month: that will do!

(102)

The *Good Person*'s gods, whose "fatal" desire (101) demands this moral/immoral (charity yet business, altruism yet survival) double bind, stem from similar avatars of metaphysical, economic law in *Saint Joan*: Mauler and his cohorts. In both plays Brecht demonstrates the collusion of religious and capitalist faiths, as his *Mother Courage* had of religious war and commerce. All three depict an abject maternal figure, yet alienate her from the "gods" in the audience and their desire to feel tragic pity.[56] However, it is through pity that Joan, Kattrin, and Shen Teh find their courage and heroism, becoming goddesslike forces of salvational praxis. With Shen Teh the double-edged sword of pity's ruthless potential—for both good and evil—becomes the sharpest. "Yet pity / Brought me such pain that ferocious rage overcame me / At the sight of misery. Then / I felt a change come over me. / My teeth turned to fangs" (100–101). Thus, according to Shui Ta, Shen Teh went away because the pitiful people of Szechwan would have made her a Dionysian sacrifice: "you'd have torn her to pieces!" (99).

In the *sparagmos* of Shen Teh by the gods, and by the people she pities, Brecht constructs an uncanny, gestic ritual. This parable play also gives a realistic depiction of split subjectivity. Like (but not as extreme as) a multiple personality disorder in which a stronger character takes control to protect more vulnerable parts of the psyche within an abused child, Shui Ta threatens to permanently displace Shen Teh toward the end of the play. For Lacan, though, such a disorder is not abnormal. It is the pervasive Oedipal condition of human subjectivity: caught between maternal desire and patriarchal law—between a lost symbiotic womb and the illusion of individuated ego. The phallic mask of her cousin, the "tobacco king," which Shen Teh must increasingly wear, demonstrates how the castrative edge of the child's mirror stage persists into adulthood.[57] But this is particularly true for the supposedly liberated, postmodern woman who, like the whore/mother Shen Teh, must choose between selling herself to the capitalist rat race or devoting her body to domestic responsibilities. If she chooses one or the other, she must bear the stigma of not embodying the full superwoman ideal. If she chooses both, she will, to some degree, be torn between them— becoming both the alienated Shui Ta and the abject Shen Teh.

This double figure must be considered, along with the earlier manifestations of her in Brecht's drama, in any adaptation of his A-effect to feminism today. For she reveals a symptomatic postmodern dilemma of feminism: whether to repress or utilize the maternal chora in fighting the abuses of patriarchy and capitalism. Iris Smith has recently argued (in *Theatre Journal*) that Brecht's "Shen Teh/Shui Ta needs to be reformulated as a fragmented subject rather than a split subject. . . . Shen Teh must exceed the sum of her parts, explode with excess and thus make of herself a subject-in-process." Smith demands (following Diamond) the adaptation, not adoption, of Brechtian dialectics through a particular idea of woman that she borrows from Kristeva. "All of Shen Teh's 'folded' desires must be made visible" (499–500). And yet, in explaining this term (a few pages earlier), Smith represses Kristeva's valorization of motherhood.[58]

Smith, following Lennox as well as Diamond, critiques Brecht's "regression to stereotyped gender roles." But in doing so, she herself stereotypes "the feminist spectator," whose pleasure is not engaged by Brecht's "ready-made dichotomies," particularly the "essentialist, mother/whore dichotomy" in plays such as *Mother Courage* (495–96). Like Case, Smith points to the "asexual mother" in that play—and in *Caucasian Chalk Circle, Good Person of Szechwan,* and *The Mother*—as being the "crux of the problem." The mother's desire is misrepresented in Brecht's drama, according to Smith, because the female subject is identified with the asexual mother (as domesticated whore): "a sexual being who willingly abandons her sexuality and self-definition for the sake of children." Of course, this problematic crux comes to its apotheosis in Shen Teh.

Yet, Smith's rejection of the Brechtian mother as "asexual" masks the variety of dialectical syntheses in the Brecht Collective's drama. The mother/whore may become: a heroic force for revolutionary change (Vlasova), a Christian yet capitalist martyr (Joan), a mother torn between saving her children and saving her business (Courage), a daughter who dies for others' children and in protest of her own mother's patriarchal sellout (Kattrin), or a mother-to-be who cannot be a good woman and still survive (Shen Teh). None of these possibilities means an abandonment of sexuality. They do mean the loss of "self-definition," however. For that is precisely their proto-postmodern character: formed by the polymorphous desires of the Other, even when the audience (as Other) includes some spectators resisting the losses of self.

The Other Audience

There are, of course, many moments of misogyny in Brecht's drama—especially in the early plays now being praised by lesbian feminists, and in those parts of later ones written by Brecht himself according to Fuegi. Yet, as Brecht's theories and drama matured, a greater sensitivity to women characters developed in his work—even if this "his" meant a repression of the Collective's chora of female (and male) coauthors. While he/they used female characters (and male ones) as gestic signifiers to point out social problems, Brecht also desired a certain degree of sympathy and psychological realism in their portrayal. In fact, Brecht's working journal, during his (and Steffin's)[59] early revisions of *The Good Person of Szechwan*, shows concern for the "strenuous efforts" of Shen Teh (Li Gung, in this initial version) when she masquerades as her male cousin. Brecht wants to emphasize that this is not an easy transformation. Thus, he has difficulty deciding how Shui Ta (Lao Go) should address the audience: "whether he ought not to do this using li gung's voice and consequently her attitude too." And yet, he feels he must demonstrate the character's "change of attitude" without making the audience a confidant for Shui Ta (CP 6:368). Only Shen Teh can have that choral intimacy with the Other's desire.

At certain, perverse moments in *Good Person*, Shen Teh must appear despite and through the alien veil of Shui Ta. Brecht's stage directions emphasize one such moment in scene 5, as Shen Teh's beloved, Yang Sun, comes to visit her tobacco shop for the first time. After hearing Sun's voice call from outside, "Shui Ta runs to the mirror with the light steps of Shen Teh and is about to arrange his hair when he sees his mistake in the mirror. He turns away with a soft laugh. Enter Yang Sun." Sun then talks with Shui

Ta in manly camaraderie, though they haggle over whether the shop will be sold so that Sun can have his dream job as flyer. This entire scene tempts the audience to voyeuristically watch for any glimpse of Shen Teh's emotion, behind the businessman's mask, as the two men barter away her economic freedom. At the beginning of the scene, Sun even tempts Shui Ta to imagine lovemaking with Shen Teh. Here the gest reveals a capitalist, homosocial intercourse—over the abject female body as sexual commodity and through the fetish object of money that one man hurriedly demands from the other (via cigars) for his promised *jouissance* of flying.

> SUN: I need the money in a hurry or not at all. And that girl isn't the kind that holds back when it comes to giving something. Just between us men, she hasn't held anything back so far.
> SHUI TA: I see.
>
> (47)

Perhaps the audience also sees—not only the capitalist gest, but also Sun's desire for Shui Ta, as the phallic mother who does not hold back. If so, Brecht is revealing more affect than his A-effect would let on(stage): the joy and terror at the heart of patriarchal consumption—and in the collective chora at the stage's edge, related to each spectator's primal fantasy of a lost omnipotent (uncastrated) mother.[60] Such perverse sympathy might arise, at a critical Brechtian distance, through both the infantile/patriarchal Sun and the maternal Shen Teh.

Early in the play, Shen Teh obtains a thousand silver dollars by selling her goodness/poverty dilemma to the (at first) sympathetic gods. She then buys the tobacco shop because of her sympathy for the poverty of its former owner.[61] Shen Teh also falls in love with Sun through pity for a man about to hang himself—and through the seductiveness of his poverty, as she says later in the play: "When I saw the holes in his shoes, I loved him very much" (69). However, after becoming pregnant by him, a fierce rage grows within her (like that of Vlasova and Courage) to protect herself, her child, and her shop—even from Sun. Thus the maternal chora and its many folds, behind the mask of Shui Ta, fights against the desire of Sun, despite her love for him. At the same time, Shui Ta struggles to hold back this loving, yet raging chora, especially as Sun makes more and more of a chauvinist pig out of himself in scene 5.

> SUN: (AMUSED) . . . You're going to appeal to her [Shen Teh's] reason? She hasn't got any reason. . . . If I put my hand on her shoulder and

FIG. 5. *The Good Person of Szechwan*, by Bertolt Brecht. Yang Sun (John Leonard) with Shen Teh (Randy Danson). Arena Stage production, directed by Garland Wright, October–November 1985. (Photograph by Joan Marcus. Courtesy of Arena Stage.)

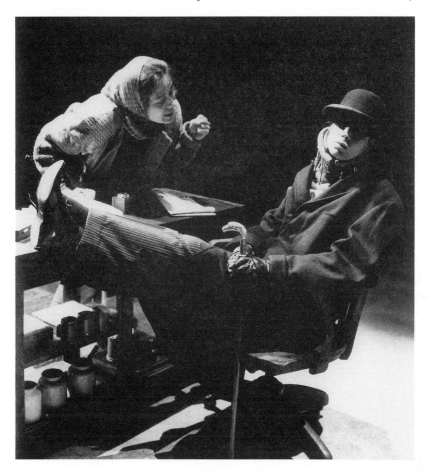

FIG. *6. The Good Person of Szechwan,* by Bertolt Brecht. Mrs. Shin (Tana Hicken) with Shui Ta (Randy Danson). Arena Stage production, directed by Garland Wright, October–November 1985. (Photograph by Joan Marcus. Courtesy of Arena Stage.)

say: "Come with me," she'll hear bells, she won't know her own mother any more.

SHUI TA: *(with difficulty)* Mr. Yang Sun!

Here Shen Teh explodes through the mask of Shui Ta, as Brecht's stage directions indicate. "He runs around like a captive animal, repeating over and over 'The shop is gone!' Then suddenly he stops still" (51).

Shen Teh's tremendous struggle to combine her feelings and reason, her maternal generosity and patriarchal business sense, the "impossible weakness" of love and the ruthless strength required for economic survival, means that "Caresses turn to strangling. A sigh of love becomes a cry of terror" (52). The distancing of Shui Ta from Shen Teh, like the gestic mask of the Brechtian actor alienating character, is fueled by abject horror, which turns into sadistic pragmatism. In the play such sadism produces capitalist success: Shen Teh's tobacco shop becomes Shui Ta's factory. But the structural parallel with Brecht's own belief in theater, as an anticapitalist instrument for social change, reveals, too, a potential instrumentalization of actor and audience at the service of the Other. Here the apparently stereotypical poles of the Good Person's character must serve as warning gests to the postmodern Brechtian theorist: binaries do not deconstruct painlessly.[62]

Ideally, the painful pleasure of theatrical sacrifice would be alienated by Brecht's epic drama. Yet, Shen Teh shows her audience a homeless child's "dirty mouth" and asks for pity—in terms that echo the traditional Catholic prayer to the Virgin Mother.

> Have you
> No compassion with the fruit
> Of your wombs? No Pity
> For yourselves, you unfortunates? Then I
> Will fight for my own at least, even if I have to
> Turn tiger. . . .
> What I have learned in the gutter, my school
> Of brutality and guile, shall
> Serve you now, my son.
>
> (74)

Shen Teh becomes a tiger, both as Madonna and as patriarchal capitalist, turning her gutter-learned abjection and feminine masochism into the successful sadism of Shui Ta, because the audience as God or Virgin Mother is lacking. The Third God even admits toward the end of the play: "our commandments seem to be fatal! I'm afraid all the moral precepts we have drawn up will have to be crossed out" (94). Yet the gods together, as judges, close the play (but not its questions) by restoring the same symbolic order and leaving—like an audience. "Let us go home. This little world / Has moved us deeply. Its joys and sorrows / Have greatly cheered and grieved us" (101).[63] They will the cathartic illusion of "the good person / Who here below bears witness to our spirit *[unserm Geist]*" (102; *Werke* 6:277)—in order to maintain her as martyr beneath them, fueling the economy of their ostensibly metaphysical theater, which Brecht parodies in showing such hollow gests. And yet, while demonstrating and questioning this oppressive illusion, Brecht's theater does not escape a similar temptation: repressing the maternal chora to produce a distanced audience.

Whatever the success today of feminism, Marxism, and deconstruction in putting the former "moral precepts" of patriarchy and capitalism under erasure, we continue sacrificing to the Other in some form, no matter how much we see it as lacking and decentered. The recent failures of communist societies all over the world and the periodic failings of our own economy, along with the continued growth of international capitalism, show that the measures taken in Brecht's drama are still significant gests— whether we stand with or against his characters' perverse traits and his theory's ideological beliefs.[64] We still tend (on either side of the politically correct battle line) to seek, mourn, and resurrect the lost victim of history at the edge of the stage: "one human being who is good and has not become wicked but only disappeared" (94). For we are that good person's lacking audience of distant gods.

Epilogue

Whether or not Nietzsche's romantic vision of a primal Dionysian chorus as lost "womb" is a correct historical recreation, the loss of ritual origins has become a primary concern in the twentieth century—as shown by certain works of modern drama and the theatrics of postmodern theory. Rituals still pervade our society: in the sacred rites of specific ethnic and religious cultures, in general civil ceremonies like voting or paying taxes, in sports events where teams represent opposing communities, and in common personal routines like TV watching and moviegoing. But while we are brought together in various forms of partial communion, through modern technology and the postmodern simulacrum, the power of such brief communal moments often reveals the loss of community in daily life. Church rituals are at best a weekly (or yearly) refuge from the loneliness of our dysfunctional families and diverse social beliefs. Civil ceremonies are meaningless habits or painful impositions. The ecstasy of sports becomes a game of profit. Movies give us merely a touch-point for passing conversations. And television, though watched by millions at once, blocks us from actual contact with other spectators—even those in the same living room.[1]

Modern drama's nostalgia for communal power shows its ties to previous periods: to theater's "birth" as an art form out of ancient and medieval rituals, to the neoclassical mimicry of Aristotelian ideals, and to the Romantic desire for a primitive sublime—despite modern styles, both realistic and antirealistic, that propose a new recovery of truth onstage. Theater's movement forward in multiple directions finds inspiration by looking back. Across the spectrum of modern experiments considered in this volume, from the sacred violence of Eliot and Artaud to the political perversity of Brecht and Genet, as well as in various postmodern theories taking their cue from Nietzsche, the edge of loss in the birth of tragedy has sparked many creative fires.

Of course, the primal ritual womb never existed until it was lost[2]—in theater's separation from it as distinct art form, with that separation viewed at a nostalgic historical distance. The "womb" is recreated, as lost, in theater's modern rebirth—as elements of ritual afterbirth are involved or repressed in each new drama onstage. Whether the aim is to incorporate or distance current communal potential (like Artaud or Brecht), loss stimulates desire, to return or reject, creating new communicative power.

From Eliot's choral experiments to more recent attempts at creating a primal chorus, as in Peter Shaffer's *Equus,* the sense of loss is so powerful that only a partial recovery of the sacred seems possible. This increases the modernist mourning for a complete order of God, community, and self (or of universal family values)—against the postmodern celebration of "diversity." At best, Eliot's martyrs bear limited communal meaning: the archbishop's transcendence needs religious believers at a sacred site, and Celia's sacrifice is distanced by the comedy of a drawing room. Even more than Eliot's Reilly, Shaffer's psychologist, Martin Dysart, rages at this modern loss of divine collective passion. Although the chorus creates an Equus noise that "heralds or illustrates the presence of Equus the God" (16), Dysart must cure his patients from such mad Equus worship, returning them to "the good Normal world where we're tethered beside them" (108). For he obeys the Apollonian god of his profession, in duty to social normality.

> The Normal is the indispensable, murderous God of Health, and I am his Priest. . . . I have talked away terrors and relieved many agonies. But also—beyond question—I have cut from them [his young patients] parts of individuality repugnant to this God, in both his aspects. Parts sacred to rarer and more wonderful Gods. (65)

Dysart's scientific faith in the normal has been profoundly disturbed by his patients' Dionysian passions and by his own postmodern glimpse of perverse, diverse gods.

Various crises of modern faith (and premonitions of the postmodern) can be seen in the work of many playwrights not covered in this book: the hollow ideal of suicide in Ibsen, the shattered pipe dreams of O'Neill, the misfires of love in Chekhov, the insubstantial order of the dreamer in Strindberg, the ebb of mythic heroes in Yeats, the mummification of small town life by Wilder, the common man's depreciation in Miller, the fragile menageries of Williams, and the loss of the author by Pirandello's characters—or, at the cusp of postmodern parody, the waiting for Godot. Beckett's minimalist tragicomedies bear modernist mourning ad absurdum, with the always again absent Godot and the "zero" outside Clov's windows and Hamm's eyes. From there—and through Genet's perverse mirrors—many postmodern playwrights have built various ethnic and gender fun-houses, recycling the ruins of lost rites and patriarchal orders. But the postmodern celebration of loss bears an undertone of modern mourning. Particularly in plays that continue to use the ritual aspects of a chorus (or a choral, narrative voice), martyred heroes, violent sacrifice, spiritual themes, and ceremonies—the postmodern death of God/self is paradoxically liberating and binding, comic and tragic, political and yet metaphysical. The originary loss of divine ritual, from modern to postmodern theater, thus returns us to more individual origins: the horrors and joys of the lost maternal body (through patriarchal reinterpretations), influencing our historical memories, polymorphous dreams, and shared art forms.

Recent currents in performance art, from body artists to monologuists to ensemble deconstructionists (like the Wooster Group), also show this concern for metatheatrical meaning within the biographical and physical. So do many postmodern scripts—even while they satirize, shatter, and recombine former metaphysical orders by recycling ritual remnants. Caryl Churchill's *Cloud Nine* rehearses the rites of Victorian colonialism in drag. In the second act, its 1970s characters experiment with a drunken chant to the mother goddess, using various ancient names, and then see the ghost of a British soldier killed in Northern Ireland. The mysterious choral voices in Marguerite Duras's *India Song* are possessed by distinct passions for each other and the story, as they narrate, question, and vocalize the characters onstage—refracting the voyeurism of the audience into multiple angles. In *The Lion and the Jewel,* Wole Soyinka depicts the mirroring mutations between cultures, as African tribal life and power rituals are penetrated by Western ideals and technology. *The Island,* by Athol Fugard, John Kani, and Winston Ntshona, recasts *Antigone* in a South African prison to create improvised rites of love, duty, betrayal, and self-sacrifice. Adrienne Kennedy's *Funnyhouse of a Negro* breaks a single autobiographical character (Sarah) into many sacrificial subjects (duchess of Hapsburg, Queen Victoria, Jesus, Patrice Lumumba) to express the metaphysical torment of incest and rape. Like Raymond in *Funnyhouse,* Ntozake Shange's Lou, in *Spell #7,* is a choral trickster who works "blk magic" upon both characters and audience, by reordering personal/historical images (especially the minstrel mask) and conducting churchlike, ironic chants: "colored & love it being colored" (52). David Henry Hwang's *M. Butterfly* unveils the seductive stereotypes of orientalism, by reenvisioning the martyred heroine of a Western opera (played by two cross-dressing males, Asian and European).

And with *Angels in America,* Tony Kushner reconceives the disparate spirits of gay and straight America, through the martyring epidemic of AIDS.

All of these dramas, in their partial use of ritual elements, invoke the maternal chora of theater and of specific personal passions. But they also depict the primal powers of an anal father: the perverse counterpart of the Father's Law in the infantile fantasy of a phallic mother.[3] The monstrous specter of patriarchy haunts the liberative loss (or deconstructive critique) of particular metaphysical orders in each of these postmodern plays. Hence, the modern ghost of tragedy—as lost, universal, ritual truth—splits into diverse tragicomic spirits, beings of cruelty and laughter, revived by the gesting postmodern sublime.[4]

Apparently, there is no avoidance of a dark god in the Other, despite differing modern and postmodern ideals. For each view sees its nemesis in the other stage—glimpsing, as if in a mirror, a horrifying loss of identity. The postmodern revolution in theater/theory, reaching back toward the lost victims of color and gender at the margins of history in order to display them as today's tragic heroes, bears just as great a power for transcendent deception as the high modernism now out of vogue. Although theater shows us the lies of life, religion, and politics, it also encourages us, at times, to ignore the lies. Yet the best theater bears an acute self-critique of the powerful passions and thoughts arising from loss.

On the other hand, the Platonic cave of the film/TV simulacrum dominates our dramatic imaginations much of the time now, seducing us into a daily mirror stage reverie, perhaps even addiction. As we "veg" in front of the collective dream screen, gaining an illusion of ego through "remote control," the Real loss of being behind the media mirror is rarely revealed. Artaud helps us to glimpse that cruelty. Genet shows us the mirror's edges. Brecht defamiliarizes the capitalist fantasy of self. Yet today's film and TV media-cracy, with its artistic mediocrity, bears an even greater power for transcendent deception than theater. The control of the camera lens and editing cuts over millions of spectators seems, in that sense, to realize Nietzsche's desire for choral, communal vision. Indeed, some works of film and television do approach a primal symbolic *sparagmos*—if only for the most astute and compassionate spectators. But as Eliot began to see in moving from *Murder* believers to *Cocktail Party* TV-viewers, our postmodern rituals of dramatic spectatorship create a vast consumer audience, spreading thin the vision. Instead of evoking the gods of the Real,[5] or showing the Other's emptiness, film and television give us stars to worship and objects to buy, making us mimetic slaves of fashion and of the pornographic free-play of imaginary violence (which may also spark real eruptions). Thus, as the historical institution of theater succumbs more and more to the mass theatric(k)s of film and television, what is being lost—from modern to postmodern—becomes a crucial wisdom, for the theaters within our minds and in our new world disorder. If we simply indulge in the dream screen, without theatrical insight, we have much more to lose.

Notes

Introduction

1. See Lyotard, *Postmodern* 81, for a comparison of modernist nostalgia and postmodern play: "modern aesthetics is an aesthetic of the sublime, though a nostalgic one. It allows the unpresentable to be put forward only as the missing contents; but the form, because of its recognizable consistency, continues to offer to the reader or viewer matter for solace and pleasure. . . . The postmodern would be that which, in the modern, puts forward the unpresentable in presentation itself; that which denies itself the solace of good forms." See also Hassan, *Postmodern* 46–83, on the "new gnosticism" in the postmodern "play of indeterminacy and immanence."

2. *Hypertheatrical* is my term, inspired by Baudrillard's theory of the "hyperreal." But I would insist, in a more Lacanian fashion, that there is still a Real to the postmodern simulacrum: the pain of loss, actual and potential.

3. Cf. Vattimo's postmodern optimism (and weak thought): "But what exactly might this loss of reality, this genuine erosion of the principle of reality, mean for emancipation and liberation?" (8). See also Baudrillard and Debord.

4. For various views of the proto-postmodern Nietzsche, see the essays collected by Koelb in *Nietzsche as Postmodernist* and by Allison in *The New Nietzsche*. See especially Koelb's introductory comparison of "Nietzsche's pursuit of 'tragedy' and Lyotard's pursuit of 'postmodernism' " (4).

5. In my chapters on T. S. Eliot, I do not consider the influence of his mother, Charlotte Eliot. But see his introduction to her historical drama, *Savonarola,* written prior to his own modernist experiments in ritual poetic theater. Sounding almost postmodern, the son suggests the hermeneutic problem of theater's lost ritual origins as a prelude to his mother's poetic license: "*no* interpretation of a rite could explain its origin. For the meaning of a series of acts is to the performers themselves an interpretation; the same ritual remaining practically unchanged may assume different meanings for different generations of performers; and the rite may even have originated before 'meaning' meant anything at all" (viii).

6. See Clément (123), who notes Lacan's concern for "the loss of ritual in modern society," as he fought against American ego-psychology.

7. See, for example, Schechner's description of *The Tooth of Crime,* as pre-

sented by his Performance Group (*Performance* 73–84). See also Grotowski, especially 120, 157–64, and the various photos of his productions.

8. See also my essay, "The Real Edges of the Screen: Cinema's Theatrical and Communal Ghosts."

9. Lacan does describe the birth of the Real along with the subject, as a phantom *lamelle*, like the placenta born with the baby: "The price of birth is the loss of connection to that organic support." But here again the role of the mother or womb is not emphasized, as it is by Kristeva, in Lacan's psychoanalytic myth about "a reservoir of psychic energy at work behind the theater of images and symptoms" (Boothby 64).

10. See Willett 218–21 on Brecht's use of *Verfremdung* rather than *Entfremdung*. See also the example of the former that Willett gives, in Brecht's words, which in my view shows a tie to the latter: "To see one's mother as a man's wife one needs an A-effect; this is provided, for instance, when one acquires a stepfather" (qtd. in Willett 221). For examples of Brecht's use of *Entfremdung*, see Brecht, *Theatre* 71, 76n—and especially 140: "The conduct of those born before us is alienated from us by an incessant evolution."

11. I take a Lacanian position on such parental blame/credit. For example, "Lacan considered the agent of psychosis to be the *unconscious* desire of the mother" (Ragland 72). Thus, even in the case of Artaud, whom Lacan actually saw as a patient and diagnosed as psychotic, the mother is not consciously at fault—though she is a prime figure in psychic etiology.

12. Cf. Pontalis 45: "The psyche's essence would be the mother in us, that part of the mother which cares for the child, on the condition that one specifies that the child creates his mother at least as much as she creates him." Thus, he also states: "the *absent* mother makes our *inside*" (46). See also Diamond, "Mimesis," on the mimetic impulse to represent maternal origins, and Peggy Phelan: "the theatre and its mother are born in their disappearance, and the offspring of their union are men" (124). Phelan responds to Diamond's feminist critique of the lie of mimesis: "*the desire* for a true referent *is* always already the true referent of mimetic theatre. The Symbolic Mother, for example, is a copy of something that never was truly there. And because she never was there, she'll never be forgotten" (126).

Chapter 1

1. For a recent view of perversion within belief, see Dollimore, "Cultural Politics" and *Sexual Dissidence*. His postmodern project is to reclaim a "perverse dynamic" for political purposes. See also Welldon 8–9, on the perverse person's "deep belief that she [male or female] is not a whole being, but her mother's part-object."

2. This recent debate on belief and community involves many other theorists as well. See, for example, Stanley Fish and his theory of "interpretive communities." For the specific relation of this to belief, see *Doing What Comes Naturally* 142–46, and also *Is There a Text in This Class?* Fish articulated his theory in opposition to Derridean deconstruction and the "implied reader" of Wolfgang Iser. See also Fish, *Doing* 319–33, for his strong distinction between theory and

belief, and Steven Mailloux, who has extended Fish's idea toward a theory of "interpretative conventions." But cf. Brinker, who makes a distinction between beliefs and artistic conventions in relation to realism, and Hirsch, who favors Brinker's "transconventional *beliefs*" over the conventionalist view he sees dominating postmodern theory (396). On the postmodern problem of community in theater, see the final chapter of Herbert Blau's *The Audience,* where he considers Derrida's idea of the "community of the question" (from the latter's essay on Emmanuel Levinas, WD 79–153). See also Blau, *Take Up* 216, on the issue of faith.

3. For the perspective of another New Critic, between Eliot's religious faith and Richards's positivism, see Cleanth Brooks's "Religion and Literature." Brooks affirms Coleridge's formula, like Eliot; but Brooks uses it to maintain a firm distinction between religious and literary belief. The former, he says, "asks something more than a temporary suspension of disbelief" (95). Brooks, like Richards (and Lyotard), sees a danger in poetry assuming the Arnoldian function of religion: "it [then] risks limiting itself and restricting its range of belief" (103). If the "provisional beliefs of poetry harden into a fixed creed," it loses a "precious freedom." Yet, like Eliot, Brooks sees a dependent interplay between the orthodoxy of religion and the perverse beliefs of literature: "even poetry subversive of religion needs it [religion]." See also Jasper (17, 136–39).

4. In 1935 Eliot drew such a battle line himself. In "Religion and Literature" he declared "the whole of modern literature" to be "corrupted" by the "new faith" of secularism (*SE* 352–54).

5. "The working man who went to the music-hall and saw Marie Lloyd and joined in the chorus was himself performing part of the act; he was engaged in that collaboration of the audience with the artist which is necessary in all art and most obviously in dramatic art" (*SE* 407). It is the poor women of Canterbury who form the chorus in *Murder in the Cathedral* and envision the saint onstage. See also Howarth 300–306.

6. This is also true of the French poststructuralists, who have had a great influence on recent American literary, performance, and cultural theory. While Barthes, Derrida, Cixous, and Irigaray critique their phallogocentric heritage, they remain tied to that parent tradition—and more specifically to the Cartesianism (and Jansenism) of their predominantly Catholic culture, though it, too, is being challenged and changed by postcolonial, multiracial influences. (Jacques Derrida, as Algerian and Jew, is emblematic of this as well.) On Eliot's own partiality toward Jansenism, as evidenced in his introduction to Pascal's *Pensées,* see Jasper 50–51.

7. See also Eliot, *After* 24. "Furthermore, the essential of any important heresy is not simply that it is wrong: it is that it is partly right. . . . [T]he more interesting heretics . . . have an exceptionally acute perception, or profound insight, of some part of the truth." This certainly applies to the heresy of avant-garde art in relation to modernism, which also involved a "hidden dialectic" of mass culture and technology within the avant-garde as it developed into postmodernism, according to Andreas Huyssen (3–15). Christianity, too, can be seen as an offshoot, heresy, and perversion of Judaism—though probably was not by T. S. Eliot. For his relationship to Judaism, see Ricks.

8. Eliot may also be responding to Richards's concluding anecdote in his 1925 essay in *The Criterion* (which was edited by Eliot): "University societies founded fifteen years ago, for example, to discuss religion, are usually found to be discussing sex to-day" ("Background" 528).

9. In an essay entitled "Belief," published six years after *Principles of Literary Criticism,* Richards continues this distinction, using the terms "verifiable belief" and "imaginative assent" (33). Once again he insists that only the latter "is needed, or, as a rule, possible" in reading poetry. A year earlier (1929), in his essay on Dante, Eliot had used similar terms, differentiating philosophical and scientific belief from "poetic *assent*" (*SE* 218)—though he changes his view on that a few years later. Jarrett-Kerr also notes this change and sides with Eliot's later view (2–4). For a recent reexamination of this debate from Richards's side (involving, too, the perspective of Wyndham Lewis), see Russo 346–51. See also Constable, who quotes at length from Richards's unpublished notebooks to detail a critique of Eliot on belief that "should disturb us" and destabilize his "seemingly secure" prestige today (225).

10. In a footnote to his essay of 1925 in *The Criterion,* Richards had pointed directly at Eliot's *The Waste Land* as exemplifying this positive, prophetic separation of poetry from belief ("Background" 520 n. 1; also *Science* 76 n. 1). Eliot responded in 1927 in *The Enemy* (two months before his *Dial* review of Richards's book, whose sixth chapter is a revision of the *Criterion* essay): "doubt and uncertainty are merely a variety of belief" ("Note" 16). This is also the year of Eliot's baptism into the Church of England.

11. Eliot describes a correlation between orthodoxy/heterodoxy and classicism/romanticism, with a preference for the former polarity as "more fundamental." He also associates the latter term of each pair with "heresy" (*After* 21). See also Anderson, who provides a broad, yet direct examination of the shift in belief from modern to postmodern, characterizing the former as objectivist and the latter as constructivist.

12. "The term, 'democracy,' . . . does not contain enough positive content to stand alone against the forces that you dislike—it can easily be transformed by them. If you will not have God (and He is a jealous God) you should pay your respects to Hitler or Stalin" (*Idea* 64). Eliot also questions the belief in capitalism, "in compound interest and the maintenance of dividends," as not enough (65).

13. On the cruelty of Foucault's theory, deriving from Nietzsche's, see James Miller.

14. Cf. Cole's theory of tragedy as the ritual of male mourning. See also Birringer's concern with "the disappearance of theater from the evolving debates on, and the theories of, postmodern art and culture" (3).

15. Lyotard advocates an anti-Hegelian dialectic, which, as David Carroll describes it, "does not have as its end the overcoming of difference and the establishment of identity, but rather the overcoming of identity and the 'figuring' of otherness" (36). On the other hand, cf. Žižek, *Sublime,* for an antipoststructuralist recuperation of Hegel's dialectics as already figuring such otherness, in its acceptance of " 'contradiction' as an internal condition of every identity" (6). Žižek thus calls Hegel "the first post-Marxist."

16. The Senate hearings on the nomination of Clarence Thomas to the

Supreme Court and Anita Hill's accusations against him are a good example (from both sides of that political battle line) of the current desire for tragic scapegoats. So are the show trials of the Menendez brothers, the Bobbitts, and O. J. Simpson. Whatever the guilt of such celebrated figures, their fetishization by the mass media turns them into greater tragic heroes (as both victims and villains). Cf. Girard.

Chapter 2

1. For a summary of such critiques, see Hardin or Friedrich 160–66. See also Hinden for a recent argument to "revive" tragic ritual theory using Nietzsche's *Birth of Tragedy*. For specific speculations on Eliot's chorus and pattern of myth in *Murder in the Cathedral* as being connected to the work of the Cambridge anthropologists, see Clark 80–81. For a critique of the Cambridge School in relation to current performance theory, see Schechner, *Performance* 1–6, 27–28, 246.

2. "Ritualization" is a term that Ronald Grimes has developed from anthropologist Erving Goffman's "interaction ritual" and paired with Victor Turner's "social drama" (Grimes, *Ritual* 10–11, 150–57; "Turner's" 91–93). These concepts describe the "unframed" (Goffman's term), "nascent" or "decadent" potential for ritual and drama in nonreligious and nontheatrical settings.

3. The original is "Alle meine Ehrfurcht . . ." (Third Essay, section 26). Kaufmann leaves out the "my." See also Harpham 216–19, on Nietzsche's own philosophical asceticism in relation to recent poststructuralist theory. Cf. James Miller 485.

4. On the significance of Dionysus and *The Birth of Tragedy* throughout Nietzsche's oeuvre, see Porter 467–71. See also Deleuze, *Nietzsche* 9–19, on the mirroring (belief/perversion) opposition between Dionysus and Christ, from *The Birth of Tragedy* onward, in relation to Hegelian dialectics. For specific parallels between Nietzsche's Dionysus/Apollo and Zarathustra, see May 160. For a deconstruction of the Dionysus/Apollo/Socrates dialectic and its apparent genetic pattern, see de Man (chap. 4). On the "crossing" of these three figures in Nietzsche's work, see Sallis.

5. In his introduction to Pascal's *Pensées,* however, Eliot implicitly aligns his own wager of belief, as a "Christian thinker," with Newman's " 'powerful and concurrent' reasons" to be "inexorably committed to the dogma of the Incarnation" (*SE* 360).

6. E. Martin Browne, who worked with Eliot on six of his seven plays, still expressed hope in 1964 for the resurrection of this movement, though Browne admits that "the movement seems to have halted" (in his forward to William Spanos's study). This is due, he says, to "a body of critics devoted to pessimist humanism or existentialism, who seem to have an unusual degree of control over the public which . . . has not the confidence to demand the satisfaction it wants" (Spanos, *Christian* vii). Even in 1985 (in his historical study of plays presented at Canterbury Cathedral), Kenneth W. Pickering still looked forward to "new generations of playwrights, performers, and audiences" of Christian drama. However, he, too, admits that the "changed attitude towards Christianity in the post-

war years makes the presentation of explicitly Christian drama to open audiences difficult" (308). See also Speaight.

7. Even in today's postmodern, antiaesthetic stage, Eagleton sees "a new kind of transcendentalism, in which desires, beliefs and interests now occupy just those *a priori* locations which were traditionally reserved for World Spirit or the absolute ego." As an example Eagleton criticizes fellow Marxist Tony Bennett, whose "self-causing, self-validating political desire is . . . in essence aesthetic and theological" (*Ideology* 382). For a quite different perspective that is also critical of (what she calls) Marxism's "faith in the perfectibility of man," see Camille Paglia. She discovers behind the Marxist "belief that economic forces are the primary dynamic in history," a Rousseauist "Romantic naturism in disguise," which tries to deny what she believes is "the perverse daemonism" of human materiality (36–37).

8. See Erich Auerbach, *Mimesis* and "Figura." For a Derridean view of *Murder in the Cathedral* that critiques Spanos's use of Auerbach, see Beehler. Cf. Wiles 147–57 on Grotowski's *figura* in relation to Brecht and Artaud, belief and audience.

9. For a study of theater as Christian incarnation of the Word, dealing with Eliot's *The Cocktail Party* (but not yet using Bakhtin), see Harris 104–6 and passim. Harris also covers Nietzsche's *The Birth of Tragedy* in relation to Grotowski and the theologian Karl Barth (133–42).

10. Cf. Harold Bloom's intentional misreading of *Murder in the Cathedral* ("Reflections" 86–87), which shows his own anxiety about Eliot's influence. See also Bloom, *Anxiety,* and Jay. See Spanos, *Repetitions,* for his discussion of the postmodern, including a brief mention of Eliot's *Family Reunion* chorus (16).

11. Cf. Blackmur 150. Cf. also Seyhan's 1981 analysis of Nietzsche's negative theology (and the role of the struggling reader) in Eliot's *Four Quartets.*

12. See also Eigen's exploration of the role of faith in psychoanalytic treatment, which compares Lacan, Winnicott, and Bion. Eigen involves, too, Derrida's belief in language as ultimate reality (428). Unfortunately though, Eigen's stress upon Bion elides important details in the theories of Lacan and Derrida. Cf. Kristeva, *In the Beginning.*

13. The most direct influence, according to Eliot, was not Brecht but Shaw's *St. Joan.* Yet the ending was designed, Eliot said, "to shock the audience out of their complacency"—through what might be seen as a Brechtian *Gestus* of the knights' "platform prose" (*Poetry* 30). See also Browne, *Making* 53, 60.

14. Cf. Schechner, *Performance* 155–66.

15. Gerald Else has attempted to counteract this "traditional" view of the origin of Greek tragedy in ritual. See in particular 10–11, for his attack upon Nietzsche's perpetuation of it, based, Else says, on an oversimplified reading of Aristotle that Nietzsche then "visionalizes." It becomes clear, however, in Else's own reading of Aristotle that he is trying to separate an ideal form of tragedy from "the actual satyrs of Greek legend and drama [who] were subhuman, 'good-for-nothing' creatures distinguished above all by braggadocio, cowardice, and lechery" (15–16). See also Silk and Stern's refutation of Else in regard to Nietzsche (147). Mason has recently, like Else (in 1967), tried to sever tragedy from religious

ritual by lessening the importance of the chorus (166). See also Toepfer 20–38. For an overview of other theorists in this debate, see Hardin.

16. Cf. Weber 65–83, who uses the term "thallus" to elaborate Freud's description of the dream navel *(Knäuel)* as being like the mycelium of a mushroom—in opposition to Lacan's return to it as a central, phallic abyss *(béance)*. On Nietzsche's Dionysus and primal chorus as "imaginary projection[s]," see Porter 483.

17. Julia Kristeva's theory of the chora takes this Greek term from Plato's *Timaeus,* where it means Receptacle (or enclosed space) of Becoming. Kristeva applies it to both the female body and linguistics, through Lacanian psychoanalysis. It thus designates both the lost, abject womb (from which the infant must separate to join the symbolic order) and the preverbal semiotic space that persists within language: "the place where the subject is both generated and negated" *(Revolution* 25–28). See also Kristeva, *Revolution* 46–59, 152; *Powers* 14–18; and Barzilai.

18. Eliot defines the term *objective correlative* as "a set of objects, a situation, a chain of events which shall be the formula of that *particular* emotion; such that when the external facts, which must terminate in sensory experience, are given, the emotion is immediately evoked" *(SE* 145). Cf. Schechner, *Performance* 286 n. 14.

19. Barish ties antitheatricalism, in Nietzsche's particular case and more generally, to anti-Semitism (414, 464–67). For Eliot's relation to anti-Semitism, see Ricks and Julius.

20. Perhaps the best theater is always impossible. See Herbert Blau's *The Impossible Theatre: A Manifesto.* Lacan has also connected the Real to the impossible. See translator's note on "Imaginary, Symbolic, Real" *(Four* 280 or *Écrits* x).

21. See Del Caro for a critique of Derrida's view of women and use of Nietzsche in *Spurs.*

22. See Guthrie 30–35, 147–48, 154. More recently, Vernant has described "the Dionysiac religion . . . [as] first and foremost the province of women" (324). Guthrie, following Dodds, insists that this religion migrated to Greece from Thrace and Phrygia, where the Asiatic mother goddess, Kybele, was worshiped (154). But Otto claims it is indigenous to Greece (52–64). Kerenyi sees its origins in Minoan Crete, which had "a single deity, a Great Goddess" (8). Detienne uses the variety of mythic origins of Dionysus to describe his distinctive presence *(parousia)* as epidemic arrival, infecting women. For archaeological evidence of a Neolithic (seventh to third millennia B.C.) earth goddess worshiping "civilization" throughout Europe, prior to the invasion of sky god worshiping, patriarchal Indo-Europeans from the East, see Gimbutas, *The Language of the Goddess* and *The Civilization of the Goddess.* See also Neumann. For recent feminist returns to the mother goddess in relation to narrative fiction, see Nina Auerbach, and Gilbert and Gubar.

23. See David Fisher for a further reading of Nietzsche through Kristeva. See also Sena, who finds the Great Mother goddess behind the mask of Nietzsche's Dionysus, as "feminine/maternal potency," both threatening and healing (201).

24. Cf. Kristeva, *Powers* 100. There she relates the "archaic Mother Goddess who actually haunted the imagination" of Judaic monotheism to the personal chora: "phantasmatic mother who also constitutes, in the specific history of each person, the abyss that must be established . . . so that such a person might learn to speak." See also her essay, "Stabat Mater" (*Tales* 234–63). For more on the mother goddess tradition within (and prior to) Judeo-Christianity, see James 201–3, 249–60; Patai; Preston (particularly the essays by Campbell and Sandstrom); and Turner and Turner. Cf. also Thomson on the "exclusion of the mother" in ancient Greek democracy (189), and the triumph of patriarchy over the matrilineal in the *Oresteia* (chap. 15).

25. Cf. Derrida's discussion of a de-phallogocentric God in Coward and Foshay's *Derrida and Negative Theology* (especially in chapter 3, Derrida's "How to Avoid Speaking: Denials"). Cf. also Marion.

26. Cf. Wiles 6–7, 29–30, concerning the translation of Aristotle's *katharsis* as "purification" rather than "purgation," in relation to Freud, Stanislavsky, and Brecht. On specific precedents to Nietzsche's Dionysian passions in the philosophical heritage of German Romanticism, see Baeumer.

27. Cf. Worthen 123–31 on the rhetorical role of the audience in relation to the *Murder* chorus (without reference to Nietzsche). See also Nietzsche's chorus of animals who try to arouse their hero, Zarathustra, to believe again in his own doctrine of eternal recurrence—as "the wheel of being" (*Zarathustra* 329). Thomas Altizer views this apotheosis of Being as a transvaluation of the "Jesus [who] stands outside Christianity" into the "new Zarathustra" (238–45). Similarly, Paul Valadier connects the dithyrambic chorus of Dionysus to Zarathustra's (255–56) and relates both figures to "the non-Pauline Jesus" (250). Cf. Stock 354–55, on the Dionysian (and animal) "fluting" of Eliot's *Murder* chorus. Both the decentering, poststructuralist Nietzsche and the (anti)theological Nietzsche can be found in the profound ambiguity of a single sentence spoken by Zarathustra's animal chorus: "The center is everywhere" (330).

28. Cf. French psychoanalyst J.-B. Pontalis's correlation of the dream to the maternal body and mental fetish (27–48).

29. In "Kant avec Sade," Lacan describes the sadist as "reject[ing] the pain of existing into the Other, but without seeing that by this slant he himself changes into an 'eternal object'" ("Kant" 65). See also Lacan, *Four* 135: "the sadist himself occupies the place of the object, but without knowing it, to the benefit of another, for whose *jouissance* he exercises his action as sadistic pervert." Lacan's view relates to Freud's that sadism and masochism are "active and passive forms" of the same perversion, "habitually found to occur together in the same individual" (*SE* 7:159). Lacan states that "sadism is merely the disavowal of masochism" (*Four* 186). See also Freud, *SE* 19:164.

30. On Nietzsche's proto-Freudian encounter in *The Birth of Tragedy* with "the disquieting interrelation between pleasure and pain," see Nagele (93).

31. Wyndham Lewis saw and disliked this link between Eliot and Richards on the point of depersonalization. For a summary and critique of Lewis's perspective, see John Paul Russo 348–49.

32. "Extimate" *(extime)* is a Lacanian neologism meaning excluded from, yet intimate to. See, for example, Ragland-Sullivan, "*Hamlet*" 35. See also Žižek,

Sublime 132, 180, for the *extimité* of *das Ding*—the *objet a* "in the very heart of the subject"—as a kernel of the Real within, yet inaccessible to, the Symbolic order.

33. Hardison's work also shows a significant divergence from Frazer and the Cambridge School. See Hardin 852–53.

34. Cf. Speaight 126–67. Eliot also situates a Latin liturgy, the blessing of candidates by the bishop, in part 2 of *The Rock* 61–64.

35. Nietzsche's father and grandfather were both Lutheran ministers. His father died when he was four years old and apparently did haunt him to some degree in later life. In *Ecce Homo* Nietzsche states: "I am, to express it in the form of a riddle, already dead as my father, while as my mother I am still living and becoming old" (222). Cf. Harpham 203.

36. Scarry's structural analysis of belief ranges from political torture, to war, to scenes of wounding in the Old Testament, where she employs a theatrical paradigm (197), to the secular fetishes of capitalism.

37. This unfolding stone-curtain-chorus, being itself a fetish, correlates also to Freud's explanation of why "pieces of underclothing" are often "chosen" as fetishes; they "crystallize the moment of undressing, the last moment in which the woman could still be regarded as phallic" (*SE* 21:155).

38. Kaja Silverman's *The Acoustic Mirror* deals with cinema rather than theater, with the maternal/female voice in the mirror stage apparatus of film. Yet my adaptation of her phrase, which she borrows from French psychoanalyst Guy Rosolato (Silverman 80), is also meant to imply the intersection of audience and performer as camera/projector at the edge of the "live" theatrical stage. Cf. Metz 74–76 on the cinematic apparatus as fetish. Feminists film theorists have described the spectator as male in relation to such a fetishistic (and voyeuristic) apparatus. See, for example, Mulvey, "Visual Pleasure," and E. Ann Kaplan (especially chapter 1, "Is the Gaze Male?"). Although I also describe the fetishistic and voyeuristic elements of theater, I would not define the spectator as one gender or the other, since I see him/her as polymorphously perverse—bearing both a feminine chora and patriarchal desire.

39. Cf. Schechner's theatrical application (*Between* 109–14) of psychoanalyst D. W. Winnicott's theory of the "transitional space" between mother and infant.

40. Breach, crisis, redress, and reintegration are phases Turner describes in social drama. Out of redress comes ritual, both in a broad and strict sense, and thence, through reflexivity, stage drama. See Turner, *From Ritual* 10, 108; Grimes, "Turner's" 80–81 or *Ritual* 174–76.

41. Cf. Grimes, *Ritual* 25–27.

42. Cf. Lyotard, *Postmodern* 23, 27, 77–82; Derrida, *Grammatology* 73, 304–15 and passim; "Living On" 146 and passim.

Chapter 3

1. See Savran 7, 52, 96, 102–32. *The Cocktail Party* did receive a more conventional off-off-Broadway production in 1988, by the Jean Cocteau Repertory, under the direction of Eve Adamson. See also Chamberlain's analysis of the paltry audiences for the West End revival in 1986. On the 1993 production of *Mur-*

der in the Cathedral by the Royal Shakespeare Company at Stratford-upon-Avon, which updated the twelfth-century martyrdom to the 1930s (when Eliot's play was originally performed) and reduced the chorus to four women, see Jones.

2. Cf. Frye 218. He describes the "chorus or chorus character" as being "the embryonic germ of comedy in tragedy."

3. Cf. Derrida, *Spurs,* on woman as untruth, and Lacan, *Feminine* 137–61, on the Woman who does not exist—though feminine *jouissance* supports the "God face" of the Other (147).

4. "Affection and hostility in the treatment of the fetish," says Freud, "run[s] parallel with the disavowal and the acknowledgement of castration" (*SE* 21:157)—i.e., belief and disbelief in the maternal phallus.

5. I use the terms *(m)other* and *(m)Other* to convey the primordial, but not sole meaning of the lost other—also in the Lacanian sense of the Other—as mother. (Cf. Ragland-Sullivan, *Lacan* 294–97 and Sprengnether 10, 233–46.) This in itself refers to one's personal history, yet I will also use the term *mother goddess* in relation to Western history with its many indigenous and marginalized Other religions characteristically involving the worship of mother earth and nature, rather than of sky gods (as in ancient Greece) or of one patriarchal God (as in Christendom). But I do not mean to homogenize this (m)Other, nor to set up a simple binary relationship. See also Lacan, *Feminine* 144, 168 and Ragland-Sullivan, *Lacan* 288–89, on "the Woman," who does not exist, as being a symptom of human belief.

6. Eliot went on to criticize this "device" (in his essay of 1951) with its demand for an "immediate transition" between individual characters and chorus (*Poetry* 33). See Browne, *Making* 127, for a director's perspective on this difficult demand.

7. For a Derridean "dis-closure" of this circle, see Beehler, "Troping." He also describes in Eliot's Eumenides a "radically Nietzschean Will to Power in the will to the reaffirmation of originating difference" (34).

8. The cathartic cure in Lacanian treatment, unlike other psychotherapies, is not a purgation of the symptom, but rather an identification with it as *sinthome* (Žižek, *Sublime* 75). Lacan used this term (the medieval French spelling of symptom) late in his career to signify a fourth order beyond Imaginary, Symbolic, and Real (Ragland 146). Žižek lists some of the associations of this neologism: "synthetic-artificial man, synthesis between symptom and fantasy, Saint Thomas, the saint." He defines it as "a certain signifying formation penetrated with enjoyment," and also points out that it is "literally our only substance, the only positive support of our being" (75). See also Ragland-Sullivan's definition: "the particularity of the *jouissance* deposited in a given subject's fiction and body" (*"Hamlet"* 31).

9. Cf. Žižek, *Sublime* 74: "When we are confronted with a patient's symptoms, we must first interpret them and penetrate through them to the fundamental fantasy as the kernel of enjoyment which is blocking the further movement of interpretation; then we must accomplish the crucial step of going through the fantasy, of obtaining distance from it, of experiencing how the fantasy-formation just masks, fills out a certain void, lack, empty place in the Other."

10. For closer parallels between *The Family Reunion* and the *Oresteia,* see Carpentier. She finds that Eliot's play is very much "modeled on the [Aeschylean]

trilogy in which the laws and customs of the old matriarchal, earth-bound religion are emphatically superseded by a patriarchal religion of the spirit in which godhead is above nature. And, like Aeschylus, Eliot confronts and resolves a matricidal impulse that is as profoundly and universally human as the oedipal impulse" (20). Cf. Thomson 229–77.

11. Cf. Kahn 12, who prefers "idolization" to "idealization" (12).

12. See also Welldon and Louise Kaplan.

13. Jessica Benjamin sees herself, and others of the "object relations tendency in American psychoanalysis," as going beyond Freud's Oedipal model, which "denies the necessity of mutual recognition between man and woman" (177–81).

14. See Sprengnether.

15. See Lacan, *Feminine* 137–47.

16. R. D. Stock also sees Harcourt-Reilly as Dionysian (355–56). Cf. Grover Smith on various aspects of shamanism in *The Cocktail Party,* and Virginia Phelan for a detailed comparison of Euripides' *Alcestis* and Eliot's play. Phelan views women as "the center" in both dramas (136).

17. According to Marcel Detienne, "Dionysos' personality is deeply colored by his status as a stranger" (10).

18. See Lacan's extension of this term (originally used by Ernest Jones), *Four* 207–29. See also Kubiak 13, on Lacanian *aphanisis* in relation to Artaud.

19. For more on the Nietzschean death of God in relation to Eliot's drama, see Spanos, *Christian* 24–25 and Scott ix, 15, 166–67.

20. Cf. Chamberlain, who judges such success as "surely deceptive," noting the very small audiences at the play's 1986 London revival and criticizing it for "never truly [having] been suited to please a wide audience" (512).

21. Leavell finds that "Celia fits Nietzsche's description of the hero even more exactly than the more obvious tragic heroes, Harry and Thomas, do in their respective plays" (124). Cf. Ward 184–85, who finds neither *Murder* nor *Family Reunion* to be "true tragedies" in the Aristotelian sense, yet sees in them "the essence of tragedy in its ritual function and communal purpose." Ward calls *The Cocktail Party* "a satyr play with a sub-plot, centered around Celia, which [also] reflects the pattern of tragedy" (205). More recently, Robin Grove has described all of Eliot's plays written between 1939 and 1958, from *Family Reunion* and *Cocktail Party* to *The Confidential Clerk* and *The Elder Statesman,* as "ritual[s] of extinction"—like *Murder in the Cathedral,* but set in "the three-walled stage-box of the genteel home" (166).

22. Cf. Savran 131–32.

23. See Sharma, especially 131–32, 140–41, for a brief analysis of Eliot's plays in relation to dramatic levels and levels of consciousness.

24. Cf. Spanos 214. He points out an "existential anguish" in the chorus's final lines of *The Family Reunion.*

25. See, in particular, Eliot, *Notes* 50. See also McCallum 139, for an analysis of Eliot's "occlusion of ethics by religion" in his later essays on culture.

26. Cf. Selmon, for a recent semiotic (though not specifically postcolonial) evaluation of Celia's death: "it is fitting that her body be eaten, for in the mouth flesh becomes word" (508).

27. See Moody 186–91, on the fear of women in Eliot's drama, from *Murder*

to *Family Reunion* and *Cocktail Party,* as related to his own marriage with Vivien(ne). See also Gibert-Maceda on the influence of various women upon Eliot's work, including that of his mother, Charlotte Eliot (who was also a dramatist/poet), as well as his wife Vivien (113).

28. For Eliot's own hysteria, with Pound as his analyst, in their collaboration upon *The Waste Land,* see Koestenbaum. He describes that text as female (115), and finds that it "lost meaning" as female and revolutionary language when Eliot surrendered it to Pound, like "the hysterical discourse of Anna O. . . . when it was exchanged between Breuer and Freud" (136).

29. Cf. Lacan, *Four* 12. "So hysteria places us, I would say, on the track of some kind of original sin in analysis. . . . The truth is perhaps simply . . . that something, in Freud, was never analysed." For a recent feminist critique, through Lacan, of Ibsenesque realism as being "itself a form of hysteria," see Diamond, "Realism" 60. She describes a parallel relationship between melodrama/realism and Charcot/Freud. Cf. also Szasz, for a medical critique (originally in 1961, without reference to Lacan) of hysteria as being the fundamental "myth of mental illness" in psychoanalysis. For a summary and repudiation of Szasz's position, see Merskey 237–40.

30. See also Sprengnether 41–54 and Jacobus 137–93.

31. Eliot continued to have that dream, at least on the musical side, despite dispensing with the chorus. In 1951 he stated: "I have before my eyes a kind of mirage of the perfection of verse drama, . . . such as to present at once the two aspects of dramatic and musical order" (*Poetry* 43). Cf. Fergusson, who gives directions for the "ideal perfection of the chorus" of *Murder in the Cathedral* (like, he says, in Wagner's *Tristan*): "the performers would make it [Eliot's chorus] come alive by understanding the music rather than by understanding poor old women" (219).

32. See Veith 1–24. Both Veith (7) and Bernheimer's introduction to *In Dora's Case* (3) quote Plato's statement that the "womb is an animal which longs to bear children."

33. See McGrath 165–66. Also, cf. Cixous and Clément, especially 3–17.

34. See Bernheimer's introduction to *In Dora's Case,* 6–8, 17. Lacan learned from his hysterics that "man's desire is the desire of the Other" and eventually described psychoanalysis as the "hystericization of discourse" (*Four* 38; *Feminine* 161 n. 6). But, as Žižek reminds, psychoanalysis "also de-hystericizes the subject." This Žižek compares to "the perverse position" (*Sublime* 181). For a critique of Lacan's position on hysteria, see David-Ménard.

35. Cf. Wade, who sees the Hindu *maya* in Eliot's play but does not refer to Nietzsche.

36. Cf. Wallace Stevens's phrase, "disillusion as the last illusion," in "An Ordinary Evening in New Haven" (468). This, particularly in relation to Eliot's play, is an apt response to the would-be demystifiers of Ibsen's and O'Neill's plays, and of recent critical theory. Cf. Blau, *To All* 2–3.

37. Cf. Sharratt (229), who has recently argued that "Eliot's work initiates a logic which can illuminate current notions of postmodernism, and that his ways of negotiating his particular cultural situation pre-echo some features of what is currently meant by postmodernism."

Chapter 4

1. I have chosen to quote from Watson's 1948 translation (of excerpts), because it reflects how Artaud's mad *écriture* was immediately transformed into conventional discourse. For a complete, yet more fragmented translation of *Van Gogh le suicidé de la société*, see *Antonin Artaud: Selected Writings* (*SW*) 483–519. Also, the 1948 translation directly influenced the work of R. D. Laing (Esslin 61; Hayman 144–45), which preceded the "schizoanalysis" of Deleuze and Guattari. (Esslin states in his preface that he has "discussed some of the implications of Artaud's psychiatric history" with R. D. Laing [7].)

2. See Esslin 107–13.

3. Cf. Greene 220–21 and Podol 518–19. See also science fiction writer Samuel R. Delany's comparison of the modernist Wagner and postmodern Artaud, with reference also to Nietzsche (74).

4. Cf. Toepfer, who criticizes both Nietzsche and Artaud for their "confused notion of an orgiastic public theatre" (38). See also Brustein 371 and Sontag xxxviii–xli.

5. Cf. Esslin 12–14, 74, 106, and Sontag lviii. See also Barber, "Foundry," Caws, and Maddox 208, for recent views of Artaud's shamanistic power.

6. See Barthes, "The Death of the Author," *Image* 142–48 and Foucault, "What Is an Author?" in *Language* 113–38.

7. Cf. Costich 54 and Esslin 71, 80, 87. Cf. also Auslander's distinction between therapeutic catharsis (with Artaud and Grotowski) and theatrical communion (according to Jacques Copeau and Peter Brook): "in Artaud's theatre this profound amelioration is achieved through purgation, not communion" (23). But Auslander limits the meaning of communion to a collective "emotional harmony" (16), as "benign" experience through "optimistic" faith (21). See also Baker-White, who disputes Auslander's emphasis upon the "individualist" rather than "collectivist" Artaud (199–200). On Grotowski's elaboration of Artaudian catharsis, see Wiles 119–57.

8. On similarities and differences between Artaud and Brecht, see Hertz, Kenny, and Nagele (chap. 5). See also Friedrich's "Deconstructed Self" and "Drama and Religion." In the latter he contrasts Artaud's work as "re-ritualization" and Brecht's as "de-ritualization" (207–12).

9. It also reflects Artaud's Catholic upbringing, according to Hayman 39–40, 67. On Artaud's gnosticism, see Hayman 87–89, Esslin 16–17, and especially Goodall, *Artaud*. Plunka also explains Artaud's gnosticism with reference to Nietzsche: "the gnostics reject the Apollonian and gravitate towards the Dionysian, the evil, dark forces of the universe. Gnostics believe that the psyche is a victim of demonic powers that relentlessly prey on the spirit in a world without divine intervention" (21). Cf. Hassan, *Postmodern* 46–83, on the "new gnosticism" of the postmodern.

10. For a highly sympathetic view of Artaudian alchemy, see Bettina Knapp's *Antonin Artaud,* and also her *Theatre and Alchemy.* For an attempt to create a systematic acting method out of Artaud's theories, see Mark Rose.

11. Of course film (and television) can also be artistically expressive at times. On the relation between Artaud's "vocal writing" and cinema, see Barthes, *Plea-*

sure 66–67. See also Kristeva, "Theatre," and Esslin 94–95. In the 1920s Artaud was quite enamored of film. See, for example, *CW* 3:21. "The human skin of things, the derm of reality—this is the cinema's first toy."

12. Cf. Hayman 94.

13. See especially Kristeva, *Revolution* 5, 103, 149–56, 186; *Powers* 25–26; *Desire* 80, 84, 132–45, 164, 191; *Tales* 235; and *Reader* 236. See also Hayman 160–62 and Goodall, "Plague" 531–32, 540.

14. See Goodall, "Plague" 534, or *Artaud* 117–18. She points to Seneca's *Oedipus* as more Artaudian (in its dwelling upon the plague) than Sophocles'.

15. For a reapplication of Deleuze and Guattari to Artaud, see Goodall, "Plague." In the end, though, she prefers Kristeva's chora (which she sees in their "body without organs") as being closer to Artaud's gnosticism (540). Yet, Goodall also distinguishes her view of Artaud from Kristeva's own (*Artaud* 37). For a critique of Deleuze and Guattari, as ignoring or romanticizing the real terror of schizophrenia, see Edwards.

16. For Artaud's *Collected Works*, Victor Corti translates *esprit* in this sentence as "mind" (*CW* 1:153), rather than Helen Weaver's translation as "spirit." See also Hayman 66, who quotes part of this sentence using "spirit" in a slightly different way.

17. See Fly for a comparison of cruelty in Artaud and Shakespeare.

18. In analyzing Blanchot's *L'arrêt de mort*, Derrida is careful to excise the traditional notion of stage presence, though the sense of it returns in a different way, as "presence*less* presence," or presence in absence ("Living On" 146). See also Derrida's relationship to negative theology, described in his three essays in Coward and Foshay.

19. In adapting Artaud's "body without organs" to anti-Oedipal schizoanalysis, Deleuze and Guattari also draw upon Nietzsche's proclamation of the death of God. But they interpret this modern loss of God as the immemorial trap of a transcendent patriarchy, subjugating its otherwise self-engendering children through mourning and guilt. Paranoiac fathers project guilt upon their sons, perpetuating the reign of the dead Father/God (275). Yet the atheistic schizoanalysis of Nietzsche and Artaud would liberate us from the structure of Oedipal belief—according to Deleuze and Guattari.

20. "The origin of theatre, such as it must be restored [by Artaud], is the hand lifted against the abusive wielder of the logos . . . against the God of a stage" (Derrida, *WD* 239). Cf. Dominque Fisher 83–107, who critiques Derrida (wrongly, I think) as "los[ing] sight of the fact that Artaud is first of all speaking about a theatrical representation" (107).

21. In a long note to "La parole soufflée," Derrida describes many similarities between Artaud's and Nietzsche's dreams of an originary theater (327 n. 31). But Derrida finds a final distinction between them in Nietzsche's desire to liberate the theater through music and dance. Cf. Goodall, *Artaud* 213–20. She accuses Derrida of substituting Nietzsche's God for Artaud's, and of occupying "the site of Artaud's discourse so as to steal it away" (217). She thus tries to save Artaud's "gnostic drama" from its poststructuralist "foreclosure" (219). For a Peircean critique of Derrida's essays on Artaud, see Smith, "Semiotics" 301–5.

22. The uterine signifier can also be seen, through the mirror of the oriental

Other, in the Hindu *yoni* (vulval icon), which corresponds to the phallic *lingam*. But note this Lacanian caveat from Ellie Ragland: "Because of the confusion between Woman and mother, woman comes to signify a totality or an essence in masculine fantasy where she is partialized, fetishized, and sought on the slope of the real, *outside* representable meaning" (193).

23. Cf. Mulvey, "Oedipus," on Laius as perverse pre-Oedipal father.

24. For a detailed examination of Freud's avoidance of the "spectral mother" throughout his career, see Sprengnether.

25. Welldon sees the Electra complex as "unnecessary" as a parallel for the Oedipus, "when Jocasta already fulfils that role" (86). But she also admits that the Jocasta myth lacks the story of maternal incest throughout early childhood, since Oedipus was given away shortly after birth (98). Thus, Welldon also develops an alternate term, the "whore/madonna complex" (110–11). Using Winnicott's terms, she characterizes the perverse mother as treating the child (particularly in the first two years of its life) as an extension of her own body—as a "transitional object." This is also characteristic of the difference between male and female perversion. "Whereas in men the act is aimed at an external part-object, in women it is against themselves: either against their bodies or against objects of their own creation—that is, their babies" (72). Cf. Louise Kaplan 199–200, and Cixous and Clément 50–52.

26. Welldon is, in fact, antiphallocentric: "why should a woman's body become a phallus in fantasy—why should it not instead represent important, complex, and uniquely feminine physical, physiological, and symbolic characteristics?" (26). See also her Kleinian valorization of the breast over the penis (31), and her exclusion of the paternal line in the "three-generational process" of becoming a mother: "a woman becomes her mother and her mother's mother" (49). Cf. Louise Kaplan 78–105, for an antiphallocentric version of the female castration complex.

27. Welldon explicitly attacks theories of sexual development "based on a need for an ever-present 'earth-mother,' a woman who has been so idealized or perhaps even idolized that her faults are overlooked." She includes in this criticism "the new feminists," who idolize Woman as "the victim of social attitudes," and thus are complicit in society's failure to accord women "any sense of responsibility for their own unique functions, deeply related to fecundity and motherhood, and liable at times to manifest themselves perversely" (86). Cf. Doane and Hodges 31–32: "as feminists, we too can fall prey [like Winnicott] to the fantasy or desire for an idealized mother."

28. This, as Hayman puts it, "made the family bonds all the closer. Surrounded for most of the time by females, the young Antonin was subjected to a bewildering alternation between maternal tenderness and disciplinarian prohibitions, between Greek pastries and unpalatable medicines" (36). Hayman also relates this female environment of Artaud's childhood to his "empathy" with the Roman emperor, Heliogabalus, "high priest of a phallic cult," who became the subject of a novel by Artaud (93). See Stout for further details on the "maternal quartet" of perverse mother, grandmother-sisters, and aunt, who surround the hero in that novel, *Héliogabale,* making him "a pawn in a matriarchal scheme"

(419). See also Jacobs for a deconstructive reading of the novel "by way of *The Theater and Its Double*" (55).

29. Jocasta does this, too, by saving the infant Oedipus from death, as the prince of Corinth, thus allowing him to become king of Thebes.

30. Hayman describes Artaud's maternal grandmother as having "a very close relationship with her grandson, often coming from Smyrna to visit the Artauds at Marseilles, while they often took holidays at Smyrna to be with her" (38). See also Esslin 15: "Artaud remained deeply attached to his two grand-mothers throughout his life. In his correspondence from the asylum at Rodez both make their appearance in the group of female figures—sometimes referred to as his daughters—whom he cherished with almost religious veneration." See, too, Knapp, *Artaud* 3–4 and Greene 15. Cf. Artaud, *SW* 540: "soot of grandma's ass, / much more than of father-mother's."

31. See also Artaud's "Letter to the Clairvoyante," *CW* 1:93–97. He idolizes this female mystic in erotic terms, with an explicit transference: "I know you are in all my vital centres and much closer to me than my mother. It is as if I were naked before you. Naked, unchaste and naked, upright, like a ghost of myself, but unashamed, for in your eyes running dizzily through my sinews, evil is really sinless" (93). He also adds a note to the general reader of this published letter: "I cannot help it. I felt like this in front of Her" (95 n. 1).

32. Artaud also used this maternal surname in 1937, in opposition to his paternal one, to identify himself (doubled) with both a false and real Jesus Christ: "I was on Golgotha two thousand years ago and my name was, as always, Artaud, and I detested the priests and God, and that was why I was crucified by the priests of Jehovah. . . . I know that filthy swine . . . who had himself accepted as resurrected in the light under the name of Jesus-Christ. When in fact he was none other than a certain M. Nalpas" (qtd. in Esslin 103).

33. For most of her career, Melanie Klein emphasized the breast and womb as primary objects of the infantile ego's initial relations. But in 1956 (a few years before her death) she recognized, along with the good/bad breast outside and innate love/hate within, "various processes of splitting, such as fragmenting the ego" (216). See also 180. For a Lacanian view of Klein's theories, see Ragland-Sullivan, *Lacan* 19–24, 35–36, 294; Ragland 23, 39, 56–58, 172; and Guéguen.

34. Deleuze and Guattari claim to take their liberative, anti-Oedipal cue from Lacan's return to the Freudian Oedipus (308–10, 328, 360). For a critique of Deleuze and Guattari's use of Lacan, see Ragland-Sullivan, *Lacan* 271–73. Artaud was actually treated by Lacan in 1938–39 at the Sainte Anne asylum in Paris. See Barber, *Artaud* 9, 99–100, on the hostility between this doctor and patient. For a recent and very detailed Lacanian analysis of Artaud's psychotic schizophrenia, see Pireddu.

35. See Juliet Mitchell's introductory note in Klein 116 on her use of the term *position* rather than *stage*. With this term Klein "substitutes a structural for a developmental notion." Thus (like Lacan's "mirror stage"), "a 'position' is an always available state, not something one passes through." While Klein describes the paranoid-schizoid and depressive positions as necessary, developmental periods that the child must "work through" (177), they are never completely left behind.

36. Cf. Deleuze and Guattari 14–15. They strongly endorse Artaud's apparently anti-Oedipal statement: "I don't believe in father or mother, / don't have papa-mama" (*SW* 550). Yet they do not quote, a few lines later in Artaud's *Here Lies,* the return of the paternal ghost.

> and above all not the mouth of being,
> sewer hole drilled with teeth
> where he's always watching himself
> the man who sucks his substance
> from me,
> to take from me a papa-mama,
> and remake himself an existence
> free of me
> on my corpse
>
> (*SW* 550–51)

In this poem, written a year before his death, Artaud shows, in my view, a desperate resistance to the Oedipal papa-mama still plaguing him, not a successful breakthrough. Cf. Pireddu 64 n. 8.

37. See also Klein 218, on "the combined parent figure, expressed in such phantasies as the mother or the mother's breast containing the penis of the father."

38. See also Klein 186, 190. Cf. Kristeva, *Tales* 33–35 and *Black Sun* 47–51.

39. See Knapp, *Artaud* 4–5, 23, for an account of Artaud's lifelong headaches in relation to his drug addiction and mysticism. See also Hayman 2–3 and Esslin 17–18, 99–100.

40. Cf. Greene 16: "Artaud knew instinctively how to use his illness to manipulate his mother for the usual childish ends."

41. See Knapp, *Artaud* 8–9 on Artaud's physical awkwardness as an actor—though this also had a spellbinding effect on spectators, particularly when he played older characters. Cf. Esslin 22, who, like Knapp, quotes from Jean Hort's description of Artaud onstage, but interprets it differently. Hayman simply quotes from Hort without comment (48). See also Anaïs Nin's description of Artaud giving a lecture in 1933: "He was enacting his own death, his own crucifixion" (qtd. in Hayman 89).

42. Cf. Artaud, *SW* 525: "It's the turn of the whole earth / against someone who has balls / in his cunt."

43. Costich also notices the "theme of incest, suggested by the young people" in this play (28).

44. In the meantime, *The Spurt of Blood* also influenced the theater of the absurd, as Knapp mentions (*Artaud* 32).

45. Cf. Knapp, *Artaud* 33. She views the knight as an "emotional weakling," because he is an "adult-boy" who still needs the nourishment of the "Nurse-Mother."

46. See Knapp, *Artaud* 33: "Switzerland, referred to by Rabelais as the Vatican of the Calvinists, is implied here."

47. Cf. Artaud, *Peyote* 13, 70, and *SW* 557, 559, 562. See also Knapp, *Artaud* 139.

48. Cf. Knapp, *Artaud* 34. She mentions that this is like a miracle play.

49. As Derrida puts it, the "rules of hieroglyphics" which Artaud finds in non-Western cosmogonies are not "controlled by the institution of the [logocentric] voice" (*WD* 191).

50. In "La parole soufflée," Derrida often performs in an Artaud-like voice, speaking his own Derridean interpretations of Artaud directly as if Artaud were speaking them—as if both minds had one voice.

51. For an archetypal, Jungian reading of dismemberment in *The Philosopher's Stone,* see Knapp, *Artaud* 106–8.

52. Cassel describes the Tarahumara "cave people," in his study of them in 1969, as "the most primitive of the North American Indians" (xi, 3). See also Artaud's condemnation of the American people for their "warlike imperialism of early America that caused the pre-Columbian Indian to be degraded" (*SW* 568). For a Jungian view of Artaud's experience with the Tarahumara, in relation to various Aztec gods, see Knapp, "Mexico." See also Arata, who uses the Mayan *Popol Vuh* to analyze Artaud's Tarahumara trip. For a gnostic interpretation, see Goodall, *Artaud* 155–64.

53. Cf. Knapp, *Artaud* 106. She relates the stone in this play to the ring (and gold) of the Nibelungs in Wagner, as the treasure of psychological identity. See also Knapp, "Mexico" 64.

54. In Ireland in 1937, only a year since his participation in the peyote ritual of the Tarahumara, Artaud began taking Communion, after two decades away from the Catholic Church. But in 1945, after a year of electroshock therapy at the Rodez asylum, he rejected Christianity again, claiming in a letter to have thrown the Eucharist out of his window (Hayman 125–29).

55. See Artaud, *SW* 567: "when they pressure me / and when they handle me / until the exit / from me / of nourishment, / of my nourishment / and its milk, / and what remains?"

56. "Defecation, the 'daily separation with the feces, precious parts of the body' (Freud), is, as birth, as my birth, the initial theft which simultaneously depreciates me and soils me. This is why the history of God as a genealogy of stolen value is recounted as the history of defecation" (Derrida, *WD* 182).

57. "Like excrement, like the turd . . . a metaphor for the penis, the work *should* stand upright. But the work, as excrement, is but matter without life, without force or form. It always collapses as soon as it is outside me. . . . Thus salvation, status, uprightness, will only be possible in an art without works. The work always being the work of death, the art without works—dance or the theater of cruelty—will be the art of life itself" (Derrida, *WD* 183). For a critique of this aspect of Derrida's analysis of Artaud, see Goodall, "Artaud's Revision" 115–17. However, Goodall fails to historicize this view of Artaud as referring to the final stage of his writings.

58. Cf. Lacan, *Four* 264.

59. Artaud also wrote an adaptation of Seneca's *Atreus and Thyestes,* which has since been lost (Greene 38). In adapting Shelley's *The Cenci,* Artaud used Stendhal's translation of a historical account from the sixteenth century (Knapp,

Artaud 112). Cf. Artaud's comment, expressing his anxiety of such influence: "I drew my play from Shelley and Stendhal, which does not mean that I either adapted Shelley or imitated Stendhal" (Blin et al. 103).

60. See *SW* 340–42, Artaud's letter to André Gide, asking him to attend a pre-production reading of *The Cenci*. "I am, therefore, expecting some very violent reactions on the part of the spectators" (340). He also articulates his patricidal desire for society: "I am attacking the social superstition of the family without asking anyone to take arms against a particular individual. The same for order, the same for justice" (341). See also Knapp, *Artaud* 113.

61. For translated excerpts from the reviews, see Blin et al. 127–41. See also Artaud's public response (142–45).

62. See also *SW* 342–44, Artaud's letter to Jean-Louis Barrault, refusing an offer of collaboration one month after *The Cenci*'s failure. "I am not the man who can stand to work closely with anyone on any kind of material, and less than ever after *The Cenci*" (343). Eight months later Artaud arrived in Mexico to seek communion with the Tarahumara. The next year he went to Ireland (from France), and returned in a straitjacket. He then began a nine-year confinement in various asylums. See Innes 95–97 on Barrault's extension of and difference from Artaud's ideas (and Eliot's).

63. For a reading of *The Cenci* using Heidegger's concept of "destining," see Snyder. He makes no mention of the lost mother/wife; yet his reference to Heidegger's "standing reserve"—as "the nebula of Chaos and Becoming" (74)—corresponds in some respects to the Kristevan chora, which I apply to Artaud.

64. Cf. Knapp, *Artaud* 115–16 and 217–18 n. 58.

65. Artaud directed the actress playing Beatrice in the *Cenci*'s premiere to face the audience between these two sentences, suggesting an appeal to that metaphysical Other as well (Blin et al. 116–17).

66. Cf. Hayman 97.

67. On the issue of silence and unspeakability in Shelley's *The Cenci*, see Kubiak 96–97, 106. On Artaud's unspeakable terror, see also 111, 129–33.

68. For a further elaboration of the stage effects in Artaud's production of *The Cenci*, see Knapp, *Artaud* 114–25, Goodall, "Artaud's Revision," and Blin et al. 108–25. See also Innes 74–77, 81–85.

69. Later in the play, Artaud makes clear the patriarchal collusion between the Cenci and the pope (*CW* 4:138, 151). See also Artaud's addresses to the pope and Dalai Lama (*CW* 1:180–81).

70. In rehearsals Artaud directed the crowd of guests to form a circle at this point (Blin et al. 122–23).

71. Cf. Cenci's Lear-like curse upon his daughter, as potential mother to their child, in Shelley's version (54–55).

72. Cf. Costich 53.

73. For a detailed comparison of Klein and Kristeva, see Doane and Hodges. Their discussion of André Green's theory of the "dead mother complex," as showing the influence of Klein/Winnicott (object relations) on Kristeva's notion of the chora, especially regarding the effects of maternal mourning, also relates to my analysis of Artaud's competition with dead siblings. In Green's theory, which Doane and Hodges critique, "the mother is not actually dead; she is self-absorbed

as a result of a loss. The child experiences her absorption as a catastrophe, as a narcissistic wound" (58).

74. Cf. Konecni. He claims to offer "empirical evidence . . . that the observation of aggressive activities . . . leads to an increase rather than a decrease of subsequent aggression" (234).

75. See Baudrillard, especially 72: "The reality of simulation is unendurable—more cruel even than Artaud's Theatre of Cruelty, which was still an attempt at a dramaturgy of life." See also 141.

76. See Artaud's reflection upon van Gogh: "That the world should be organized under the command of its own womb" (*SW* 497). See also the conclusion of Derrida's second essay on Artaud: "why it is *fatal* that, in its closure, representation continues" (*WD* 250).

77. "Simulation [today] is . . . the generation by models of a real without origin or reality: a hyperreal" (Baudrillard 2).

Chapter 5

1. For a recent theological view of Jean Genet's postmodern sainthood, in relation to Sartre, Heidegger, Deleuze and Guattari, see Wyschogrod (chap. 7). See also Gitenet, who calls Genet's theater "the sacred in action" (174); Driver, who finds in Genet's drama "the unity of a moral—yes, a saintly—enterprise" (45); and Pucciani, who calls Genet "a religious writer" (43). Pucciani views *The Maids* as a neoclassical morality play, although as a "tragedy inverted. He [Genet] is Racine turned inside out" (58–59). But cf. Nachman, who condemns "the moral void in Genet's aestheticism" (363). This derives, according to Nachman, from Genet's "lack of a family," indicative of "what is being lost" in a postmodern world (370). Cook also criticizes Genet's immorality. Yet Federman finds him to be a genuine "moralist" (145).

2. For a recent, philosophical examination of Genet in relation to Sartre, Heidegger, and Pirandello, see Dobrez (chaps. 9, 10, 11, 13). See also Nelson, who attempts to show that "*The Balcony* goes beyond Sartre and his associates" (61)—although Nelson focuses, like Sartre, on the reality/illusion binary.

3. Guicharnaud sees "Genet's disgust with Western theatre, especially its frivolity and triviality" as being "closely related to Artaud's theories" (98). See also Marowitz 177–78, Cetta 7–9, Innes 112–15, Savona 157, and Plunka, *Rites* 132–40.

4. Dort states that "Genet takes precisely the opposite course from Artaud: while the latter takes exception to rehearsal, in that it is repetition, diminution and disguise, Genet makes it the very object of his theater; he stages it and exalts it." Dort reverses the inheritance argument of Brustein: "Artaud take[s] up where Genet left off" (119). See also Federman 136–37, Dobrez 286–89, Innes 112–15, and Plunka, *Rites* 140–43 (where he also compares Genet and Brecht).

5. Cf. Todd 13–15. She describes the doubling of Genet and Derrida, as authors, texts, and signatures. Derrida "is, then, Genet's son as well as his father and mother" (15). Cf. also Bickel 174–75. She defines "two basic lines" of Genet criticism: existentialist and Dionysian, i.e., Sartrean and Derridean (or, one might

say, modern and postmodern). On Derrida's difference from Kristeva in relation to Genet, see Hill 147.

6. Derrida's flower, via Genet, becomes a figure for deconstruction itself: "Practical deconstruction of the transcendental effect is at work in the structure of the flower" (*Glas* 15).

7. Cf. Sartre 617, 620, 624–25. Federman, while siding with Blin on the Artaud/Genet debate (136–37), praises the revelation of a hate that binds in Genet's theater, through the "contradiction between . . . the real action and the imaginary seduction of the spectator" (138). Hassan discovers (especially in *The Maids*) that "levels of reality pull apart, showing the mad perspectives of a play that calls the reality of the audience into question by denying its own" (*Dismemberment* 199). Regarding *The Balcony*, Hassan sees the reality of the spectators becoming imaginary like the play. "The audience itself dwells in one of the brothel's 'studios'" (201–2). Piemme also views the audience of this drama as playing "the role of traveller in an ultimate scenario imagined by Genet" (171).

8. Chaudhuri's semiotic analysis of Genet's drama would shift the focus from an exhausted "mirror as theme or symbol" to a new view of mirror-play "in the signifying space" (6). For a semiotic analysis of Genet's novels, see Oswald.

9. See Ragland-Sullivan, *Lacan* 132, on Lacan's critique of the Sartrean Imaginary. See also 181: "Lacan placed reality on the *moi* slope of Imaginary (fantasmatic) perception and, consequently, did not claim fixedness or verifiability as properties of reality."

10. See Cixous and Clément, *Newly Born Woman,* the French title of which is *La jeune née,* homophonous for "La Genet." See also Cixous, "Laugh of the Medusa" 255–56, and Running-Johnson, "The Medusa's Tale." For Cixous's critique of patriarchal stage space, see her "Aller," and MacCannell 175–83. Though taking a Jungian view, Lewis Cetta's book on Genet also prefigures the concern of American feminists with a revolutionary mother goddess in Genet's work. Cetta connects the revolutionary power of "Genet's beloved outlaws" to the mythic stature of his lost mother.

11. Witt views Bachofen's version of the Great Mother as "a more fruitful source of comparison" than Cetta's use of Joseph Campbell's theories (176). But like Cetta, Witt identifies figures of the Great Mother in Genet's plays: particularly her "non-Western force" with Felicity in *The Blacks* and Kadidja, Warda, and the Mother (of Said) in *The Screens* (Witt 176–77). See also Running-Johnson's essay on *The Maids.* She refers to Irigaray's view of the Lacanian mirror (961–62, 964), but uses Cixous's "Medusan space located beyond the mirror" (963) more prominently. For a selection of Bachofen's work, introduced by Joseph Campbell, see *Myth, Religion, and Mother Right.*

12. In the queen of Genet's *The Blacks* (who should be played by a black actress wearing a white mask, according to Genet), Witt sees "the presence of the power of African matriarchy behind the institutions of patriarchy" (176). The Great revolutionary Mother also appears in *The Balcony*'s queen: "The subservience of whore to client is turned inside out when the whore-mother Irma plays the role of queen, as is the subservience of black to white when the queen removes her white mask." In *The Screens,* too, "it is the mothers, in their eternal form, that have the last word" (179).

13. See Running-Johnson, "The Medusa's Tale," for a sympathetic summary of Cixous's nostalgic idealization of the mother's voice in feminine writing, including Genet's. Cf. Ragland-Sullivan's critique of French feminists (and Deleuze and Guattari) who idealize the rebellious Imaginary: "The Imaginary must by sought, then, not just as a separate category, but at the join between Real events and Symbolic naming" (*Lacan* 156). See also Savona 153–61 on the "political matricide" as well as patricide—and subversive maternal voice—in Genet's drama.

14. In his foreword to a new edition of *The Maids* (1954), Genet still expressed great admiration for the Mass: "I know of nothing more theatrically effective than the elevation of the host" ("Note" 39). Cf. White 11–31. He speculates, contra Sartre, that Genet's love of ritual and life of crime shows the influence of his very religious foster mother, her friendship with the local priest (with whom Genet identified), and little Jean's loss of maternal affection when his foster brother returned home at the end of World War I.

15. See also Stewart, "Toward a New Chronology," and Stewart and McGregor, "Genet's Psychiatric Examination of 1943," for further attacks upon the historicity of Genet's autobiographical accounts, which supported his Sartrean self-image, as a "legend he was seeking to create" ("Genet's Psychiatric" 797). See also Plunka 1–19.

16. Cf. Plunka, *Rites,* especially 144–46. He uses Victor Turner's theory of the "liminal" stage in rites of passage (with only a brief mention of Lacan's mirror stage [42]) to analyze Genet's plays as creating "communitas" in the theater through the character's "metamorphosis."

17. On the terms *ideal ego* and *ego ideal,* see Ragland-Sullivan: "In 'Group Psychology and the Analysis of the Ego' (1921), he [Freud] referred to the narcissistic investment in self as an 'ideal ego,' and the objects toward whom ego libido flows as 'ego ideals'" (*Lacan* 31). See also 54: "Freud confused both [ideal ego and ego ideal] as objects of Desire, representing wish fulfillment. Lacan's efforts have gone in the opposite direction; he tries to maintain a distance between the ideal ego and ego ideals (alter ego) and to separate both of these from the mechanism of desiring."

18. Cf. Plunka, *Rites* 148–49, on the initial negative reviews of *Deathwatch* in Paris, New York, and London, which criticized the play for glorifying criminality.

19. See also Genet, *Prisoner of Love,* and his interview with Hubert Fichte.

20. Lacan's three orders of Real, Imaginary, and Symbolic are "in-mixed" dimensions (Ragland-Sullivan, *Lacan* 190), for which he drew three overlapping rings, tied in a "Borromean knot." See also Alan Sheridan's note on these three orders, especially concerning the Real as "that which is lacking in the symbolic order, the ineliminable residue of all articulation, the foreclosed element, which may be approached, but never grasped: the umbilical cord of the symbolic" (Lacan, *Four* 280 or *Écrits* x).

21. See also Genet, "Note" 37: "One can only dream of an art that would be a profound web of active symbols capable of speaking to the audience a language in which nothing is said but everything portended." He goes on to explain his attempt to reach this ideal in writing for the stage: "I attempted to effect a dis-

placement that . . . would bring theatre into the theatre. . . . I hope thereby . . . [for] the advantage of signs as remote as possible from what they are meant first to signify, though nevertheless attached to them in order, by this sole link, to unite the author with the spectator" (38). Implicit references to both Artaud and Brecht might be seen in such statements, but they are also genuinely Genet.

22. See Ragland-Sullivan, *Lacan* 188: "The 'real' Real is both beyond and behind Imaginary perception and Symbolic description." See also Ragland-Sullivan, "Lacan" 108, for another formulation of this en route to her analysis of *The Maids*.

23. Cf. the end of Genet's interview with Fichte (94). Also, midway through that interview Genet says: "When I am talking to you here in front of the microphone, I am not completely sincere. I want to give a certain image of myself" (78).

24. *The Maids* repeatedly illustrates the attitude of Nietzschean *ressentiment* (in *On the Genealogy of Morals*): the slave's deep envy of the master's "nobility"—to the point of a reactive "Will to Power" over the master. For example, the maid Solange: "Now we are Mademoiselle Solange Lemercier, that Lemercier woman. The famous criminal. . . . I am not a maid. I have a noble soul" (95). Solange here assumes the gaze of the Nietzschean slave's "venomous eye of *ressentiment*," which sees "the noble, powerful man" as "evil" (40), but she also turns it upon herself, in mirror stage *jouissance,* assuming both nobility and evil, in the gaze of the Other (maid and audience). This reminds one, too, of Genet's own rise to evil nobility as famous criminal and artistic genius, invited to dinner by the French president at the Palace of the Champs-Elysees (Hassan 180).

25. Cf. Ragland-Sullivan, "Lacan" 114–15. She critiques a master/slave reading of *The Maids* as "Sartre's interpretation" and finds instead that the maids are attempting to escape "psychic suffocation" by identifying with Madame.

26. Cf. Walker, who tries to rescue a Marxist message in *The Balcony* by analyzing Genet's different versions of 1956, 1960, 1962, and 1968. Cf. also Shevtsova, who shows a deconstruction of the theater/society binary in the same play, making it "an allegory of capitalist society . . . [and] the politics of repression." But her nihilistic conclusion is the opposite of Walker's search for revolutionary hope. "We—actors who are also spectators—have nothing left but empty signs" (Shevtsova 42).

27. Cf. Ragland-Sullivan, "Lacan" 106–15. See also Derrida, *Glas* 54: "each maid asks the other to carry her within herself, like Madame's penis."

28. Cf. Straus 104–6. He gives a similar analysis of the bishop's mirror-staged *je/moi* split. See also Genet's comment in the Fichte interview: "Standing before the work of art I lose the feeling of being 'myself,' the feeling of my 'self,' more and more. But when confronted with subversive events, my 'self,' my 'social self' grows, becoming stronger and stronger" (72). See Ragland-Sullivan, *Lacan* 53, for an explanation of how Lacan splits the Freudian "superego" between the identificatory *moi* and social *je.*

29. This theatrical glimpse of the Real is repeated in Irma's words and actions at the end of *The Balcony*: "facing the audience," she tells it to "go home" to a reality "falser than here" (96).

30. Genet is careful to insist on a white audience for *The Blacks,* even sym-

bolically—with a token white spectator, white masks given to the black spectators, or a white mask on a dummy in the audience (4).

31. Cf. Federman, who calls *The Blacks* "an inverted ceremony of exorcism"
(143).

32. For Genet's attitude toward Brecht, see "Hubert Fichte" 72. Genet criti-
cizes both Brecht's *Galileo* and his alienation ideal of the cigar-smoking spectator.
See also the comparisons between Genet and Brecht made by Taubes (85) and
Bickel (169–70).

33. Cf. Genet, "Note" 39–40. "No doubt one of the functions of art is to substitute the efficacy of beauty for religious faith. At least, this beauty should have
the power of a poem, that is, of a crime."

34. See also Dean, *Self* 42–57.

35. See also Ragland-Sullivan, "Lacan" 113–14. Cf. Sartre 617.

36. See also the "Translator's Note" (by Alan Sheridan) on *desire:* "Lacan
has linked the concept of 'desire' with 'need' *(besoin)* and 'demand' *(demande)*.
. . . There is no adequation between the need and the demand that conveys it;
indeed it is the gap between them that constitutes desire, at once particular like
the first and absolute like the second. Desire (fundamentally in the singular) is a
perpetual effect of symbolic articulation" (*Four* 278). This relates, too, to my discussion here of the "need" of the chief of police for the outside rebellion and for
the perverse impersonation of him by Roger in *The Balcony*. The gap between
this need and the chief's demand to become a Symbolic (explicitly phallic [78])
and Imaginary hero-figure in the brothel is graphically demonstrated by Genet
when Roger as chief castrates himself (93).

37. See Lacan's discussion of psychoanalytic transference, specifically: "it is
in the space of the Other that he [the subject] sees himself and the point from
which he looks at himself is also in that space" (*Four* 144).

38. For a more extensive discussion of laughter in *The Screens*, see Blau,
"Comedy." See also Genet's description of Palestinian women whom he knew
during his years with the PLO (after writing *The Screens*): "The women . . . added
to all their virtues a dimension that seemed to subtend a great peal of laughter"
(*Prisoner* 4).

39. Cf. Genet's discussion in the Hubert Fichte interview (83) of ritual passage in relation to his own writings. Genet also analyzes the "beauty" of an actual
murder he once witnessed as being in its "revolt." He says that his own "impulse
to murder has been channeled into a poetic impulse" (82).

40. Cf. Pontalis's theory of the dream as "maternal body," as well as "private
theatre," which the analyst, in "the role of spectator," penetrates paternally
(29–37).

41. See Green 11–15, for his analysis of Artaud's theories.

42. One might argue, on the other hand, that cinema does create a barrier
between performance/audience space and the outside world, through similar
"chambers" and screens. See my essay, "The Real Edges of the Screen."

43. Cf. Guicharnaud 109. He sees Said and his wife ruling in the afterlife,
with the mother below them hierarchically.

44. Or, one might say, "deconstructed." Cf. Derrida, *Glas* 116–17. See also
White 492–95, on the violent demonstrations against Genet's play and its depic-

tion of the Algerian War, by right-wing spectators in the premiere production at the Paris Odéon in 1966.

45. On Genet's life after his terrorist associations, from 1980 to his death in 1986, see Ménager.

46. For a defense of Lacan against Irigaray, see Ragland-Sullivan, *Lacan* 273–80, 294–95.

47. Cf. Lacan, *Feminine* 96–97, 155–56, for his discussion of feminine homosexuality and spiritual "hommosexuality."

Chapter 6

1. While she praises Brecht's early, homosexual plays, Case heartily condemns "the rise of the asexual mother figure and the Epic style" in Brecht's later drama, beginning with *The Mother* (72). "This gender-specific, sexless, instrumentalized mother figure serves to stop the exploration of new images for men and women" (73). (See also Wright's argument that the early Brecht is the most postmodern—i.e., more like Lyotard, with the later Brecht being more like Habermas [*Postmodern Brecht* 90].) Diamond, though, values the *Gestus* so highly that she believes it to be purified of both perversity and mortality, redemptively giving "no fetishization and no end to signification" (90). She then promises a recovery of lost women dramatists through her gestic feminist criticism (90–91), without analyzing the mourning and refetishizing that such exhumation involves. For an earlier criticism and more recent praise of Brecht's female characters, see Lennox and Pollock, respectively. Both see in such characters a powerful subversiveness which is of use to today's feminism (Lennox 84; Pollock 85–86). See also Smith, "Brecht," which reapplies Brecht's theories, adjusted by feminism, to his later plays.

2. See, for example, the letters by Andersen, Davis, and Hassig in the November 1994 issue of *Communications from the International Brecht Society.* Andersen calls Fuegi's scholarship "shocking" and points out specific errors. Davis finds "Fuegi perverse, in this case, rather than Brecht" (12). Hassig complains of Fuegi "misusing" their collaborative work on a documentary film about Ruth Berlau—as Fuegi claims Brecht did to Berlau and others. Cf. Völker, *Brecht* 346–47, on Berlau's personal relations with Brecht and her split personality (like that of the Good Person of Szechwan). For a brief version of Fuegi's attack on Brecht, see Fuegi, "The Zelda Syndrome: Brecht and Elisabeth Hauptmann." Cf. Calabro 7–19.

3. Cf. Fuegi, *Brecht* 74: "Though he can kill off other women at a great rate in his world of metaphor . . . his mother is left psychically unburied; perhaps thereby she remains unlost."

4. See Wiles 6–7, 29–30, on the translation of Aristotle's *katharsis* as "purification" rather than "purgation," in relation to Freud, Stanislavsky, and Brecht.

5. See Brecht, *Theatre* 69–76, and 132, for his views on theater "for pleasure or for instruction."

6. See Willett's note in *Brecht on Theatre* 42. I use his translation of "gest"

for Brecht's *Gestus,* which means: "both gist and gesture; an attitude or a single aspect of an attitude, expressible in words or actions."

7. Cf. Sokel, for a non-Lacanian analysis of the "split characters" in Brecht's plays. See also Wiles 73, 104–6. He adapts Sokel's theory to describe the "schizoid" Brechtian actor, particularly in relation to *The Measures Taken.*

8. For further similarities between Lacan and Brecht, see Bishop. See also Wright, *Postmodern Brecht,* particularly 35 and 55–57.

9. Cf. Brustein 277–78.

10. Cf. Friedrich, "Deconstructed Self," particularly 289–92. He states that *The Measures Taken* "uncannily presaged the [Stalinist] purges and showtrials soon to come; and furthermore, it prefigured the postmodern preoccupation with the deconstruction of the self"—which he opposes (289). See also Esslin 144, Wiles 91–93, Brooker 191–215, and Calabro 2–6.

11. Cf. Barthes, "Diderot, Brecht, Eisenstein" (*Image* 69–78) and "Brecht and Discourse." On Barthes and Brecht in relation to ritual, see Blau, "Myth."

12. Cf. Wright, *Postmodern Brecht* 19: "Contrary to popular belief, *Verfremdung* does not do away with identification but examines it critically."

13. In his brief poem, "The Moment before Impact," Brecht describes the gap between an actor's spoken word and the audience's reception of it (*Poems* 342). On the split within the audience produced by Brecht's drama, see also *Theater* 132. For a psychological critique of Brecht's anti-Aristotelian alienation effect, see Konecni.

14. This, in my view, says much about the value of the non-Western Other to Brecht, Kristeva, and Western culture in general. But it does not convey the full meaning of that other culture, or rather cultures, to themselves—although it is significant in their various relationships to the West, from the other side of the mirror. See Spivak 136–41, for a criticism of Kristeva's projections upon the Chinese.

15. Cf. Woodward's argument in favor of grief (contra Freud and via Barthes) as something to be sustained "between mourning and melancholia" (96).

16. On the gender of the semiotic chora, see Moi 11–12. Kristeva's use of the term "abject" (as adjective, verb, and noun) relates to the powerful emotive force of the chora, suggesting both its rejection (repression) and its horrifying return, as lost primal object. See, for example, *Powers* 15: "The abject is the violence of mourning for an 'object' that has always already been lost." For a summary of Kristeva's views on abjection, see Gross 86–93.

17. Cf. Barthes, "Diderot, Brecht, Eisenstein," *Image* 69–78. See also Jameson, "Imaginary and Symbolic in Lacan" 102: "the Brechtian attack on 'culinary' theater . . . can best be understood as an attempt to block Imaginary investment and thereby to dramatize the problematical relationship between the observing subject and the Symbolic Order or history."

18. Cf. Irigaray, *Speculum* 227: "So woman has not yet taken (a) place."

19. Cf. Wright, *Postmodern Brecht* 31. She gives a characteristic, though in my view too simple, answer. "Brecht's aesthetic is based upon a view of the text that has become mandatory in poststructuralist theory: the text as site of production, involving author, reader, and an Other, which for Brecht is history."

20. Hayman states that Brecht went to "a kindergarten run by barefoot fri-

ars" (7). Völker, *Brecht* 5, concurs. However, Fuegi insists that it was known as the Barefoot School because it had originally been run by mendicant friars; yet by the time Brecht went there, it "had long since become a Protestant institution" (*Brecht* 5).

21. See Jesse (18 and passim), who traces further influences of the Bible and Lutheranism on Brecht's early work. See also Dickson 129–44 and Murphy. The latter traces Brecht's penchant for dialectical thinking, even prior to his Marxism, to the "Catholic-Protestant dialectic at home," where the Bible began its formative influence on his later literary work (4). Völker, *Brecht* 6, on the other hand, insists that "Religion played no great part either at school or at home."

22. See also Fuegi, *Brecht* 4. He mentions the young Brecht's intimacy with certain servants, who might have worn the cast-off clothing of his mother. One in particular, Marie Miller, while dressing and undressing Brecht and his brother, "would sometimes hide objects in her underclothes for them to find." Fuegi associates Brecht's perverse intimacy with, yet loss of such mother substitutes—even before the death of his mother—with his adult fear of abandonment by women lovers: "He would always try and hang on to a relationship, denying any loss."

23. Brecht has the grandfather read from the Bible, provoking the girl's comment. The passage he reads uses the command form of *to break*, which is "Brecht" in German: "Break bread for the hungry and have compassion for them as they suffer" (*Werke* 1:10; my translation).

24. See Knopf 12–13 for a brief summary and analysis (in German) of this play, which is rarely included in Brecht collections or commentaries. See also Murphy, chapter 2.

25. Berthold Brecht, Bertolt's father, wrote a history of the paper factory where he worked. But he was often too busy there to spend much time with his children. While Bertolt's mother wrote poetry, his father mocked this inclination in their son. "Do you know the difference between me and my son? I'm a poet's dad and he's a dud poet [*Dichtervater . . . fader Dichter*]." See Hayman 6–7 and (for original sources) Frisch and Obermeier 20–23. This joking, yet fateful riddle seems to demand, like an oracle, not only that the Oedipal father be eliminated, but also that a substitute father be found in order for Brecht to find success. It is also significant that the young Brecht, christened "Eugen Berthold," eventually took the middle name, the *Nom du Père*, as his own, yet altered its ending to a sharper and more alliterative consonant. Cf. Esslin 4. Hayman also states that Brecht's father "inflamed his anticonformism" (33). See, for example, the argument between Brecht and his father about bolshevism (Hayman 62). See also Fuegi, *Brecht* 18, on the "emotional distance" of Brecht senior and his sons from their dying wife and mother (according to Walter, one of the sons).

26. Similar lines occur in an earlier poem, but spoken by the mother. "Then, naturally, she cries and says: But the washing! And that I'd soon have her under the sod at this rate / And the day would come when I'd want to claw it up to get her back once more / But it would be too late by then, and I'd start finding out / How much she'd done for me" (*Poems* 16). Cf. "Song about the Woman" (42–43). Brecht had Baal's mother say this to him, too, in the play's second draft. But Brecht cut her out of the play entirely after the death of his own mother. See Hayman 31–32 and Brecht, *CP* 1:356.

27. Cf. Derrida, "Fors," for his ruminations on Nicolas Abraham and Maria Torok's theory of how incorporation forms a "crypt" within the ego: "Sealing the loss of the object, but also marking the refusal to mourn, such a maneuver is foreign to and actually opposed to the process of introjection. I pretend to keep the dead alive, intact, *safe (save) inside me,* but it is only in order to refuse, in a necessarily equivocal way, to love the dead as a living part of me, dead *save in me,* through the process of introjection, as happens in so-called 'normal' mourning" (71). See also Lukacher 88–93.

28. For examples, see Hayman 59 and 62.

29. Cf. Blau, *To All* 94. Cf. also Speirs, who describes Baal as being "able to rejoice in the fact that in dying he is living, that death, as Hofmannsthal put it, is a 'great God of the soul'" (23). I would point, however, to the great goddess of the soul (or psyche)—the encrypted maternal *chora*—as incestuous source of Baal's death-drive *jouissance*. (For another critique of Speirs's view of *Baal,* see Tatlow 42–43.)

30. Her first name was Sophie, like a lover/victim of Brecht's Baal. Cf. Hayman 55–57 on Brecht's guilt for not expressing his love for his mother before her death, and his continued "brooding" after it.

31. Cf. Hayman 34, who relates this line to Brecht's own fears, expressed in a letter to Caspar Neher, that Paula Banholzer (Brecht's girlfriend) had become pregnant.

32. Cf. Hayman 30–31, on the oratorio Brecht began at the age of twenty about the mother and God. The mother complains that her womb is cursed by the son's sinfulness. But God commends the son's anger and defiance.

33. An intermediary father figure, particularly in relation to *Baal,* would be Frank Wedekind, whom Brecht idolized onstage and imitated physically after the playwright/actor's death in 1918. In 1919 he named his first-born son (by Paula Banholzer) "Frank." See Hayman 26–28 and 48.

34. See also Esslin, *Brecht* 141, 150–51, and 181. Cf. Hayman 35–36, who connects the young Brecht's Baal-like lust for Nature, and his death-wish yearning to return to the mother's womb, with his need to prove to her that he is not a wastrel—and the sense of purpose he finds later in Marxism.

35. Cf. Brecht, *Theatre* 105, where he calls the "pomp of the Fascists, taken at face value, . . . a hollow gest." But he also opens the face of this hollow gest by refocusing the scene upon a mournful edge: "men strutting instead of walking, a certain stiffness, a lot of colour, self-conscious sticking out of chests, etc. All this could be the gest of some popular festivity, quite harmless, purely factual and therefore to be accepted. Only when the strutting takes place over corpses do we get the social gest of Fascism." See also Smith, "Brecht" 492–93.

36. This phrase is inspired by Kristeva's essay on modern theater's mirage semiology: "the new locus of representation no longer develops out of a mechanical mixture of actors and audience, but by a different articulation of semiotic and symbolic elements . . . where the crises of the speaking would be recognizable" ("Modern" 134).

37. While Esslin takes Brecht at his word that he not only "patched people up in order to ship them back to the front," but also "opened the man's skull and tinkered with his brains" (qtd. in Esslin, *Brecht* 7); Fuegi disputes this. "There is

not a shred of evidence that Brecht did amputations or performed brain surgery" (*Bertolt* 7–8). Fuegi insists that Brecht was stationed at "a clinic for patients with venereal disease" (*Brecht* 44).

38. When he published this poem in his *Manual of Piety,* a parody of popular religious manuals, Brecht also made the dedication to Christian Grumbeis, "born . . . in Aichach" (11). But see also the note by Hugo Schmidt, which states that there is no record of such a person in the city registry of Aichach (282).

39. Fuegi insists that Elisabeth Hauptmann wrote 80 percent of *He Who Says Yes* and "a substantial portion" of *The Measures Taken* (*Bertolt* 71). She even published her own version of the Nō play *Taniko*—"under her own name"— prior to those other two "Brecht" versions (*Brecht* 245). Yet, Fuegi makes the matter even more confusing by ascribing *Taniko* to Seami, rather than to Zenchiku (Seami's son-in-law), as Waley does. Hayman, like Waley, ascribes the play to Zenchiku, and says of *Der Jasager:* "About three quarters of Brecht's script consists of Elisabeth Hauptmann's 1929 translation of Waley's English, but Brecht took the secularization even further" (150).

40. Brecht also saw Kabuki performed in Berlin in 1930–31 (Hayman 150–51). Cf. Nagele 118, 125–26 on the secularization of Nō ritual in Brecht's *Lehrstücke.*

41. Another example of this, toward the end of Brecht's life, is the performance of *The Trial of Lucullus* in East Berlin in 1951. Brecht was having trouble pleasing the Party with this play. So the audience was told that the court of the dead (and its verdict) should be identified in the play with "posterity" (Esslin 163). Thus, the shades onstage, mirroring the spectators (and judgment of the Party), also reflected a future audience/Other. Cf. Suvin's essay, "The Mirror and the Dynamo," in *Brecht and Beyond* 112–30.

42. Cf. Waley's introduction, where he describes the historical development of Nō drama out of ritual perversity within Shinto mythology (15).

43. At the end of his life, Brecht stated that *The Measures Taken* was the form theater would take in the future (Völker, *Brecht* 190). See note 10 here. See also Hayman 152–53, who points to the similarity between this play and Eliot's *Murder in the Cathedral*—in their common attempt to evoke a religious sense of duty and in their use of biblical rhythms.

44. See Fuegi, *Brecht* 261. Again he attributes this play to Hauptmann's work as well as Brecht's: "Formally, *Die Mutter,* or *The Mother,* borrows heavily from the stage devices Hauptmann had introduced to the collective from her work with the Japanese medieval drama"—i.e., with *Taniko.*

45. Work on *St. Joan* began in 1930, a year before *The Mother,* but it was completed after. According to Fuegi, "surviving records of the play *[St. Joan]* give an unusually clear picture of how it came into being," as a collective work by Elisabeth Hauptmann, Emil Burri, and Brecht (262). See also Knopf 107, who finds that much of the preparatory work was done by Brecht's colleagues, including the plot construction *[Aufbau der Fabel].* Cf. McCullough 99, who attributes *St. Joan* to those three authors, plus "H. Borchardt," and *The Measures Taken* to Brecht, "S. Dudlow, [and] H. Eisler."

46. Cf. Parmalee, who describes the "negative influence" of *Major Barbara* on *Saint Joan* (69).

47. Mauler sees her at this point as having "lived for twenty years"; but at

the end of the play (at her death), her age is announced as twenty-five (*Saint Joan* 43, 122).

48. Joan still imitates Christ, however, in her conversion to violence: "Are you trying to turn God's house into a barn?" (*Saint Joan* 75). Cf. Frederic Grab's introduction, which shows a relationship (and distinction) in Brecht's reading of *Das Kapital* to the play's depiction of economic laws as inscrutable, and from his Leninism to Joan's violent conversion (14–15).

49. Cf. Parmalee, who also says of *Saint Joan*: "Even martyrdom is perverted" (63).

50. The final lines of the *Saint Joan* chorus, with Mauler joining in, parody the famous lines (236–42) from part 1 of Goethe's *Faust,* to which Freud also refers in his essay on the uncanny. With Brecht's play, Joan's sacrifice parallels that of Margaret in *Faust,* though no redemptive voice speaks at her death. But Brecht's double-souled chorus transcends her despair, albeit gestically, as Faust (with Mephistopheles) does Margaret's. Marx's *Das Kapital* also parodies *Faust* in describing the capitalist's double-souled breast, as Parmalee has pointed out (69). See also Suvin 131–65. Cf. Fuegi, *Brecht* 263, who sees "two souls" battling throughout the play: Hauptmann's Joan Dark and Brecht's Mauler.

51. Fuegi sees in Mother Courage the ruthlessness of Brecht's own writing (and character); whereas "Kattrin reflects the values of [Margarete] Steffin and [Ruth] Berlau"—his unacknowledged coauthors (*Brecht* 381).

52. Cf. Bryant-Bertail 58: "Through a feminist reading, the irony of Kattrin's life and death turns upon Brecht as well as upon Mother Courage."

53. Mother Courage becomes a hollow, gestic fetish at the end of the play, but her wagon figures as such much earlier. Concerning scene 5, Brecht remarks: "A change has taken place in Courage. She has sacrificed her son to the wagon and now she defends the wagon like a tigress" (*CP* 5:363). The wagon thus becomes a metonymic substitute for her own absent phallus (her child). At the end of the play, with all of her children gone, she says, as she harnesses herself to it instead of them: "I hope I can pull the wagon alone. I'll manage, there isn't much in it" (210). She thus joins herself to her hollow fetish in place of each lost child.

54. Of course, Fuegi views this split character as exemplifying the women coauthors masked by Brecht's name. "The play shouts the agony of [Margarete] Steffin, who lived much of her life as an author wearing a male disguise" (*Brecht* 389). Hauptmann and Berlau also worked on the play (431).

55. Cf. Knust, "East-West" 76. He focuses on the epilogue's appeal to the audience, rather than to the gods, as a prime example of Brecht's perverse adaptation of Strindberg's *A Dream Play,* in using oriental myths and motifs for *The Good Person of Szechwan.* See also Knust, "Brecht's Dream-Playing" 216–18.

56. Shen Teh expresses her desire for other gods, bearing a better economic order, in her address to the audience between scenes 4 and 5 (*CP* 6:46). See also her beseeching of the audience in scene 7 to help a homeless child: "A citizen of tomorrow is asking you for a today!" (71). Cf. Berckman on the function of utopian hope in Brecht's drama, and particularly in *Good Person.* Cf. also Suvin 112–65.

57. Cf. Wright, "*Good Person.*" She uses Lacan and psychoanalyst Joan Riv-

ierre to examine the "dual masquerade" of Shen Teh/Shui Ta. "As a woman, then, Shen Te is already implicated in a masquerade. . . . The appearance of her male half, Shui Ta, is a defence against the failure of this masquerade" (118).

58. After calling Brecht's female characters "stunted" in their sexual identities, and claiming that his males are not similarly castrated ("foreshortened") Smith turns to Kristeva for support. Here Smith quotes the phrase, "a being of folds," as Kristeva's description for "woman" (496)—without indicating its original biological and religious context in "Stabat Mater" (Kristeva, *Tales* 234–63). Cf. Irigaray's view of woman (similar to, though not cited by, Smith's essay) as feminine surface rather than maternal volume. Irigaray rejects the "privileging of the maternal over the feminine," through which woman (whose sex is not one) "renounces the pleasure that she gets from the *nonsuture of her lips*" (*This Sex* 30).

59. Fuegi cites Brecht's diary for evidence of Steffin's role as coauthor: "on June 11, 1940, Brecht wrote, 'i go through word for word with Grete for the xth time *Good Person [Woman] of Se[t]zuan.*' Only when Grete was present was there any real progress on this or any other of the major projects" (*Brecht* 388).

60. Cf. Laura Mulvey's recent reexamination of the Oedipus myth. She points behind Kristeva's pre-Oedipal mother to the "even more 'unspeakable'" threat of the primal, pre-Oedipal father. "Perhaps desire for and fear of a powerful mother and the misogyny it generates conceals something even more disturbing, desire for and fear of a violent father" ("Oedipus" 48). Cf. MacCannell. See also Fuegi, *Brecht* 532: "Nowhere in this landscape [of Brecht's work] is there a loving or genuinely present father, or indeed a biological mother who does not by default or design allow her children to be slaughtered."

61. The tobacco shop may reflect Brecht's own ancestral desires, since his family had owned one in Achern. See Lunn 17–18, for a Marxist analysis of this biographical detail in relation to the Brecht-Lukács debate of the 1930s.

62. Cf. Reinelt on the parallels and differences between Brecht's alienation effect and deconstruction—in relation to feminist criticism.

63. What Manheim here translates as "moved us deeply" is originally: "Hat uns sehr gefesselt" (*CP* 6:101; *Werke* 6:276). *Fesseln* means both to fascinate and to chain or shackle. Thus, this phrase encapsulates Brecht's entire critique of Aristotelian catharsis. In the next line, however, there is also a hint of the indelible ritual chora at the edge of Brecht's dais. "Cheered" is actually *erquickt* (*Werke* 6:277) from the German for "quicken," also meaning "refresh" or "revive." So, the joys and sorrows of the pregnant Shen Teh also cause a quickening pain in her metaphysical chorus and audience.

64. Recently, there has also been much interest in Brecht's later theory of "naïveté," which he devised to replace, yet also clarify, the alienation effect. See, for example, Terry Eagleton's brief essay "Brecht and Rhetoric." Eagleton points, as a model for theory today, to the childlike Brechtian actor who "press[es] perversely on to interrogate the whole form of social life" (170–71). This relates, I would argue, to Freud's fetishist who, despite knowing better, holds onto the common childhood belief in the phallic mother (*SE* 21:152–57). See also Schoeps's recent essay, particularly as he uses Brecht's theory of naïveté to explain the empathetic goodness of certain female characters (195–96). I would connect this

development in Brecht's theory of theater, and in his visionary child heroines (from Joan Dark, to Kattrin, to Simone Machard), with a further sublimation of the abject chora. On the many dreams and materialist visions in Brecht's drama, see Knust, "Brecht's Dream-Playing." On Brecht's ultimate resignation within a womblike space, see Brustein 277–78. See also Rouse, on Brecht's postwar theory and praxis with his Berliner Ensemble.

Epilogue

1. Cf. Bennett 83–85: "modern drama aims typically at the production of ceremony," which he defines as "a limited communal action"—distinct from the experience of film. On the different limits to the evocation of belief in theater or film, see Blau, *Blooded* 123: "We hardly think of a suspension of disbelief at the movies, whereas there is always on stage a compromising incompatibility between the corporeal body and the *mise en scène.*"

2. Cf. Ragland 103: "lost primordial objects were never possessed in the first place." See also 103–5, 117–19, 163, 172–73.

3. See Žižek, *Enjoy* 124–28. See also Mulvey, "Oedipus" 48.

4. Cf. Žižek, *Enjoy* 123: "it is as if the universal and particular paradoxically *exchange places.*"

5. See Lacan, *Four* 45.

Bibliography

Ackroyd, Peter. *T. S. Eliot.* London: Hamish Hamilton, 1984.

Allison, David B., ed. *The New Nietzsche.* Cambridge: MIT Press, 1985.

Altizer, Thomas J. J. "Eternal Recurrence and Kingdom of God." In Allison 232–46.

Andersen, Jan. "My Notes about an Interview, a Film, and a Book by John Fuegi." *Communications from the International Brecht Society* 23, no. 2 (1994): 15–18.

Anderson, Walter Truett. *Reality Isn't What It Used to Be.* San Francisco: Harper, 1990.

Arata, Luis O. "In Search of Ritual Theater: Artaud in Mexico." In Plunka, *Antonin Artaud* 80–88.

Artaud, Antonin. *Selected Writings.* Ed. Susan Sontag. Trans. Helen Weaver. New York: Farrar, Straus and Giroux, 1976.

———. *Collected Works.* 4 vols. to date. London: Calder and Boyars, 1968.

———. *The Peyote Dance.* Trans. Helen Weaver. New York: Farrar, Straus and Giroux, 1976.

———. *The Theater and Its Double.* Trans. Mary Caroline Richards. New York: Grove, 1958.

———. "Van Gogh, the Suicide Provoked by Society." Trans. Peter Watson. *Horizon* 17 (Jan. 1948): 46–50.

Auerbach, Erich. "Figura." *Scenes from the Drama of European Literature: Six Essays.* Minneapolis: University of Minnesota Press, 1984.

———. *Mimesis: The Representation of Reality in Western Literature.* Trans. Willard R. Trask. Princeton: Princeton University Press, 1953.

Auerbach, Nina. *Woman and the Demon: The Life of a Victorian Myth.* Cambridge: Harvard University Press, 1982.

Augustine. *Confessions.* Trans. Henry Chadwick. Oxford: Oxford University Press, 1991.

Auslander, Philip. "'Holy Theater' and Catharsis." *Theater Research International* 9, no. 1 (1984): 16–29.

Bachofen, Johann Jakob. *Myth, Religion, and Mother Right: Selected Writings of J. J. Bachofen.* Trans. Ralph Manheim. Princeton: Princeton University Press, 1967.

Baeumer, Max L. "Nietzsche and the Tradition of the Dionysian." *Studies in Nietzsche and the Classical Tradition.* Ed. James C. O'Flaherty et al. Chapel Hill: University of North Carolina Press, 1976. 165–89.

Baker-White, Robert. "Artaud's Legacy in the Collectivist Avant-Garde: Community and Representation in Works by Grotowski, Chaikin, and Schechner." In Plunka, *Antonin Artaud* 199–221.

Barber, Stephen. *Antonin Artaud: Blows and Bombs.* London: Faber, 1993.

———. "A Foundry of the Figure: Antonin Artaud." *Artforum* 26, no. 1 (1987): 88–95.

Barish, Jonas. *The Antitheatrical Prejudice.* Berkeley and Los Angeles: University of California Press, 1981.

Barthes, Roland. "Brecht and Discourse: A Contribution to the Study of Discursivity." *The Rustle of Language.* Trans. Richard Howard. New York: Hill and Wang, 1986. 212–22.

———. *Image—Music—Text.* Trans. Stephen Heath. New York: Hill and Wang, 1977.

———. "On Brecht's *Mother.*" *Critical Essays.* Trans. Richard Howard. Evanston, Ill.: Northwestern University Press, 1972. 139–42.

———. *The Pleasure of the Text.* Trans. Richard Miller. New York: Hill and Wang, 1975.

Barzilai, Shuli. "Borders of Language: Kristeva's Critique of Lacan." *PMLA* 106 (1991): 294–305.

Bataille, Georges. *Literature and Evil.* Trans. Alastair Hamilton. London: Calder and Boyars, 1973.

Baudrillard, Jean. *Simulations.* Trans. Paul Foss, Paul Patton, and Philip Beitchman. New York: Semiotext(e), 1983.

Beckett, Samuel. *Proust.* New York: Grove, 1957.

Beehler, Michael T. "*Murder in the Cathedral:* The Countersacramental Play of Signs." *Genre* 10 (fall 1977): 329–38.

———. "Troping the Topic: Dis-Closing the Circle of *The Family Reunion.*" *Boundary* 2 8, no. 3 (1980): 19–42.

Benjamin, Jessica. *The Bonds of Love: Psychoanalysis, Feminism, and the Problem of Dominance.* New York: Random, 1988.

Benjamin, Walter. *Illuminations.* Ed. Hannah Arendt. Trans. Harry Zohn. New York: Schocken, 1969.

———. *The Origin of the German Tragic Drama.* Trans. John Osborne. London: NLB, 1977.

———. *Understanding Brecht.* Trans. Anna Bostock. London: NLB, 1972.

Bennett, Benjamin. *Theater as Problem: Modern Drama and Its Place in Literature.* Ithaca, N.Y.: Cornell University Press, 1990.

Berckman, Edward M. "The Function of Hope in Brecht's Pre-Revolutionary Theater." *Brecht Heute/Brecht Today* 1 (1971): 11–26.

Bernheimer, Charles, and Claire Kahane, eds. *In Dora's Case: Freud—Hysteria—Feminism.* New York: Columbia University Press, 1985.

Bickel, Gisele A. Child. "Crime and Revolution in the Theater of Jean Genet." In Hopkins and Aycock 169–80.

Birringer, Johannes. *Theatre, Theory, Postmodernism.* Bloomington: Indiana University Press, 1991.

Bishop, Philip E. "Brecht, Hegel, Lacan: Brecht's Theory of Gest and the Problem of the Subject." *Studies in Twentieth Century Literature* 10, no. 2 (1986): 267–88.

Blackmur, R. P. *Form and Value in Modern Poetry*. Garden City, N.Y.: Doubleday, 1952.

Blau, Herbert. *The Audience*. Baltimore: Johns Hopkins University Press, 1990.

———. *Blooded Thought: Occasions of Theatre*. New York: PAJ, 1982.

———. "Comedy since the Absurd." *Modern Drama* 25 (1982): 545–68.

———. *The Impossible Theatre: A Manifesto*. New York: Macmillan, 1964.

———. "The Myth of Ritual in the Marketplace of Signs." *The Play and Its Critic: Essays for Eric Bentley*. Ed. Michael Bertin. New York: University Press of America, 1986. 305–39.

———. *Take Up the Bodies: Theater at the Vanishing Point*. Urbana: University of Illinois Press, 1982.

———. *To All Appearances: Ideology and Performance*. New York: Routledge, 1992.

Blin, Roger, et al. "Material on Antonin Artaud's *Les Cenci*." *Drama Review* 16 (1972): 90–145.

Bloch, Ernst. *The Utopian Function of Art and Literature: Selected Essays*. Trans. Jack Zipes and Frank Mecklenburg. Cambridge: MIT Press, 1988.

Bloom, Harold. *The Anxiety of Influence: A Theory of Poetry*. London: Oxford University Press, 1975.

———. "Reflections on T. S. Eliot." *Raritan* 8, no. 2 (1988): 70–87.

Boal, Augusto. *Games for Actors and Non-Actors*. Trans. Adrian Jackson. London: Routledge, 1992.

Boothby, Richard. *Death and Desire: Psychoanalytic Theory in Lacan's Return to Freud*. London: Routledge, 1991.

Brecht, Bertolt. *Poems*. Ed. John Willett and Ralph Manheim. London: Methuen, 1976.

———. *Brecht on Theatre*. Ed. and trans. John Willett. New York: Hill and Wang, 1964.

———. *Collected Plays*. Ed. Ralph Manheim and John Willett. 9 vols. New York: Random, 1971–74.

———. *Gesammelte Werke*. 20 vols. Frankfurt: Suhrkamp, 1967.

———. *Manual of Piety*. Trans. Eric Bentley. New York: Grove, 1966.

———. *The Measures Taken and Other Lehrstücke*. Trans. Carl Mueller, Ralph Manheim, and Wolfgang Sauerlander. London: Methuen, 1977.

———. "Notes on Stanislavski." *Stanislavski in America*. Ed. Erika Munk. New York: Hill and Wang, 1966. 124–36.

———. *Saint Joan of the Stockyards*. Trans. Frank Jones. Bloomington: Indiana University Press, 1969.

———. *Werke*. 30 vols. Frankfurt: Suhrkamp, 1989.

Brinker, Menachem. "Verisimilitude, Conventions, and Beliefs." *New Literary History* 14, no. 2 (1983): 253–67.

Brooker, Peter. *Bertolt Brecht: Dialectics, Poetry, Politics*. London: Croom Helm, 1988.

Brooks, Cleanth. "Religion and Literature." *Sewanee Review* 82, no. 1 (1974): 93–107.

Brooks, Peter, and Joseph Halpern, eds. *Genet: A Collection of Critical Essays.* Englewood Cliffs, N.J.: Prentice-Hall, 1979.

Browne, E. Martin. "The Christian Presence in the Theater." *The Climate of Faith in Modern Literature.* Ed. Nathan A. Scott Jr. New York: Seabury, 1964. 128–41.

———. *The Making of T. S. Eliot's Plays.* London: Cambridge University Press, 1969.

Brustein, Robert. *The Theatre of Revolt: An Approach to Modern Drama.* Boston: Little, Brown, 1962.

Bryant-Bertail, Sarah. "Women, Space, Ideology: *Mutter Courage und Ihre Kinder.*" In Fuegi, Bahr, and Willett 43–61.

Calabro, Tony. *Bertolt Brecht's Art of Dissemblance.* Wakefield, N.H.: Longwood Academic, 1990.

Carlson, Marvin. *Theories of the Theatre: A Historical and Critical Survey, from the Greeks to the Present.* Ithaca, N.Y.: Cornell University Press, 1984.

Carpentier, Martha C. "Orestes in the Drawing Room: Aeschylean Parallels in T. S. Eliot's *The Family Reunion.*" *Studies in Twentieth Century Literature* 35, no. 1 (1989): 17–42.

Carroll, David. *Paraesthetics: Foucault, Lyotard, Derrida.* New York: Methuen, 1987.

Case, Sue-Ellen. "Brecht and Women: Homosexuality and the Mother." In Fuegi, Bahr, and Willett 62–74.

Cassel, Jonathon F. *Tarahumara Indians.* San Antonio: Naylor, 1969.

Caws, Mary Ann. "Madness in a (M)other Tongue: Artaud's Address." *French Forum* 14, no. 1 (1989): 65–73.

Cetta, Lewis T. *Profane Play, Ritual, and Jean Genet: A Study of His Drama.* Birmingham: University of Alabama Press, 1974.

Chamberlain, Lesley. "Through a Cocktail Glass Darkly." *Modern Drama* 31 (1988): 512–19.

Chang, Han-Liang. "Hallucinating the Other: Derridean Fantasies of Chinese Script." Working paper, Center for Twentieth Century Studies—University of Wisconsin, Milwaukee, 1988.

Chasseguet-Smirgel, Janine. *The Ego Ideal.* Trans. Paul Barrows. London: Free Association, 1985.

Chaudhuri, Una. *No Man's Stage: A Semiotic Study of Jean Genet's Major Plays.* Ann Arbor, Mich.: UMI Research, 1986.

Churchill, Caryl. *Cloud Nine.* New York: Routledge, 1991.

Cima, Gay Gibson. *Performing Women: Female Characters, Male Playwrights, and the Modern Stage.* Ithaca, N.Y.: Cornell University Press, 1993.

Cixous, Hélène. "Aller à la mer." *Modern Drama* 27 (1984): 546–48.

———. "The Laugh of the Medusa." Trans. Keith Cohen and Paula Cohen. *New French Feminisms: An Anthology.* Ed. Elaine Marks and Isabelle de Courtivron. Amherst: University of Massachusetts Press, 1980. 245–64.

Cixous, Hélène, and Catherine Clément. *The Newly Born Woman.* Trans. Betsy Wing. 1975. Minneapolis: University of Minnesota Press, 1986.

Clark, David R., ed. *Twentieth Century Interpretations of "Murder in the Cathedral."* Englewood Cliffs, N.J.: Prentice-Hall, 1971.

Clément, Catherine. *Syncope: The Philosophy of Rapture.* Trans. Sally O'Driscoll. Minneapolis: University of Minnesota Press, 1994.

Cole, Susan Letzler. *The Absent One: Mourning Ritual, Tragedy, and the Performance of Ambivalence.* University Park: Pennsylvania State University Press, 1985.

Collins, Jerre, J. Ray Green, Mary Lydon, Mark Sachner, and Eleanor Honig Skoller. "Questioning the Unconscious: The Dora Archive." In Bernheimer and Kahane 243–53.

Constable, John. "I. A. Richards, T. S. Eliot, and the Poetry of Belief." *Essays in Criticism* 49, no. 3 (1990): 222–43.

Cook, Rufus. "Quest for Immobility: The Identification of Being and Non-Being in Jean Genet's *The Balcony.*" In Hopkins and Aycock 115–28.

Corlett, William. *Community without Unity: A Politics of Derridean Extravagance.* Durham, N.C.: Duke University Press, 1989.

Costich, Julia F. *Antonin Artaud.* Boston: Twayne, 1978.

Coward, Harold, and Toby Foshay. *Derrida and Negative Theology.* Albany: State University of New York Press, 1992.

David-Ménard, Monique. *Hysteria from Freud to Lacan.* Trans. Catherine Porter. Ithaca, N.Y.: Cornell University Press, 1989.

Davis, R. G. "Letter about John Fuegi." *Communications from the International Brecht Society* 23, no. 2 (1994): 12–13.

Dean, Carolyn. "Law and Sacrifice: Bataille, Lacan, and the Critique of the Subject." *Representations* 13 (winter 1986): 42–62.

———. *The Self and Its Pleasures: Bataille, Lacan, and the History of the Decentered Subject.* Ithaca, N.Y.: Cornell University Press, 1992.

Debord, Guy. *Society of the Spectacle.* Trans. Donald Nicholson-Smith. Detroit: Black and Red, 1983.

Delany, Samuel R. *Wagner-Artaud.* New York: Ansatz, 1988.

Del Caro, Adrian. "The Pseudoman in Nietzsche; or, The Threat of the Neuter." *New German Critique* 50 (spring–summer 1990): 135–56.

Deleuze, Gilles. *Nietzsche and Philosophy.* Trans. Hugh Tomlinson. New York: Columbia University Press, 1983.

———. "The Schizophrenic and Language." Trans. Josué V. Harari. *Textual Strategies: Perspectives in Post-Structuralist Criticism.* Ed. Josué V. Harari. Ithaca, N.Y.: Cornell University Press, 1979. 277–95.

Deleuze, Gilles, and Félix Guattari. *Anti-Oedipus: Capitalism and Schizophrenia.* Trans. Robert Hurley, Mark Seem, and Helen R. Lane. Minneapolis: University of Minnesota Press, 1983.

de Man, Paul. *Allegories of Reading: Figural Language in Rousseau, Nietzsche, Rilke, and Proust.* New Haven: Yale University Press, 1979.

Derrida, Jacques. "Fors." Trans. Barbara Johnson. *Georgia Review* 31, no. 1 (1977): 64–116.

———. *Glas.* 1974. Trans. John P. Leavey Jr. and Richard Rand. Lincoln: University of Nebraska Press, 1986.

———. "Living on—Border Lines." Trans. James Hulbert. *Deconstruction and Criticism.* New York: Continuum-Seabury, 1979. 75–176.

———. Of Grammatology. Trans. Gayatri Chakravorty Spivak. Baltimore: Johns Hopkins University Press, 1976.

———. Spurs: Nietzsche's Styles. Trans. Barbara Harlow. Chicago: University of Chicago Press, 1978.

———. "Structure, Sign, and Play in the Discourse of the Human Sciences." The Languages of Criticism and the Sciences of Man. Ed. Richard Macksey and Eugenio Donato. Baltimore: Johns Hopkins University Press, 1970. 247–72.

———. Writing and Difference. Trans. Alan Bass. Chicago: University of Chicago Press, 1978.

Detienne, Marcel. Dionysos at Large. Trans. Arthur Goldhammer. Cambridge: Harvard University Press, 1989.

Diamond, Elin. "Brechtian Theory/Feminist Theory: Toward a Gestic Feminist Criticism." Drama Review 32, no. 1 (1988): 82–94.

———. "Mimesis, Mimicry, and the True-Real." Modern Drama 32 (1989): 59–72.

———. "Realism and Hysteria: Toward a Feminist Mimesis." Discourse 13, no. 1 (1990–91): 59–92.

Dickson, Keith A. Towards Utopia: A Study of Brecht. Oxford: Clarendon Press, 1978.

Doane, Janice, and Devon Hodges. From Klein to Kristeva: Psychoanalytic Feminism and the Search for the "Good Enough" Mother. Ann Arbor: University of Michigan Press, 1992.

Dobrez, L. A. C. The Existential and Its Exits: Literary and Philosophical Perspectives on the Works of Beckett, Ionesco, Genet, and Pinter. London: Athlone, 1986.

Dollimore, Jonathan. "The Cultural Politics of Perversion: Augustine, Shakespeare, Freud, Foucault." Genders 8 (summer 1990): 1–16.

———. Sexual Dissidence: Augustine to Wilde, Freud to Foucault. Oxford: Clarendon, 1991.

Dort, Bernard. "Genet: The Struggle with Theater." In Brooks and Halpern 114–28.

Driver, Tom F. Jean Genet. New York: Columbia University Press, 1966.

Duras, Marguerite. India Song. Trans. Barbara Bray. New York: Grove, 1976.

Eagleton, Terry. Against the Grain: Essays 1975–1985. London: Verso, 1986.

———. The Ideology of the Aesthetic. Cambridge: Basil Blackwell, 1990.

Edwards, Lee R. "Schizophrenic Narrative." Journal of Narrative Technique 19, no. 1 (1989): 25–30.

Eigen, Michael. "The Area of Faith in Winnicott, Lacan, and Bion." International Journal of Psycho-Analysis 62 (1981): 413–33.

Eliot, Charlotte. Savonarola: A Dramatic Poem. London: R. Cobden-Sanderson, 1926.

Eliot, T. S. After Strange Gods: A Primer of Modern Heresy. London: Faber, 1934.

———. The Complete Poems and Plays, 1909–1950. New York: Harcourt, 1971.

———. The Idea of a Christian Society. New York: Harcourt, 1940.

———. "Literature, Science, and Dogma." Dial 82, no. 3 (1927): 239–43.

———. "A Note on Poetry and Belief." Enemy 1 (Jan. 1927): 15–17.

———. Notes towards the Definition of Culture. London: Faber, 1948.

———. *Poetry and Drama*. Cambridge: Harvard University Press, 1951.

———. Review of *The Philosophy of Nietzsche*, by A. Wolf. *International Journal of Ethics* 26, no. 3 (1916): 426–27.

———. *The Rock*. New York: Harcourt, 1934.

———. *Selected Essays*. New York: Harcourt, 1932.

———. *The Use of Poetry and the Use of Criticism*. London: Faber, 1933.

Else, Gerald F. *The Origin and Early Form of Greek Tragedy*. Cambridge: Harvard University Press, 1967.

Esslin, Martin. *Artaud*. London: John Calder, 1976.

———. *Brecht: A Choice of Evils*. 4th ed. London: Methuen, 1984.

Euripides. *Three Plays of Euripides: Alcestis, Medea, The Bacchae*. Trans. Paul Roche. New York: Norton, 1974.

Federman, Raymond. "Jean Genet: The Theater of Hate." In Brooks and Halpern 129–45.

Fergusson, Francis. *The Idea of Theater*. Princeton: Princeton University Press, 1949.

Fish, Stanley. *Doing What Comes Naturally*. Durham, N.C.: Duke University Press, 1989.

———. *Is There a Text in This Class? The Authority of Interpretive Communities*. Cambridge: Harvard University Press, 1980.

Fisher, David H. "Nietzsche's Dionysian Masks." *Historical Reflections/ Reflexions Historiques* 21, no. 3 (1995): 515–36.

Fisher, Dominique D. *Staging of Language and Language(s) of the Stage*. New York: Peter Lang, 1994.

Fletcher, John, and Andrew Benjamin, eds. *Abjection, Melancholia, and Love: The Work of Julia Kristeva*. London: Routledge, 1990.

Fly, Richard. "Shakespeare, Artaud, and the Representation of Violence." *Essays in Literature* 16, no. 1 (1989): 3–12.

Foucault, Michel. *The History of Sexuality*. Vol. 1. Trans. Robert Hurley. New York: Random, 1978.

———. *Language, Counter-Memory, Practice*. Trans. Donald F. Bouchard and Sherry Simon. Ithaca, N.Y.: Cornell University Press, 1977.

Freud, Sigmund. *The Standard Edition of the Complete Psychological Works of Sigmund Freud*. Ed. James Strachey. 24 vols. London: Hogarth, 1953–74.

Friedrich, Rainer. "The Deconstructed Self in Artaud and Brecht: Negation of Subject and Antitotaliterianism." *Forum for Modern Language Studies* 26, no. 3 (1990): 282–97.

———. "Drama and Ritual." *Drama and Religion*. Ed. James Redmond. Cambridge: Cambridge University Press, 1983. 159–223.

Frisch, Werner, and K. W. Obermeier. *Brecht in Augsburg: Erinnerungen, Texte, Fotos*. Berlin: Suhrkamp, 1976.

Frye, Northrop. *The Anatomy of Criticism*. Princeton: Princeton University Press, 1957.

Fuegi, John. *Bertolt Brecht: Chaos according to Plan*. Cambridge: Cambridge University Press, 1987.

———. *Brecht and Company: Sex, Politics, and the Making of Modern Drama*. New York: Grove, 1994.

———. "The Zelda Syndrome: Brecht and Elisabeth Hauptmann." In Peter Thomson 104–16.

Fuegi, John, Gisela Bahr, and John Willett, eds. *Brecht: Women and Politics*. Detroit: Wayne State University Press, 1983.

Fugard, Athol, John Kani, and Winston Ntshona. *The Island*. In *Modern Drama*. Ed. W. B. Worthen. Orlando: Harcourt, 1995. 664–74.

Genet, Jean. *Le Balcon*. London: Methuen, 1982.

———. *The Balcony*. Trans. Bernard Frechtman. Rev. ed. New York: Grove, 1966.

———. *The Blacks: A Clown Show*. Trans. Bernard Frechtman. New York: Grove, 1960.

———. "Hubert Fichte Interviews Jean Genet." *Gay Sunshine Interviews*. Vol. 1. Ed. Winston Leyland. San Francisco: Gay Sunshine, 1978.

———. *Letters to Roger Blin: Reflections on the Theater*. Trans. Richard Seaver. New York: Grove, 1969.

———. *The Maids* and *Deathwatch*. Trans. Bernard Frechtman. New York: Grove, 1954.

———. "A Note on Theater." *Drama Review* 7, no. 3 (1963): 37–41.

———. *Prisoner of Love*. Trans. Barbara Bray. London: Picador-Pan, 1989.

———. *The Screens*. Trans. Bernard Frechtman. New York: Grove, 1962.

———. *The Thief's Journal*. Trans. Bernard Frechtman. New York: Grove, 1964.

Gibert-Maceda, M. Teresa. "T. S. Eliot on Women: Women on T. S. Eliot." *T. S. Eliot at the Turn of the Century*. Ed. Marianne Thormählen. Lund, Sweden: Lund University Press, 1990. 105–19.

Gilbert, Sandra M., and Susan Gubar. *Sexchanges*. Vol. 2 of *No Man's Land: The Place of the Woman Writer in the Twentieth Century*. New Haven: Yale University Press, 1989.

Gimbutas, Marija. *The Civilization of the Goddess*. San Francisco: Harper, 1991.

———. *The Language of the Goddess*. San Francisco: Harper, 1989.

Girard, René. *Violence and the Sacred*. Trans. Patrick Gregory. Baltimore: Johns Hopkins University Press, 1977.

Gitenet, Jean. "Profane and Sacred Reality in Jean Genet's Theatre." In Brooks and Halpern 172–77.

Goodall, Jane. *Artaud and the Gnostic Drama*. Oxford: Clarendon, 1994.

———. "Artaud's Revision of Shelley's *The Cenci*: The Text and Its Double." *Comparative Drama* 21, no. 2 (1987): 115–26.

———. "The Plague and Its Powers in Artaudian Theater." *Modern Drama* 33 (1990): 529–42.

Green, André. *The Tragic Effect: The Oedipus Complex in Tragedy*. Trans. Alan Sheridan. Cambridge: Cambridge University Press, 1979.

Greenblatt, Stephen. *Renaissance Self-Fashioning: From More to Shakespeare*. Chicago: University of Chicago Press, 1980.

Greene, Naomi. *Antonin Artaud: Poet without Words*. New York: Simon, 1970.

Grimes, Ronald L. *Ritual Criticism: Case Studies in Practice, Essays on Its Theory*. Columbia: University of South Carolina Press, 1990.

———. "Victor Turner's Social Drama and T. S. Eliot's Ritual Drama." *Anthropologica* 27, nos. 1–2 (1985): 79–99.

Gross, Elizabeth. "The Body of Signification." In Fletcher and Benjamin 80–108.

Grotowski, Jerzy. *Towards a Poor Theatre*. New York: Simon and Schuster, 1968.

Grove, Robin. "Pereira and After: The Cures of Eliot's Theater." *The Cambridge Companion to T. S. Eliot*. Ed. A. David Moody. Cambridge: Cambridge University Press, 1994. 158–75.

Guéguen, Pierre Gilles. "On Fantasy: Lacan and Klein." *Newsletter of the Freudian Field* 6, nos. 1–2 (1992): 67–75.

Guicharnaud, Jacques. "The Glory of Annihilation: Jean Genet." In Brooks and Halpern 98–113.

Guthrie, W. K. C. *The Greeks and Their Gods*. Boston: Beacon, 1955.

Hardin, Richard F. "'Ritual' in Recent Criticism: The Elusive Sense of Community." *PMLA* 98, no. 5 (1983): 846–62.

Hardison, O. B. *Christian Rite and Christian Drama in the Middle Ages*. Baltimore: Johns Hopkins University Press, 1965.

Harpham, Geoffrey Galt. *The Ascetic Imperative in Culture and Criticism*. Chicago: University of Chicago Press, 1987.

Harris, Max. *Theater and Incarnation*. New York: Macmillan, 1990.

Hassan, Ihab. *The Dismemberment of Orpheus*. 2d ed. Madison: University of Wisconsin Press, 1982.

———. *The Postmodern Turn*. Columbus: Ohio State University Press, 1987.

Hassig, Rudy. "Use and Misuse of a Cooperation." *Communications from the International Brecht Society* 23, no. 2 (1994): 14–15.

Hayman, Ronald. *Artaud and After*. Oxford: Oxford University Press, 1977.

———. *Brecht: A Biography*. London: Weidenfeld and Nicolion, 1983.

Hertz, Uri. "Brecht/Artaud." *Third Rail* 5 (1982): 29–35.

Hill, Leslie. "Julia Kristeva: Theorizing the Avant-Garde?" In Fletcher and Benjamin 137–56.

Hinden, Michael. "Drama and Ritual Once Again: Notes toward a Revival of Tragic Theory." *Comparative Drama* 29, no. 2 (1995): 183–202.

Hirsch, E. D., Jr. "Beyond Convention?" *New Literary History* 14, no. 2 (1983): 389–97.

Hopkins, Patricia M., and Wendell M. Aycock, eds. *Myths and Realities of Contemporary French Theater: Comparative Views*. Lubbock: Texas Tech Press, 1985.

Howarth, Herbert. *Notes on Some Figures behind T. S. Eliot*. London: Chatto and Windus, 1965.

Huyssen, Andreas. *After the Great Divide*. Bloomington: Indiana University Press, 1986.

Hwang, David Henry. *M. Butterfly*. New York: Penguin, 1986.

Innes, Christopher. *Avant Garde Theatre*. London: Routledge, 1993.

Irigaray, Luce. *This Sex Which Is Not One*. Trans. Catherine Porter. Ithaca, N.Y.: Cornell University Press. 1985.

———. *Speculum of the Other Woman*. Trans. Gillian C. Gill. Ithaca, N.Y.: Cornell University Press, 1985.

Iser, Wolfgang. *The Implied Reader: Patterns in Prose Fiction from Bunyan to Beckett*. Baltimore: Johns Hopkins University Press, 1974.

Jacobs, Carol. *The Dissimulating Harmony.* Baltimore: Johns Hopkins University Press, 1978.

Jacobus, Mary. *Reading Woman: Essays in Feminist Criticism.* New York: Columbia University Press, 1986.

James, E. O. *The Cult of the Mother-Goddess: An Archaeological and Documentary Study.* London: Thames and Hudson, 1959.

Jameson, Fredric. "Imaginary and Symbolic in Lacan." *The Ideologies of Theory: Essays 1971–1986.* Vol. 1. Minneapolis: University of Minnesota Press, 1988. 75–115.

———. *The Political Unconscious: Narrative as a Socially Symbolic Act.* Ithaca, N.Y.: Cornell University Press, 1981.

Jarrett-Kerr, Martin. *Studies in Literature and Belief.* London: Rockliff, 1954.

Jasper, David. *The Study of Literature and Religion.* London: Macmillan, 1989.

Jay, Gregory S. *T. S. Eliot and the Poetics of Literary History.* Baton Rouge: Louisiana University Press, 1983.

Jesse, Horst. "The Young Bertolt Brecht and Religion." *Communications of the International Brecht Society* 15, no. 2 (1986): 17–27.

Jones, Emrys. "*Murder in the Cathedral* at Stratford." *T. S. Eliot at the Turn of the Century.* Ed. Marianne Thormählen. Lund, Sweden: Lund University Press, 1990. 146–61.

Julius, Anthony. *T. S. Eliot, Anti-semitism, and Literary Form.* Cambridge: Cambridge University Press, 1995.

Kahane, Claire. "Hysteria, Feminism, and the Case of *The Bostonians.*" *Feminism and Psychoanalysis.* Ed. Richard Feldstein and Judith Roof. Ithaca, N.Y.: Cornell University Press, 1989. 280–97.

Kahn, M. Masud R. *Alienation in Perversions.* London: Hogarth, 1979.

Kaplan, E. Ann. *Women and Film.* New York: Methuen, 1983.

Kaplan, Louise J. *Female Perversions.* New York: Doubleday, 1991.

Kennedy, Adrienne. *Funnyhouse of a Negro.* In *Adrienne Kennedy in One Act.* Minneapolis: University of Minnesota Press, 1988. 1–23.

Kenner, Hugh. *The Invisible Poet: T. S. Eliot.* London: Methuen, 1965.

Kenny, Neil. "Changing the Languages of Theater: A Comparison of Brecht and Artaud." *Journal of European Studies* 13, no. 3 (1983): 170–86.

Kerenyi, C. *Dionysos: Archetypal Image of Indestructible Life.* Trans. Ralph Manheim. Princeton: Princeton University Press, 1976.

Klein, Melanie. *The Selected Melanie Klein.* Ed. Juliet Mitchell. New York: Free Press–Macmillan, 1986.

Knapp, Bettina L. *Antonin Artaud: Man of Vision.* Chicago: Swallow, 1980.

———. "Mexico: The Myth of *Renovatio.*" *Substance* 50 (1986): 61–68.

———. *Theater and Alchemy.* Detroit: Wayne State University Press, 1980.

Knopf, Jan. *Brecht-Handbuch.* Stuttgart: Metzlersche, 1980.

Knust, Herbert. "Brecht's Dream-Playing: Between Vision and Illusion." In Mews 209–23.

———. "East-West Encounters in Brecht's Szechwan Play." *Comparative Literature East and West: Traditions and Trends.* Ed. Cornelia N. Moore and Raymond A. Moody. Honolulu: University of Hawaii Press, 1989. 78–80.

Koelb, Clayton. *Nietzsche as Postmodernist: Essays Pro and Contra.* New York: SUNY Press, 1990.

Koestenbaum, Wayne. *"The Waste Land:* T. S. Eliot's and Ezra Pound's Collaboration on Hysteria." *Studies in Twentieth Century Literature* 34, no. 2 (1988): 113–39.

Konecni, Vladimir J. "Psychological Aspects of the Expression of Anger and Violence on the Stage." *Comparative Drama* 25, no. 3 (1991): 215–41.

Kristeva, Julia. *In the Beginning Was Love: Psychoanalysis and Faith.* Trans. Arthur Goldhammer. New York: Columbia, 1987.

———. *Black Sun: Depression and Melancholia.* Trans. Leon S. Roudiez. New York: Columbia University Press, 1989.

———. *Desire in Language: A Semiotic Approach to Literature and Art.* Trans. Leon. S. Roudiez. New York: Columbia University Press, 1980.

———. *The Kristeva Reader.* Ed. Toril Moi. New York: Columbia University Press, 1986.

———. "Modern Theater Does Not Take (a) Place." Trans. Alice Jardine and Thomas Gora. *Sub-Stance* 18–19 (1977): 131–34.

———. "On the Melancholic Imaginary." Trans. Louise Burchill. *Discourse in Psychoanalysis and Literature.* Ed. Shlomith Rimmon-Kenan. London: Methuen, 1987. 104–23.

———. *Powers of Horror: An Essay on Abjection.* Trans. Leon S. Roudiez. New York: Columbia University Press, 1982.

———. *Revolution in Poetic Language.* Trans. Margaret Waller. New York: Columbia University Press, 1984.

———. *Tales of Love.* Trans. Leon S. Roudiez. New York: Columbia University Press, 1987.

———. "Within the Microcosm of 'The Talking Cure.'" Trans. Thomas Gora and Margaret Waller. *Interpreting Lacan.* Ed. Joseph H. Smith and William Kerrigan. New Haven: Yale University Press, 1983. 33–48.

Krutch, Joseph Wood. "The Tragic Fallacy." *The Modern Temper: A Study and a Confession.* New York: Harcourt, 1929. 115–43.

Kubiak, Anthony. *Stages of Terror: Terrorism, Ideology, and Coercion as Theatre History.* Bloomington: Indiana University Press, 1991.

Kushner, Tony. *Angels in America, Part One: Millennium Approaches.* New York: Theatre Communications Group, 1992.

Lacan, Jacques. *Écrits: A Selection.* Trans. Alan Sheridan. New York: Norton, 1977.

———. *Feminine Sexuality.* Trans. Jacqueline Rose. New York: Norton, 1985.

———. *The Four Fundamental Concepts of Psycho-Analysis.* Ed. Jacques-Alain Miller. Trans. Alan Sheridan. New York: Norton, 1978.

———. "Kant with Sade." Trans. James B. Swenson Jr. *October* 51 (winter 1989): 55–104.

Leavell, Linda. "Nietzsche's Theory of Tragedy in the Plays of T. S. Eliot." *Twentieth Century Literature* 31, no. 1 (1985): 111–26.

Lennox, Sara. "Women in Brecht's Works." *New German Critique* 14 (spring 1978): 83–96.

Lukacher, Ned. *Primal Scenes: Literature, Philosophy, Psychoanalysis.* Ithaca, N.Y.: Cornell University Press, 1986.

Lunn, Eugene. "Marxism and Art in the Era of Stalin and Hitler: A Comparison of Brecht and Lukacs." *New German Critique* 1, no. 3 (1974): 12–44.

Lyotard, Jean-François. *Driftworks.* New York: Semiotext(e), 1984.

———. *The Postmodern Condition: A Report on Knowledge.* Trans. Geoff Bennington and Brian Massumi. Minneapolis: University of Minnesota Press, 1984.

MacCannell, Juliet Flower. *The Regime of the Brother: After the Patriarchy.* London: Routledge, 1991.

Maddox, Donald. "Antonin Artaud and a Semiotics of Theater." *Romanic Review* 76, no. 2 (1985): 202–15.

Mailloux, Stephen. *Interpretive Conventions: The Reader in the Study of American Fiction.* Ithaca, N.Y.: Cornell University Press, 1982.

Marion, Jean-Luc. *God without Being: Hors-texte.* Trans. Thomas A. Carlson. Chicago: University of Chicago Press, 1991.

Marowitz, Charles. "The Revenge of Jean Genet." *The Encore Reader: A Chronicle of the New Drama.* Ed. Charles Marowitz, Tom Milne, and Owen Hale. London: Methuen, 1965. 170–78.

Mason, H. A. *The Tragic Plane.* Oxford: Clarendon, 1985.

May, Keith M. *Nietzsche and the Spirit of Tragedy.* London: Macmillan, 1990.

McCallum, Pamela. *Literature and Method: Towards a Critique of I. A. Richards, T. S. Eliot, and F. R. Leavis.* London: Gill and Macmillan, 1983.

McCullough, Christopher. "Saint Joan of the Stockyards." In Peter Thomson 96–103.

McGrath, William J. *Freud's Discovery of Psychoanalysis: The Politics of Hysteria.* Ithaca, N.Y.: Cornell University Press, 1986.

Ménager, Serge Dominique. "Remembrance of Genet's Passing: Jean Genet's Tomb." *Theoria* 72 (Oct. 1988): 17–22.

Merskey, Harold. *The Analysis of Hysteria.* London: Cassell, 1979.

Metz, Christian. *The Imaginary Signifier: Psychoanalysis and the Cinema.* Bloomington: Indiana University Press, 1982.

Mews, Siegfried, ed. *Critical Essays on Brecht.* Boston: G. K. Hall, 1989.

Miller, Arthur. "Tragedy and the Common Man." *The Theater Essays of Arthur Miller.* Ed. Robert A. Miller. New York: Viking, 1978. 3–7.

Miller, James. "Carnivals of Atrocity: Foucault, Nietzsche, Cruelty." *Political Theory* 18, no. 3 (1990): 470–91.

Minich-Brewer, Mária. "Performing Theory." *Theatre Journal* 37, no. 1 (1985): 13–30.

Moi, Toril. Introduction to *The Kristeva Reader,* by Julia Kristeva. New York: Columbia University Press, 1986. 1–22.

Moody, A. David. *Tracing T. S. Eliot's Spirit.* Cambridge: Cambridge University Press, 1996.

Mulvey, Laura. "The Oedipus Myth: Beyond the Riddles of the Sphinx." *Psychoanalysis and Cultural Theory: Thresholds.* Ed. James Donald. New York: St. Martin's, 1991. 27–50.

———. "Visual Pleasure and Narrative Cinema." 1975. *Narrative, Apparatus, Ideology: A Film Theory Reader.* Ed. Philip Rosen. New York: Columbia University Press, 1986. 198–209.

Murphy, G. Ronald. *Brecht and the Bible.* Chapel Hill: University of North Carolina Press, 1980.

Nachman, Larry David. "Genet: Dandy of the Lower Depths." *Salmagundi* 58–59 (1982–83): 358–72.

Nagele, Rainer. *Reading after Freud: Essays on Goethe, Holderlin, Habermas, Nietzsche, Brecht, Celan, and Freud.* New York: Columbia University Press, 1987.

Nelson, Benjamin. "*The Balcony* and Parisian Existentialism." *Drama Review* 7, no. 3 (1963): 60–79.

Neumann, Erich. *The Great Mother.* Trans. Ralph Manheim. 2d ed. Princeton: Princeton University Press, 1972.

New American Bible, The. New York: P. J. Kenedy and Sons, 1970.

Nietzsche, Friedrich. *The Birth of Tragedy* and *The Case of Wagner.* Trans. Walter Kaufmann. New York: Random, 1967.

———. *On the Genealogy of Morals* and *Ecce Homo.* Trans. Walter Kaufmann. New York: Random. 1967.

———. *Thus Spoke Zarathustra.* In *The Portable Nietzsche.* Trans. Walter Kaufmann. New York: Penguin, 1976. 103–439.

Oswald, Laura. *Jean Genet and the Semiotics of Performance.* Bloomington: Indiana University Press, 1989.

Otto, Walter F. *Dionysus: Myth and Cult.* Trans. Robert B. Palmer. Bloomington: Indiana University Press, 1965.

Paglia, Camille. *Sexual Personae.* New Haven: Yale University Press, 1990.

Parmalee, Patty Lee. "Saint Joan of the Stockyards." In Mews 62–76.

Patai, Raphael. *The Hebrew Goddess.* 3d ed. Detroit: Wayne State University Press, 1990.

Phelan, Peggy. *Unmarked: The Politics of Performance.* London: Routledge, 1993.

Phelan, Virginia B. *Two Ways of Life and Death: "Alcestis" and "The Cocktail Party."* New York: Garland, 1990.

Pickering, Kenneth W. *Drama in the Cathedral: The Canterbury Festival Plays, 1928–1948.* Worthing, West Sussex: Churchman, 1985.

Piemme, Michele. "Scenic Space and Dramatic Illusion in *The Balcony.*" In Brooks and Halpern 161–76.

Pireddu, Nicoletta. "The Mark and the Mask: Psychosis in Artaud's Alphabet of Cruelty." *Arachne* 3, no. 1 (1996): 43–65.

Pizzato, Mark. "The Real Edges of the Screen: Cinema's Theatrical and Communal Ghosts." *Spectator* 16, no. 2 (1996): 71–89.

Plato. *Timaeus* and *Critias.* Trans. Desmond Lee. New York: Penguin, 1977.

Plunka, Gene A. "Antonin Artaud: The Suffering Shaman of the Modern Theater." In Plunka, *Antonin Artaud,* 3–36.

———, ed. *Antonin Artaud and the Modern Theater.* Rutherford, N.J.: Fairleigh Dickinson University Press, 1994.

———. The Rites of Passage of Jean Genet. Rutherford, N.J.: Fairleigh Dickinson University Press, 1992.

Podol, Peter L. "Contradictions and Dualities in Artaud and Artaudian Theater: The Conquest of Mexico and the Conquest of Peru." Modern Drama 26, no. 4 (1983): 518–27.

Pollock, Della. "New Man to New Woman: Women in Brecht and Expressionism." Journal of Dramatic Theory and Criticism 4, no. 1 (1989): 85–105.

Pontalis, J.-B. Frontiers of Psychoanalysis: Between the Dream and Psychic Pain. Trans. Catherine Cullen and Philip Cullen. New York: International Universities, 1981.

Porter, James I. "The Invention of Dionysus and the Platonic Midwife: Nietzsche's Birth of Tragedy." Journal of the History of Philosophy 33, no. 3 (1995): 467–97.

Preston, James J., ed. Mother Worship: Themes and Variations. Chapel Hill: University of North Carolina Press, 1982.

Pucciani, Oreste F. "Tragedy, Genet, and The Maids." Drama Review 7, no. 3 (1963): 42–59.

Ragland, Ellie. Essays on the Pleasures of Death: From Freud to Lacan. New York: Routledge, 1995.

Ragland-Sullivan, Ellie. "Hamlet, Logical Time, and the Structure of Obsession." Newsletter of the Freudian Field 2, no. 2 (1988): 29–45.

———. "Jacques Lacan, Literary Theory, and The Maids of Jean Genet." Psychological Perspectives on Literature: Freudian Dissidents and Non-Freudians. Ed. Joseph Natoli. Hamden, Conn.: Shoe String, 1984. 100–119.

———. Jacques Lacan and the Philosophy of Psychoanalysis. Urbana: University of Illinois Press, 1986.

Ramas, Maria. "Freud's Dora, Dora's Hysteria." In Bernheimer and Kahane 149–80.

Reinelt, Janelle. "Rethinking Brecht: Deconstruction, Feminism, and the Politics of Form." Essays On Brecht/Versuche Über Brecht. Ed. Marc Silberman et al. Madison, Wis.: International Brecht Society, 1980.

Richards, I. A. "A Background for Contemporary Poetry." Criterion 3, no. 12 (1925): 511–28.

———. "Belief." Complementarities: Uncollected Essays. Cambridge: Harvard University Press, 1976.

———. Principles of Literary Criticism. New York: Harcourt, 1926.

———. Science and Poetry. New York: Norton, 1926.

Ricks, Christopher. T. S. Eliot and Prejudice. London: Faber, 1988.

Rose, Jacqueline. "Introduction-II." Feminine Sexuality. By Jacques Lacan. 27–57.

Rose, Mark V. The Actor and His Double. Chicago: Actor Training and Research Institute, 1986.

Rouse, John. Brecht and the West-German Theatre. Ann Arbor, Mich.: UMI, 1989.

Running-Johnson, Cynthia. "Genet's 'Excessive' Double: Reading Les Bonnes through Irigaray and Cixous." French Review 63, no. 6 (1990): 959–66.

―――. "The Medusa's Tale: Feminine Writing and 'La Genet.'" *Romanic Review* 80, no. 3 (1989): 483–95.

Russo, John Paul. *I. A. Richards: His Life and Work*. Baltimore: Johns Hopkins University Press, 1989.

Sallis, John. *Crossings: Nietzsche and the Space of Tragedy*. Chicago: University of Chicago Press, 1991.

Sartre, Jean-Paul. *Saint Genet: Actor and Martyr*. 1952. Trans. Bernard Frechtman. New York: George Braziller, 1963.

Savona, Jeannette L. *Jean Genet*. New York: Grove, 1983.

Savran, David. *The Wooster Group, 1975–1985: Breaking the Rules*. Ann Arbor, Mich.: UMI Research, 1986.

Scarry, Elaine. *The Body in Pain: The Making and Unmaking of the World*. New York: Oxford University Press, 1985.

Schechner, Richard. *Between Theater and Anthropology*. Philadelphia: University of Pennsylvania Press, 1985.

―――. *Performance Theory*. Rev. ed. New York: Routledge, 1988.

Schoeps, Karl-Heinz. "From Distancing Alienation to the Intuitive Naiveté: Bertolt Brecht's Establishment of a New Aesthetic Category." *Monatshefte* 81, no. 2 (1989): 186–98.

Scott, Nathan A., Jr. *The Broken Center: Studies in the Theological Horizon of Modern Literature*. New Haven: Yale University Press, 1966.

Selmon, Michael. "Logician, Heal Thy Self: Poetry and Drama in Eliot's *The Cocktail Party*." *Modern Drama* 31, no. 4 (1988): 495–511.

Sena, Marylou. "Dionysos as Antidote: The Veils of Maya." *Research in Phenomenology* 24 (1994): 189–205.

Seyhan, Azade. "Nietzsche and Eliot: The Dialectic Vision as Revealed in the Hermeneutic Cycle." *Selecta* 2 (1981): 24–27.

Shaffer, Peter. *Equus*. New York: Penguin, 1977.

Shakespeare, William. *King Lear*. London: Routledge, 1972.

―――. *The Tragedy of Hamlet, Prince of Denmark*. New York: NAL, 1963.

Shange, Ntozake. *Spell #7*. In *Three Pieces*. New York: St. Martin's, 1981. 3–52.

Sharma, H. L. *T. S. Eliot: His Dramatic Theories*. New Delhi: S. Chand, 1976.

Sharrat, Bernard. "Eliot: Modernism, Postmodernism, and After." *The Cambridge Companion to T. S. Eliot*. Ed. A. David Moody. Cambridge: Cambridge University Press, 1994. 223–35.

Shelley, Percy Bysshe. *The Cenci*. New York: AMS, 1975.

Shevtsova, Maria. "The Consumption of Empty Signs: Jean Genet's *The Balcony*." *Modern Drama* 30, no. 1 (1987): 35–45.

Shusterman, Richard. *T. S. Eliot and the Philosophy of Criticism*. New York: Columbia University Press, 1988.

Silk, M. S., and J. P. Stern. *Nietzsche on Tragedy*. Cambridge: Cambridge University Press, 1988.

Silverman, Kaja. *The Acoustic Mirror: The Female Voice in Psychoanalysis and Cinema*. Bloomington: Indiana University Press, 1988.

Smith, Grover. "Eliot and the Shamans." *T. S. Eliot at the Turn of the Century*. Ed. Marianne Thormählen. Lund, Sweden: Lund University Press, 1990. 162–80.

Smith, Iris. "Brecht and the Mothers of Epic Theater." *Theatre Journal* 43 (1991): 491–505.

———. "The Semiotics of the Theater of Cruelty." *Semiotica* 56, nos. 3–4 (1985): 291–307.

Snyder, Marc. "Antonin Artaud's *Les Cenci:* Toward a Metaphysics of Destining." *Constructions* 1984:67–76.

Sokel, Walter H. "Brecht's Split Characters and His Sense of the Tragic." *Brecht: A Collection of Critical Essays.* Ed. Peter Demetz. Englewood Cliffs, N.J.: Prentice-Hall, 1962. 127–37.

Sontag, Susan. Introduction to *Antonin Artaud: Selected Writings.* New York: Farrar, Straus and Giroux, 1976. xvii–lix.

Soyinka, Wole. *The Lion and the Jewel.* In *Collected Plays 2.* London: Oxford University Press, 1974.

Spanos, William V. *The Christian Tradition in Modern British Verse Drama: The Poetics of Sacramental Time.* New Brunswick, N.J.: Rutgers University Press, 1967.

———. *Repetitions: The Postmodern Occasion in Literature and Culture.* Baton Rouge: Louisiana State University Press, 1987.

Speaight, Robert. *Christian Theatre.* New York: Hawthorn, 1960.

Speirs, Ronald. "Baal." In Mews 19–29.

Spivak, Gayatri Chakravorty. *In Other Worlds: Essays in Cultural Politics.* New York: Methuen, 1987.

Sprengnether, Madelon. *The Spectral Mother: Freud, Feminism, and Psychoanalysis.* Ithaca, N.Y.: Cornell University Press, 1990.

Steiner, George. *The Death of Tragedy.* New York: Knopf, 1961.

Stevens, Wallace. *The Collected Poems of Wallace Stevens.* New York: Knopf, 1981.

Stewart, Harry E. "Jean Genet's Childhood in Alligny-en-Morvan." *Romance Notes* 27, no. 1 (1986): 107–11.

———. "Jean Genet's Favorite Murderers." *French Review* 60, no. 5 (1987): 635–43.

———. "Toward a New Chronology: Jean Genet's Life and Works in 1939." *French Review* 61, no. 1 (1987): 60–64.

Stewart, Harry E, and Rob Roy McGregor. "Jean Genet's Psychiatric Examination in 1943." *French Review* 62, no. 5 (1989): 793–802.

Stock, R. D. *The Flutes of Dionysus: Daemonic Enthrallment in Literature.* Lincoln: University of Nebraska Press, 1989.

Stout, John C. "Modernist Family Romance: Artaud's *Heliogabale* and Paternity." *French Review* 64, no. 3 (1991): 417–27.

Straus, Todd. "Being-as-Actor in Ionesco and Genet: A Psycho-Theatrical Reading." *French Forum* 10, no. 1 (1985): 97–108.

Suvin, Darko. *To Brecht and Beyond.* Totowa, N.J.: Barnes, 1984.

Szasz, Thomas. *The Myth of Mental Illness.* Rev. ed. New York: Harper, 1974.

Tatlow, Anthony. "Mastery or Slavery? (On Brecht's Early Plays)." In Mews 30–44.

Taubes, Susan. "The White Mask Falls." *Drama Review* 7, no. 3 (1963): 84–92.

Thiher, Allen. "Jacques Derrida's Reading of Artaud: 'La Parole soufflée' and 'La Clôture de la représentation.'" *French Review* 57, no. 4 (1984): 503–8.

Thomson, George. *Aeschylus and Athena: A Study in the Social Origins of Drama*. New York: Grosset and Dunlap, 1968.

Thomson, Peter, ed. *The Cambridge Companion to Brecht*. Cambridge: Cambridge University Press, 1994.

Todd, Jane Marie. "Autobiography and the Case of the Signature: Reading Derrida's *Glas*." *Comparative Literature* 38, no. 1 (1986): 1–19.

Toepfer, Karl. *Theatre, Aristocracy, and Pornocracy: The Orgy Calculus*. New York: PAJ, 1991.

Turner, Victor. *Dramas, Fields, and Metaphors: Symbolic Action in Human Society*. Ithaca, N.Y.: Cornell University Press, 1974.

———. *From Ritual to Theater: The Human Seriousness of Play*. New York: PAJ, 1982.

Turner, Victor, and Edith Turner. *Image and Pilgrimage in Christian Culture*. New York: Columbia University Press, 1978.

Valadier, Paul. "Dionysus versus the Crucified." In Allison 247–61.

Vattimo, Gianni. *The Transparent Society*. Trans. David Webb. Baltimore: Johns Hopkins University Press, 1992.

Veith, Ilza. *Hysteria: The History of a Disease*. Chicago: University of Chicago Press, 1965.

Vernant, Jean Pierre. *Myth and Thought among the Greeks*. London: Routledge, 1983.

Völker, Klaus. *Brecht: A Biography*. Trans. John Nowell. New York: Continuum-Seabury, 1978.

———. *Brecht Chronicle*. Trans. Fred Wieck. New York: Continuum-Seabury, 1975.

Wade, Stephen. "The Orchestration of Monologues: *The Cocktail Party* and a Developing Genre." *Agenda* 23, nos. 3–4 (1986): 202–9.

Waley, Arthur. *The No Plays of Japan*. New York: Grove, 1957.

Walker, David H. "Revolution and Revisions in Genet's 'Le Balcon.'" *Modern Language Review* 79 (1984): 817–30.

Ward, David. *T. S. Eliot between Two Worlds*. London: Routledge, 1973.

Weber, Samuel. *The Legend of Freud*. Minneapolis: University of Minnesota Press, 1982.

Welldon, Estela V. *Mother, Madonna, Whore: The Idealization and Denigration of Motherhood*. New York: Guilford, 1988.

White, Edmund. *Genet: A Biography*. New York: Knopf, 1993.

Wilder, Thornton. *Three Plays*. New York: Harper, 1957.

Wiles, Timothy J. *The Theater Event: Modern Theories of Performance*. Chicago: University of Chicago Press, 1980.

Willett, John. *Brecht in Context*. New York: Methuen, 1984.

Wimsatt, W. K., Jr., and Monroe C. Beardsley. "The Intentional Fallacy." *The Verbal Icon: Studies in the Meaning of Poetry*. By Wimsatt. Lexington: University of Kentucky Press, 1954. 3–18.

Winnicott, D. W. *Playing and Reality*. London: Routledge, 1989.

Wischenbart, Ruediger. "Jean Genet: The Intellectual as Guerrilla." Interview. Trans. Gitta Honegger. *Performing Arts Journal* 9, no. 1 (1985): 38–46.

Witt, Mary Ann Frese. "Mothers and Stories: Female Presence/Power in Genet." *French Forum* 14, no. 2 (1989): 174–86.

Woodward, Kathleen. "Freud and Barthes: Theorizing Mourning, Sustaining Grief." *Discourse* 13, no. 1 (1990–91): 93–110.

Worthen, W. B. *Modern Drama and the Rhetoric of Theater.* Berkeley and Los Angeles: University of California Press, 1992.

Wright, Elizabeth. "*The Good Person of Szechwan:* Discourse of a Masquerade." In Peter Thomson 117–27.

———. *Postmodern Brecht: A Re-Presentation.* London: Routledge, 1989.

Wyschogrod, Edith. *Saints and Postmodernism: Revisioning Moral Philosophy.* Chicago: University of Chicago Press, 1990.

Yeats, W. B. *The Collected Plays of W. B. Yeats.* New York: Macmillan, 1935.

Žižek, Slavoj. *Enjoy Your Symptom! Jacques Lacan in Hollywood and Out.* New York: Routledge, 1992.

———. *The Sublime Object of Ideology.* London: Verso, 1989.

Index